Intervention-Research

A volume in
Research in Management Consulting
Anthony F. Buono, *Series Editor*

Intervention-Research

From Conceptualization to Publication

edited by

Anthony F. Buono
Bentley University

Henri Savall
ISEOR and University Jean Moulin Lyon 3

Laurent Cappelletti
French Conservatory of Arts and Crafts (Le Cnam)

IAP
INFORMATION AGE PUBLISHING, INC.
Charlotte, NC • www.infoagepub.com

Library of Congress Cataloging-in-Publication Data

A CIP record for this book is available from the Library of Congress
http://www.loc.gov

ISBN: 978-1-64113-288-6 (Paperback)
978-1-64113-289-3 (Hardcover)
978-1-64113-290-9 (ebook)

Printed in the United States of America

CONTENTS

INTRODUCTION

Anthony F. Buono

This volume continues to build on the relationship between the Research in Management Consulting series and the intervener-researchers at the Socio-Economic Institute for Firms and Organizations (ISEOR) in Ecully, France, extending that partnership to our recent work with the French Foundation for Management Education (FNEGE). Founded in 1968, FNEGE is dedicated to closing the gap between the teaching and practice of management in France. As part of the Foundation's multifaceted activities—which range from seminars and an advanced training initiative for French doctoral students to joint programs with international organizations an associations—FNEGE partnered with ISEOR to sponsor a series of workshops on developing high quality intervention-research. This volume is one of the results from that endeavor.

As we have noted in previous RMC volumes, for those not familiar with the work of ISEOR and the SEAM framework a bit of background is in order. The Socio-Economic Approach to Management (SEAM) is an integrative intervention model that encompasses the qualitative, quantitative, and financial dimensions of organizational life. Emerging from Henri Savall's seminal work on organizational intervention and his long-term

Intervention Research, pages ix–xiii

collaboration with Véronique Zardet (e.g., Savall, 1975; Savall & Zardet, 1987, 2004) , SEAM is a scientific approach to consultancy that focuses on uncovering the *dysfunctions* and *hidden costs* that exist in organizations, "hidden" in the sense that they are not captured by traditional accounting methods and financial analyses. Through focused intervention that encompasses the entire organization—what the ISEOR team refers to as the HORIVERT approach (combining horizontal and vertical intervention)—the underlying goal is to enhance organizational performance by attacking the "TFW virus." According to Savall, Zardet, and their colleagues, this virus, which is a lingering vestige of the early work by Frederick Taylor, Henri Fayol, and Max Weber, has sufficiently infiltrated our thinking about management and organization to the point where we are falling well short of our own potential. The resultant *dysfunctions* this virus unleashes creates *hidden costs* that lead to the *noncreation of potential*, readily destroying a firm's *value-added* possibilities.

While this brief description reflects the essence of ISEOR's approach to intervention, capturing that endeavor in ways that are acceptable to academic audiences and approachable to the practitioner world presents a different challenge. As Savall's opening chapter in this volume underscores, intervention-research brings the researcher and practitioner closer together, allowing them to explore the realities of organizational life in ways that capture information that is not officially recorded in company files, providing them with the opportunity to validate such findings. Through the resulting dialogue, the intervener-researcher is able to uncover insights that are not easily or directly accessible to most organizational members, external stakeholders, or even to more traditional researchers who typically "pass through" an organization, often at "arms-length." This latter orientation has been criticized as simply "hanging out" in practice (Dingwall, 1997) and equated to little more than "sitting on the fence" as a researcher (Ramage, 1995). As Savall points out, in contrast to such traditional approaches to research, the intervener-researcher "*directly observes phenomena* that no [organizational] database is taking into account."

INTERVENTION-RESEARCH: FROM CONCEPTUALIZATION TO PUBLICATION

As suggested above, while such intervention-research helps to uncover valuable insight into organizational dynamics and performance, the challenge of capturing and disseminating that insight is entrenched in the underlying rigor-relevance debate (e.g., Kieser & Leiner, 2009). Although we have witnessed increased calls for "actionable knowledge," this ideal, unfortunately, remains a rather elusive concept (cf. Aldag, 2012; Bartunek & Egri, 2012;

Nielsen, Buono, & Poulfelt, 2017) as critics contend either that rigorous academic research falls well short of relevance to the practitioner world or research that proves to be valuable to practitioners falls short of the rigor expected in academic life. This volume is intended to help bridge that divide.

Following Savall's opening discussion of qualimetric methodology (i.e., the integration of qualitative, quantitative, and financial data) and the nature of intervention-research, Véronique Zardet examines various research-intervention tools and approaches, drawing on ISEOR's work on socioeconomic enquiry. Jean-Michel Plane then looks at the role of intervention-research in the production of knowledge, drawing on an intervention in an Information Technology (IT) production department in a large insurance company to illustrate the underlying dynamics.

The next five chapters examine the ways in which intervention research can be initiated in a broad array of contexts. Florence Noguera looks at the principles and practices of intervention research in the human resource management arena, followed by Laurent Cappelletti's analysis of the dynamics underlying the process of negotiating an intervention-research engagement, exploring the ideal underlying this approach as scientific consultancy. As Cappelletti suggests, within the intervention-research paradigm the client organization is not only a traditional consultancy customer but also a "scientific observation area." Thierry Nobre and Isabelle Barth continue this focus in two different contexts. Nobre explores how researchers without the support of a well-developed research laboratory (such as ISEOR) can still engage client organizations in the intervention-research process, examining the need to reframe the typically subtle relationship between research, knowledge, and publication. Barth takes this dynamic in a different direction, looking at the challenges of engaging in intervention-research within one's own organization, treating it as a scientific observation area. Finally Marc Bonnet concludes this section by illustrating how intervention-research can be used to combat functional illiteracy in the workplace and contribute to our general body of knowledge, drawing on two chapters in a book published by the French Ministry of Employment.

The next section in the volume contains nine chapters that examine and illustrate the intervention-research publication process. My introductory chapter provides an overview of the challenges, subtleties, and nuances associated with publishing intervention research, from ways to conceptualize the iterative nature of practice-scholarship in creating actionable knowledge, to the different challenges associated with early and latter research stages, to the nuts and bolts of the publication and review process. The eight chapters that follow provide specific examples and deconstruction of peer-reviewed intervention-research journal articles.

In Chapter 10, Henri Savall shares his experience publishing intervention-research, drawing on a co-authored article that appeared in the

Organizational Research Methods (ORM) journal. The ORM article was based on a content analysis of reviewer comments/evaluations of intervention-research articles, which he uses to illustrate the rigor-relevance debate in management research and the main quality criteria that emerge in the peer review process. In the next six chapters, the contributors similarly share their experiences, illustrating how intervention-research was used in their work with companies and organizations and how that work was ultimately published in well-respected academic journals: Véronique Zardet (*Gérer et Comprendre* [Managing and Understanding]), Jean-Michel Plane (*Journal of Business Ethics*), Florence Noguera (*Human Resources Management*), Laurent Cappelletti (*Management Accounting Quarterly*), Thierry Nobre (*Accounting, Control & Auditing Review*), Marc Bonnet (*Society and Business Review*), and Isabelle Barth (*Revue Internationale de Psychosociologie et de Gestion des Comportements Organisationnels* [International Review of Psychosocial and Management of Organizational Behaviors]).

In the concluding section, co-editors Henri Savall and Laurent Cappelletti share and reflect on the various questions and comments raised by participants in the FNEGE-hosted workshops we've conducted over the past two years.

In addition to Savall and Cappelletti, I would like to, once again, add my personal thanks to my ISEOR and FNEGE colleagues for their support and contribution to a core objective of the RMC series—an attempt to capture the true blending of theory and practice in our organizational interventions in ways that are geared to and accessible by both academics and practitioners. Throughout my editorship of the RMC series, my ongoing goal has been to enhance our understanding of the potential and pitfalls of management consulting and the consultancy process, striving to provide insight into the dynamics and processes associated with successful intervention in today's complex and ever-changing organizations—and to share that (actionable) knowledge and insight with a broad array of practical scholars and scholarly practitioners. This volume is dedicated to that inquisitive audience.

REFERENCES

Aldag, R. J. (2012). Bump it with a trumpet: On the value of our research to management education. *Academy of Management Learning & Education, 11*(2), 285–292.

Bartunek, J. M., & Egri, C. P. (2012): Introduction: Can academic research be managerially actionable? What are the requirements for determining this? *Academy of Management Learning & Education, 11*(2), 244–246.

Dingwall, R. (1997). Accounts, interviews and observations. In G. Miller & R. Dingwall (Eds.), *Context and method in qualitative research*, pp. 51–65. London, England: SAGE.

Kieser, A., & Leiner, L. (2009). Why the rigor–relevance gap in management research is unbridgeable. *Journal of Management Studies, 46*(3), 516–533.

Nielsen, R., Buono, A.F., & Poulfelt, F. (2017, August). *At the knowledge interface: Developing co-created research competency.* Paper presented at the Academy of Management annual meeting, Atlanta, GA.

Ramage, M. (1995). *Hanging around doesn't mean sitting on the fence.* Cooperative Systems Engineering Group. Computing Department, Lancaster University. Technical Report: CSEG/13.

Savall, H. (1975). *Enrichir le travail humain: l'évaluation économique* [Job enrichment: An economic evaluation]. Paris, France: Dunod.

Savall, H., & Zardet, V. (1987). *Maîtriser les coûts et les performances cachés: Le contrat d'activité périodiquement négociables* [Mastering hidden costs and performance: The periodically negotiable activity contract]. Paris, France: Economica.

Savall, H., & Zardet, V. (2004). *Recherche en sciences de gestion: Approche qualimétrique—Observer l'objet complexe.* [Research in management sciences: The qualimetric approach—Observing the complex object]. Paris, France: Economica.

PART I

FRAMING THE INTERVENTION-RESEARCH CHALLENGE

CHAPTER 1

QUALIMETRIC INTERVENTION-RESEARCH

Integrated Epistemology and Generic Constructivism

Henri Savall

Research work relies on *scientific observation.* Science's progress reflects the evolution of realized progress in methods and instruments with a rigorous and accurate observation of the studied object. The history of the life and natural sciences stresses the importance given by researchers to scientific observation. It seems that in the human and social sciences, which includes economics and management studies, one did not necessarily grant the same importance to the rigorous observation of studied facts or phenomenon. Interpretation, often founded on the distant intellectual speculation of observable phenomenon, is hypertrophied in most widespread scientific practices in a wide range of disciplines.

Intervention Research, pages 3–27

IMPORTANCE OF SCIENTIFIC OBSERVATION IN MANAGEMENT SCIENCES

Intervention-research constitutes an epistemology and a research methodology based on the *intensification* of scientific observation by the researcher. It aims at raising the level of scientificity of research in the human, social and management sciences. Within this context, management science work consists of describing, explaining, and prescribing or forecasting, as the case may be, the studied phenomenon.

The *Raw Materials* of Scientific Work

Scientific research in the management sciences typically relies on a number of data sources, including: (a) documents written by organization's actors (with concerns about their accessibility because they are not in public access); (b) what actors are saying during their activities, which influence their practices (*oral discourse* and its volatile nature); and (c) what actors are actually doing during their activities (*observable acts* assuming one is able to be close enough to observe them). If we admit that Management Science is proposing to study actor *practices* linked to organizational performance, one might consider that the concept of practice covers these three observable objects: written documents, oral expression, and acts.

This concept of practice corresponds with an object that is mainly *incorporeal*, that immediately constitutes a methodological issue the management science researcher is observing. A rigorous research methodology implies that (a) the researcher *gets access in proximity to the actors-witnesses* of management practices, (b) these witnesses are willing to express themselves in the researcher's presence, (c) the researcher rigorously captures what the actors are saying, and (d) the researcher chooses investigation techniques that reduce subjectivity *bias* introduced by the always specific relation between researchers and actors.

Research works that rely only on existing *databases* or *questionnaires* ignore these fundamental and sensible epistemological questions. Indeed, using databases, if we judge the academic literature in Management Science, is not submitted to a preliminary and critical examination of *the quality of the raw material* used by the researcher, that is to say, the data's reliability, consistence, authenticity, and even sincerity. The reading of roughly a thousand papers published in high-ranked academic journals suggests that this question is rarely posed by the authors in a critical analysis of their very own methodology, neither sanctioned by reviewers. Using questionnaires gets those same epistemological weaknesses and limits.

Intervention-research aims at addressing these limits, with a lot of modesty, because erasing bias is proved impossible. However, by taking into account these biases and the *combination* of different research methodologies, the intervener-researcher is attempting to be *careful* and *modest* in analyzing an interpreting results. Intervention-research allows researchers to get *really* close to actors, to *make them speak*, to collect *in written form* their expression of facts and phenomena that are not reworded by the company, and after, to *make them validate* the written result of their expression. By dialoguing with the actors, the researcher collects "exclusive" documents that are not easily or directly accessible to most actors of the company, external people, and, less again to researchers who are far way or only passing through. By their presence, researchers are able to *directly observe phenomena* that no database is taking into account.

When intervention-research is practiced as *cumulative* and with *teamwork*, it allows researchers to create exclusive data bases, due to the researcher's *interaction* with organizational actors, owners of precious information that are interesting for the researcher and, for the major part, are deep in the actors' *memory*. These materials could not be collected by other process than constructive interaction between the researcher and actors, through a *knowledge coproduction process* (see Figure 1.1).

The heart of intervention-research is the *data*, and the process allows the intervener to *extract information* that remains inaccessible through simple *data-mining* methods that are never given to people. The researcher has to deserve it and obtain it through interactive scientific work. Information that interests the researcher relies at *gaze-state*, that is to say very instable

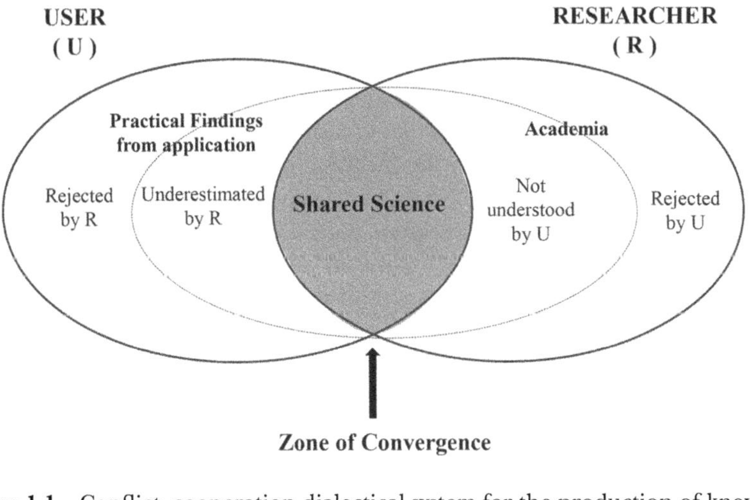

Figure 1.1 Conflict–cooperation dialectical system for the production of knowledge of scientific intent.

and difficult to work with, in *mind-set* and *memory* of the *actors-witnesses* of the facts and phenomena to be studied. When researchers take notes from the field, they give *materiality* and visibility to this "hidden" information. It enhances their degree of authenticity and significance and gives them stability for the research process. When researchers write what actors did not write elsewhere, it allows them to create *worthy research material.* When *databases* are built from such materials they also rise to a higher quality level than other databases. Arkhipoff (1985), mathematician and administrator of French Institute of Statistics and Economic Studies (INSEE), showed the fragility of the known data used by statisticians that only lead to quantified results and are—without any prudence—spread to all of society. As he has written, "Switching from Company Accountability to Nation one is far away to be as simple that people could sometimes imagine." This movement implies simultaneously the left-siding of initial microeconomics data and the existence of an area of indetermination, a source of a lack of precision. So there is an issue of the accountability degree of precision and a distinction between accountability rigor and precision of the numbers considered. Those difficulties are not exclusively proper to National Accountancy, but are already present in the problematic of corporate account consolidation.

HISTORY OF QUALIMETRIC-BASED INTERVENTION-RESEARCH

Following a decade of macroeconomic research on crisis theory and underemployment (Savall, 1973, 1975, 2011), I have concluded that the macroeconomic approach could not sufficiently highlight the value-creation process. In 1972, Malinvaud's research team (Carré, Dubois, & Malinvaud, 1972) by studying in great detail French Growth over 30 years, demonstrated that *grosso modo,* the half of value-creation calculated according econometric models, did not explain the variation of capital and labor quantities, applying the classic formula $Y = f(K * L)$, where the production overall value Y is a function of capital and labor quantities. There was an *unexplained deposit* that represented 50% of the overall value produced. American economist Solow (1956), among others, had detected a considerable gap in a former publication.

I would establish two deductions from it. First, one essential variable is missing in this traditional formula, rather admitted from various forms from classical economists, including Marxists, neoclassicals, and Keynesians. And that measurement tools such as National Accounting, set on businesses accountabilities, do not allow one to detect and to measure this unknown variable.

Reconstructive Criticism of National Accounting and Company Accounting

From what I understood, based on scientific progress accompanied by historic progress of measuring tools, I decided to penetrate the mystery of the 50% unexplained value. My work hypothesis was to change the level of analysis and observing point, by going into companies in order to observe processes and phenomena that go with value-creation. Indeed, national accounting relies on results of private and public organization accounting. So, we had to admit that the model of National and Organization Accountability was incomplete and that a rigorous scientific exposé was needed to discover other variables that helped to explain value-creation. Thus, I created *qualimetric-based intervention-research* in order to better study phenomena and measure value-creation inside organizations. This methodology creates a more relevant database than econometric models that are unfit to measure the finer aspects of complex problematics that generate economic value-creation.

It was also convenient to qualify the deposit related to unmeasured variables. That is why I proposed the concept of *hidden costs and performance.* The idea was quite simple, the observer, researcher or actor perceives some *visible* elements but not others that are *hidden.* Research, being a discovery process of new knowledge, I oriented our work to explore, identify and use the *hidden costs-performance* that were ignored in the Economic and Management Sciences literatures (Boje & Rosile, 2003; Perroux, 1979; Savall, 1975, 1979).

Action-Research and the Sociotechnical Approach: Two Sources in Organizational Science

Being conscious of the limits of observation methods, which remain *rough* and *distant* in the macroscopic approach of economics, and also being conscious of the theoretical deadlock, which confines the production function(that bestows privilege on quantities of capital and labor), I was searching in a nearby discipline for a methodology that fostered closer observation. *Work sociology* gave perspectives, starting from the critical approach of Georges Friedmann, and relayed by Jean-Daniel Reynaud, Michel Crozier, and Alain Touraine to their disciples of the Lyon School of Sociology, such as Philippe Bernoux or Jean Ruffier. These researchers came to the field of *scientific observation* within organizations and elaborated descriptive and explicative theories of observed situations (see Schein, 1994; Weick, 1999).

In the same perspective, the *sociotechnical school* was developing, since WWII, an interesting methodological approach, *action-research* whose target was transforming work situations. Experiments and publications were steered according to an open-systems approach (Emery & Trist, 1960, 1969) and mainly fed by work at the London Tavistock Institute and several experimentations in Scandinavian countries. The *ontological* dimension of research was clearly expressed—the need to improve working situations.

The sociotechnical approach was presenting a considerable lacuna, a deliberate conception of *economic performance* considered as a *constraint* and not as one of the essential dimension of the purpose of the studied work situation. This constituted an *epistemological obstacle* to developing the sociotechnical approach and action-research. Some recent and remarkable publications are pushing us toward a new ontological trend (Van de Van & Johnson, 2006) on useful characteristics of research on Management Science for practitioners. Researchers from the Action-Research School are quite in midstream: they have properly chosen closed-observation in order to study phenomena related to work situations. However, they still are attached to the *neutrality paradigm of researcher*, supposed to be a *sine qua non* situation of scientificity.

From these two pertinent approaches—action-research as methodology and the sociotechnical approach as a theory—I decided to enrich both by *integrating* two fundamental elements. First, the choice of investigation methods and analysis instruments as well as their rigor constitute a main component of theoretical construction. Second, the *economic* dimension is an essential element of work situations and the functioning of organization that constitutes their *existence* and their short-, mid-, and long-term performance. Intervention-research was thus born from action-research, by deepening the question of the impossible neutrality (supposed objectivity) of the researcher. Intervention-research fully assumes its *non*-neutrality and the consequences for limits of the research's objectivity. This methodology comes close to an approach that I qualified as *generic constructivism*, situated between positivism and constructivism, trying to exceed the relative superficiality of the first and the specific features of the second. This perspective was born in cognitive psychology (Piaget, 1988), from research on the construction of individual knowledge. Generic constructivism responds to the needs of Management Science research, whose main elaborating perimeter and transmission vector of knowledge is not the individual but the team or the organization (Savall, 1979; Savall & Zardet, 2003).

GENERIC CONSTRUCTIVISM: THE EPISTEMOLOGICAL PILLAR OF QUALIMETRIC INTERVENTION-RESEARCH

The practice of intervention-research by ISEOR researchers in approximately 2,000 organizations and applied in a variety of research topics builds on three principles that determine the epistemology of the type of research method: interactive-cognitivity, generic contingency, and contradictory intersubjectivity.

Interactive-cognitivity refers to the fact that the *collective* construction of knowledge results in an interactive process between two and more actors, each one holding a piece of knowledge and contributes, through successive *interactions*, to build up a shared knowledge between actors from a team or an organization. This dynamic justifies the necessity of a partnership between the researcher and the scientific observation field.

Generic contingency reflects the reality that although each situation is contingent on a number of variables, deep analysis reveals a generic component that we find in other situations, for example, as we find the same atom in different molecules. The principle of generic contingency is also subject to conditions of additivity of components from a sum, in other words, posing that [1 + 1 = 2] presupposes that the two terms are homogeneous.

Finally, *contradictory intersubjectivity* stands for the interactive process that allows two and more actors, starting from subjective and different points of view, to build, through iterations over time, a common and acceptable representation. Since objectivity is *impossible* especially in human and social sciences, this conventional representation, not being "objective," allows one to create a platform of knowledge from scientific intention that could be used by certain actors in a space and determined time.

Our concept of *generic constructivism* is based on these three principles (see Figure 1.2). It allows, by successive replication of intervention-researches in

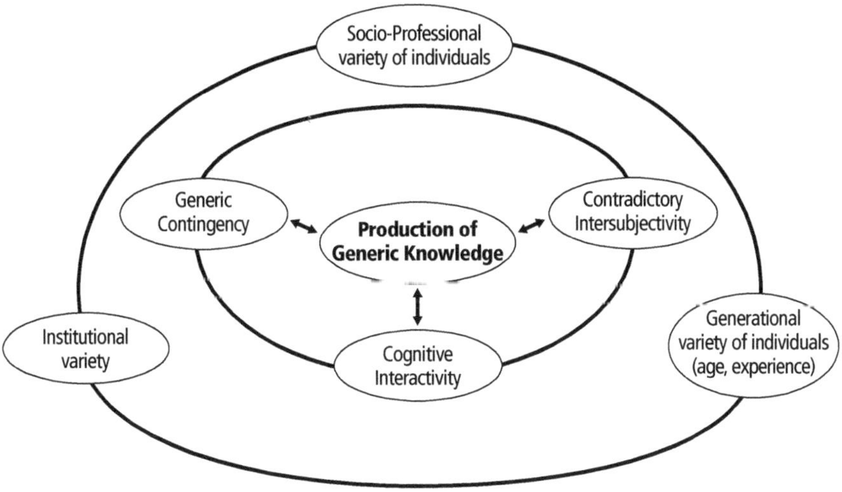

Figure 1.2 Integrating the variety of individual actors and groups into a generic knowledge production system.

situations always specific, to extract generic knowledges that could be transposed to other situations (see Kwesiga & Pattie, 2006, on the epistemological importance of replication). How could we know that knowledge is generic and not only specific or local? If actors are using it, one could say that this knowledge as a certain value. Knowledge is a convention since there will be an innovation recognized by the two communities—the researchers and the practitioners. Given the *dominant stream* of positivism, which is quantitative and logico-deductive, when we practice intervention-research, we have the charge to prove its scientificy. This proof must be robust, given the methodological traceability and the epistemologic foundations that are the key-points of intervention-research.

An Example of a Qualimetric Intervention-Research Product: Socioeconomic Theory of Organizations

The socioeconomic theory of organizations has been supported by a sociotechnical approach, by striving to complete and deal with in-depth criticisms of working organizations and propose new concepts and management models that integrate social and economic variables of organizations. Building the socioeconomic theory of organizations was based on a significant number of successive experimentations, being possible through the qualimetric intervention-research method and a certain stability of the research team (Savall, 1974; Savall & Zardet, 1987, 2008).

Studied Objects and Knowledge Construction: The Contribution of Qualimetrics

Scientific research is an activity that aims to produce new knowledge on identified products, whether new or not well studied issues. However, the word research may engender a *semantic confusion.* In the researchers' universe, *publishing* is associated with research, while research is better understood as a process, one of its expected products might be an academic publication. So, research refers to a production process that constitutes a *learning process* of new knowledge by the scientific-oriented investigator. Artificial intelligence proposes three interesting concepts: a *knowledge database* constituted by a *fact base* and *a rules base.* Indeed, knowledge consists of establishing a link between the different components of the material or incorporeal studied object (or evocated by actors). The simple statement "If A then B" is useful to represent a scientific *knowledge structure.* Thus, the well-known rule: *if* one heats pure water to 100° Celsius and *if* the atmospheric pressure is at 760 mm of mercury, *then liquid* water becomes gaseous *steam.*

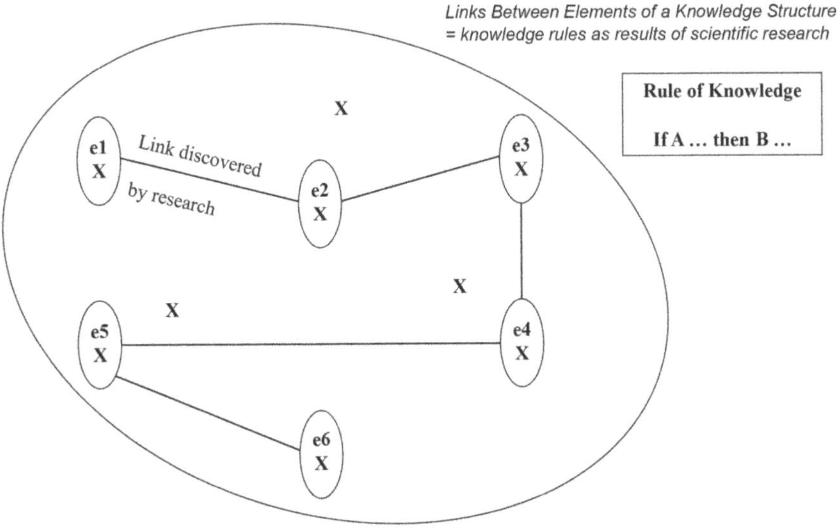

Figure 1.3 Links between elements of a knowledge structure.

Scientific work consists of determining the components of a knowledge structure as well as the *links* between these components (see Figure 1.3). The epistemological rigor invites us to overcome an *overly analytic* approach to knowledge, that is, a knowledge structure confined to a small number of components and links. Scientific progress consists of extending this tight field of knowledge in a more *holistic* vision that is considered more relevant.

The statement of knowledge consists of providing a *representation* of a fact or a phenomena spotted in a surrounding universe. A holistic representation of the studied object needs a continuum of qualitative (key-words), quantitative (key-numbers) and financial (numbers in monetary units) information—which we termed *qualimetric* as out conception of scientific-based representation. Meanwhile, a deplorable tradition tends to separate numbers and letters, people gifted in mathematics and people gifted in the arts, and quantitative and qualitative research (Savall, 1986a, 1986b; Gephart, 1988, 2004; Hammersley, 1992; Rynes, 2004; Savall, Bonnet, & Péron, 2004; Savall, Bonnet, Zardet, & Péron, 2007; Seale, 1999; Zardet & Krief, 2013). Qualimetrics consists of gathering these components that have been artificially separated, according to its underlying principle—a *key-word needs a number to make sense and a number needs a key-word to make sense.* Even a mathematical statement uses a combination of words, signs, and numbers.

A qualimetric intervention-research systematically uses a *qualimetric representation* in order to formulate the collected data and the results obtained by the investigation process. The qualimetric approach offers a rich span of qualitative, quantitative, and financial components that allow the researcher to better represent the observed objects and the theoretical statements produced by the research. This qualimetric approach of intervention-research constitutes progress in formulating scientific-based representations. It also facilitates the dialogue between researchers from interrelated fields and actors during the intervention-research process. Indeed, some researchers or actors are more sensitive to the literary statement and others more comfortable within numerical measurement. Representing an object by a *combination of key-ideas and key-numbers* allows one to take into account nuances and subtleties that an acceptable representation of complex facts and phenomena impose.

It is fully convenient to pinpoint the linguistic *obstacles* caused by the *polysemy* of words used as well as by the researchers and the actors. Indeed, we often use words in different ways, in their lexical register and as part of our own communication strategy. As such, this calls for preventive measures in communicating between researchers and actors. Thus the word *experimental* design, in current the world of economists and management modeling, can reflect a simulation *in vitro* made on a computer without a rigorous observation of studied situations. In contrast, true experimental methodology, built on Claude Bernard's works, evokes and refers to real situations studied *in vivo*, in living organizations full of actors in flesh and bones. The "real" is composed in sense of Aristotle by physical and virtual phenomena.

Research results also depend upon the *glance* that holds the researcher on the studied object, which could be relatively superficial, consisting of

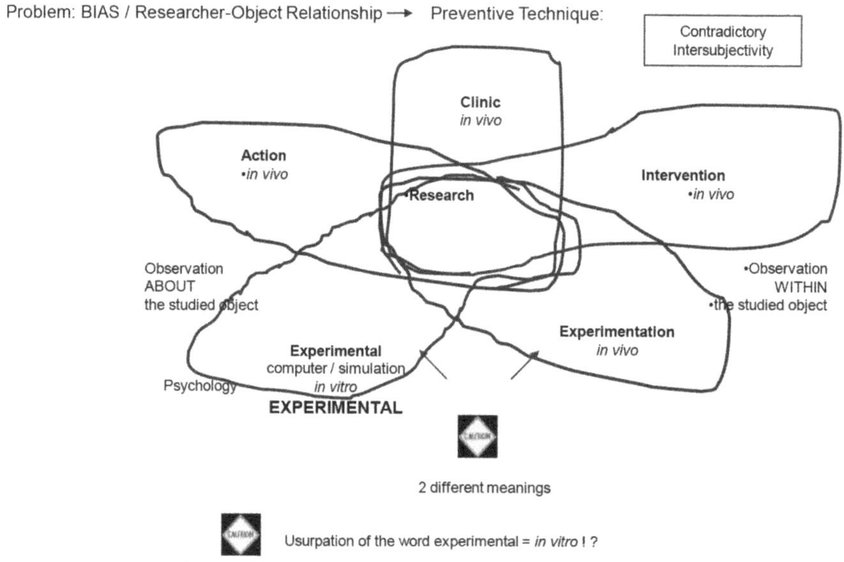

Figure 1.4 Conscious or unconscious semantic confusion?

skimming over the object without any plan to transform it (see Figure 1.4). In this case, a *contemplative* approach from the researcher is favored. On the contrary, one could deepen the knowledge of the material or incorporeal object by penetrating it, transforming (under condition of scientific *ethic*) in order to better know its properties, which can be revealing due to the researcher's intervention. The *positivist* stream exacerbates the *neutrality* of the researcher as a panacea synonym of scientificity. On the contrary, qualimetric intervention-research deliberately transforms some features of the studied object in order to better reveal its properties. The science of *Life and Nature* did not proceed in some other way. Physicists transformed the studied matter, as well as the chemist or biologist. In essence, these disciplines practice in a way that we call intervention-research (Moisdon, 1984, 2014; Savall, 1979; Savall & Fière, 2014). It is not acceptable, without any discussion, that the human and social sciences are considered *different by nature* from the science of Life and Nature, especially if we consider human biology, that is to, say medicine. This difference is a *petition of principle,* which has never been demonstrated.

Quality of the Relationship Between Research and the Field of Scientific Observation

The quality of the relationship between the researcher and actors of scientific observation field is a key factor in the quality of the research. The creation of scientific-based knowledge results from a back and forth interaction between the field of scientific observation and the researcher's lab, from alternating between observation sequences *in situ* and from detachment regarding the field that allows a refection stage with the proper distance. This process implies a periodical return of the researcher inside the organization, in order to organize *successive iterations* that enhance progressively the quality of collected information. Intervention-research cannot be satisfied with a limited, punctual stay of the researcher with the organizational actors. It implies a certain *longitudinality* that is necessary for the application of the three principle that found the *epistemological quality* of information analyzed by the scientific–oriented researcher: cognitivity interactivity, contradictory intersubjectivity, and generic contingency (Savall & Zardet, 1996, 2004, 2011).

Practicing intervention-research reveals the importance of the *legitimacy of the researcher* within the organization(s) that constitutes the field of the research, allowing their *proximity* with actors as *co-producers* of the knowledge. It matters that the intervener-researcher closes an *agreement* with the welcoming organization (Benghozi, 1990; Savall, 1979; Savall & Zardet, 2013). This *intervention-research agreement* determines the conditions of the collaboration and the reason for the researcher within the organization (see following chapter by Véronique Zardet). It might be subject to payment and produce a retribution for the researcher or laboratory, or be conducted free of charge. In this case, the cost for the company is not null, because the value of the time spent by actors collaborating with the researcher is always assumed by the company and is a part of the production cost of the research. The agreement results from a peer to peer discussion between the researcher and the company's CEO. The relationship between the field of scientific observation and the research is situated in a framework of *transparency*. The researcher's presence in the field is not clandestine nor discreet, it has been contractualized.

The Essential Tool of Scientific Work: The Hypothesis Concept

A *key-idea* elaborated by the researcher could cast in two positions, according to the state of research progress. First, it could constitute a *hypothesis*, a *dynamic* tool in scientific work process, a statement that steers the dynamic of the research. If the demonstration is achieved, the key-idea will get the status of a *scientific result or statement* that corresponds to one of the objectives of the research. The concept of hypothesis has been accepted by researchers from the *positivist* stream and holders of the *logico-deductive* approach. Some of these individuals are pushing researchers from other streams by forcing them to use the word *proposition* in place of hypothesis, in order that this one would be reserved for the positivist stream and its followers.

Yet qualimetric intervention-research considers that the hypothesis is an unavoidable tool to build a scientific statement. One only has to consider that the hypothesis is not fixed, that it evolves and is milestoned—its formulation is linked to a certain stage of the research process. Indeed, the dynamic of research makes researchers discover information that could drive them to pre-validate a hypothesis and continue the demonstration, invalidate and abandon it, or reformulate the initial one. Thus, the hypothesis comes with the learning process and knowledge creation by the researcher (see Figure 1.5). As such, the "final" hypothesis, which emerges at the beginning of the ending stage of the research, is likely to be different from the initial one, because it will be enriched by the intermediary results capitalized during the knowledge creation process, according to the researcher's discoveries.

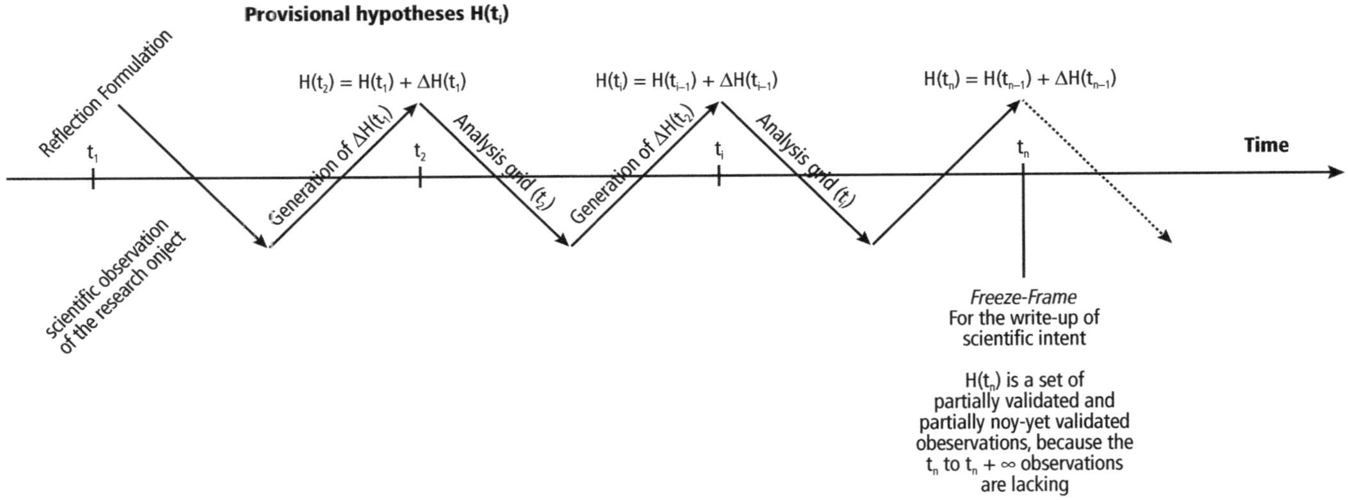

Figure 1.5 Heuristic process of laboratory–field alternation.

Modesty of the Researcher and Respect for Its Predecessors: The Academic Literature Analysis

The intervener-researcher does not ignore the fact that other researchers have treated the same object or closely related ones. The academic knowledge expressed by other researchers in books and articles helps to position the discoveries of the researcher regarding previous work in the field. The difficulty from an epistemological rigor point of view relies on the fact that the traceability of methodologies used by authors is limited, quite inexistent in some papers, even in highly ranked journals. Indeed, researchers know their own methodology and process through which they get their results, but typically do not have the same degree of knowledge about the methods that lead a peer to the statement found in literature.

Given that intervention-research favors scientific observation, the intervener-researcher is invited to sketch out the *hard core* of the research, emerging from fieldwork, and segment it into *themes* and *subthemes.* This constitutes a nomenclature that, as a "fishing net," allows one to seek materials in the academic literature that will *position* one's own research results with respect to those of other researchers. Around this hard core is a *thematic periphery of external bibliography* that consists of making an inventory of *pertinent* materials extracted from the literature. Thus, the researcher, by discovering interesting observations on the chosen object periodically takes into account what other researchers have written on the research thematic. The knowledge obtained by the researcher, thus favored in phasing of the research, avoids the risks of exegesis and scholasticism, by highlighting the results of research gained by direct observation of the studied object. Physicists, chemists, and biologists no matter do differently.

The stake of this option is the quality of *scientific progress* in management science, because researchers have intensified their progress since they enhanced their methods and tools of *experimentation.* For example, in a FNEGE barometer (Lamarque & Dubois, 2015, 2017), the first theme among needs expressed by companies focuses on customer relationships. This issue has not sufficiently been studied by the French management science researcher community. As this example suggests, there are two universes partially disjointed, one of identified issues by companies and organization, and those in which researchers have spontaneously invested their focus on.

The tool *thematic periphery* allows one to positon the results of the researcher by crossing the existing literature and identifying *proximities* and *gaps* or contradictions, then elaborating a scientific discussion and notifying, in all modesty, the limits and perspectives of the research (see Figure 1.6).

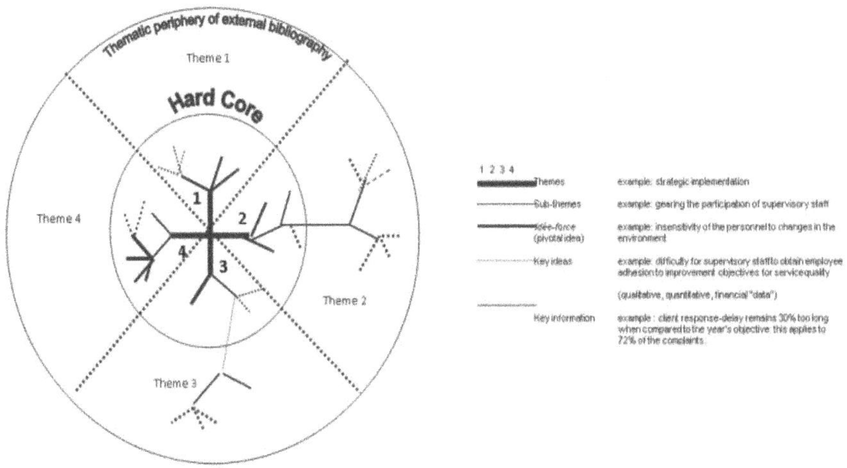

Figure 1.6 Arborescent tree-form of the endogenous construction of a scientific discourse and its positioning in relation to other authors.

Importance of Qualimetric Content Analysis in Intervention-Research

The profusion of collected data that allows intervention-research enables one to enrich and upgrade the method of *content* analysis, an approach well-known to researchers (Neuendorf, 2002). From qualitative information, *verbatims* or key-ideas expressed by actors or discovered in documents can be fused into *synthesis key-ideas* then pivotal-ideas more and more generic, and then classified into a nomenclature elaborated by the researcher. In a second step, *key-numbers* collected or elaborated by the researcher, will be associated with the generic key-ideas, producing a qualimetric view that provides a more satisfying *representation* of the studied object (see Figure 1.7).

Going deeper into the content analysis method lead us to classify the key-words, units at the base of qualitative information, in two categories. The first one includes *themes* and corresponds to the notion of *variable* in the quantitative sphere. The second consists of *ideas* that correspond to the notion of *value* of the variable in quantitative approach.

Research results constituted by *rules of knowledge* are synthetized as thematic *arborescence* in which are located *pivotal ideas.* Themes are divided into subthemes that contain key ideas and *verbatim.* Such representation of the studied object might be done at the beginning of the research with key ideas that the status of hypotheses, which corresponds to *an expectation of rules of knowledge* if the demonstration finishes. The arborescence will be

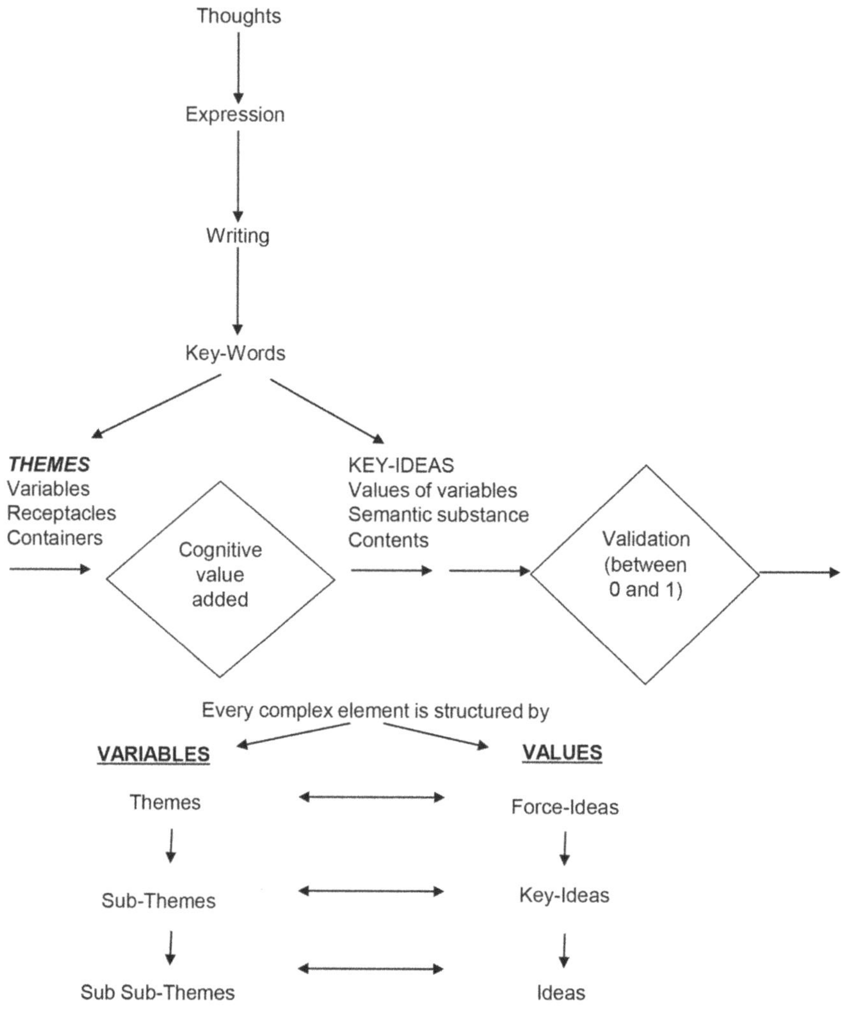

Figure 1.7 Process for the elaboration of cognitive value added: Structuring themes and key-ideas through content analysis then validation.

modified at the end of the research, representing one or several *validated rules of knowledge*. The gap between the beginning and the end of the research constitutes a value added that contributes to scientific progress (see Figure 1.8).

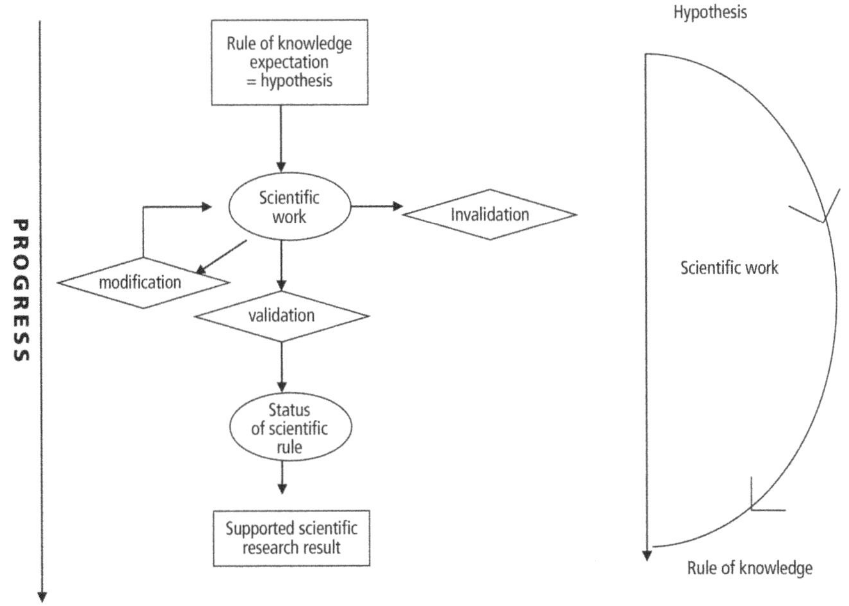

Figure 1.8 Value-added by scientific work: Process to evolve from an expectation to a proven rule of knowledge.

ANALOGY BETWEEN MANAGEMENT SCIENCE INTERVENTION-RESEARCH AND RESEARCH IN MEDICAL SCIENCE

Numerous intervention-researches have been carried out in the healthcare industry by ISEOR researchers. The analogy emerged from our proximity with healthcare professionals and our cooperation with research in human biology. Progress in medical science is useful to explain and justify in terms of the scientific interest of intervention-research. In management science there is a lack of consensus on many important concerns, while in biology research protocols are well established, rigorous, and practiced by the overwhelming majority of researchers (Thiébaut, 2010).

The *transformative* dimension of intervention-research consists of modifying the state of the studied object in order to realize observations. The analysis of those variations of state allows one to extract the knowledge of certain *properties* of the studied object. These insights are not accessible to the "traveling" observer, limited to superficial observation methods that one could qualify as *contemplative.* Physicists, chemists, or biologists know that they will discover the essential characteristics of the studied object only by handling, using fitted observation tools, or injecting reactive substances in order to create common knowledge and deserve the name of scientific research that calls for *sustainable progress* for mankind. We thought that the notion of anthropocentric science allows a kind of analogy between human and social science (whose economy and management belong) and medical science (Savall & Fière, 2014).

Another common point is *longevity*. Indeed, research in human biology and medical science focuses on patient longevity that allows one to define, from an *ontologic* point of view, life conditions that are *deontologically* acceptable in terms of autonomy and dignity. Thus, the key-spot of the pertinence of researches in human biology is the *survival-development* of the individual, that is to say, its capacity to extend one's life expectancy in terms of physiologic autonomy and social dignity. By analogy, the essential orientation of management science might be defined as extending an organization's life expectation and its social (*dignity*) and economic (*resources autonomy*) performance.

The working hypothesis that inspired ISEOR's work is that *transformative* and qualimetric intervention-research presents analogies with medical research. So we began with 30 intervention-research projects in the healthcare industry with interviews with medical researchers. Transformative research consists of defining the life conditions of a preferable state that will never be considered as an absolute optimum but rather as a relative optimum, which could be realized "here and now"—with, of course, modesty by the scientific researcher. The transformative approach of intervention-research consists of creating new knowledge that allows companies and organizations, singular human communities, to be managed in order to create a sustainable best-being. As for medical research, management science intervention-research is practiced with a double systematic meaning: dispensing care in order to improve the health condition of a company or organization, and simultaneously, discovering new diseases or variations of known diseases, validating the effectiveness, efficiency and pertinence of management methods, tools and practices regarding sustainable performance expected by company actors as for researchers that accompany them.

More than 44 years of transformative intervention-researches has allowed ISEOR to establish the role of a "back-and-forth" interaction between the laboratory and the scientific observation field (SOF) that creates *innovative knowledge,* sometimes exploratory, sometimes validating, according to the stage of progress of scientific-based knowledge applied to the studied object. Interaction with the *scientific observation field* is essential because the actor gets and holds, more or less consciously, information and knowledge useful to the researcher. This why cooperation between actors and researchers in the company or organization (the social observation field) is so important. In the perspective of epistemological rigor, the scientific intervention-research process consists of active cooperation, conscious and deliberated, in a knowledge *co-creation* system.

For the management science researcher (or more generally human and social sciences researchers), the studied object is living, actively and consciously, an *object-subject* whose cooperation is necessary for scientific work effectiveness. By contrast, physicists and chemists deal with more inert objects that seem not to be conscious. This difference may explain the success of the positivist approach that ramps up during the second part of the 19th century, an era of great progress in the *life and natural Sciences.* Even without rigorous analysis, the fact that the human and social sciences are by nature different from the life and natural sciences is partly explained by the relative delay of the social sciences (including management sciences) in noticing progress in the other sciences.

Human biology (medicine) is also conditioned by the limits of experimentation, being half-way between those two categories of science that history had overly differentiated. The risk for the social sciences is to lose the main scientific feature whose first condition is *observing, resisting against theoretical innovation,* perpetrating the transfer of theories and concepts without sufficient *critical spirit* from the learner and applier. This dynamic can create a risk for *mainstream* theory resurgence, with the threat of reducing scientific-based theories into ideologies, by failing to cultivate *conceptual and theoretical innovation.* The naturally not-demonstrated postulate of the fundamental difference of the social sciences and life sciences is enabling academically admitted and maintained research methods that are superficial, in essence, not developing sufficient rigor and a deep observation of the studied object.

Validation of elaborated knowledge is done by experimentation (internal validation) and replication (external validation). In the ISEOR research program (Savall 1975, 1979; Savall & Zardet, 1987, 2008; Savall, Zardet, & Harbi, 2004), the identification of dysfunctions and hidden cost-performance was carried out with rigorous, in-depth, longitudinal observation and study of 1,854 companies and organizations from 42 countries and 72 different sectors of activity. Roughly 110,000 people were involved in organizational change actions as research partners. This program, carried out with nearly 600 researchers, made it possible to identify that, despite the differences in countries, sectors, size and legal status of companies and organizations (for-profit, public sector), there were similar *pathologies* that permanently threatened their survival-development capacity and the jobs of the concerned actors.

One important key of intervention-research consists of determining three levels of hypotheses, with different and complementary natures: descriptive, explicative, and prescriptive.

- The notion of *descriptive hypothesis* reflects modesty of the researcher in the description of an object, because researcher could propose a different description.
- The *explanatory hypothesis* consists of stating explanations and interpretations regarding phenomena, which is usually appreciated in the researcher community.
- The *prescriptive hypothesis* constitutes the highest level of this epistemology. It includes recommendations about next steps at the end of the scientific work. According to some researchers, paradoxically, this kind of hypothesis does not belong in research.

The *central hypothesis*, which sets out the essence of the demonstration that researcher wishes to make, is a tree of descriptive, explanatory, and prescriptive hypotheses. Thus the management science researcher will prescribe how one could modify the situation observed in a change project. Similarly, in medical research, does the patient-actors agree to take the drug? How will the effects be assessed? Research can stop at the *diagnosis* stage, or from the *project* without experimentation, or from the *implementation*, or even up to the qualitative, quantitative and financial *evaluation* of the experimentation results (see Figure 1.9). What is required in this

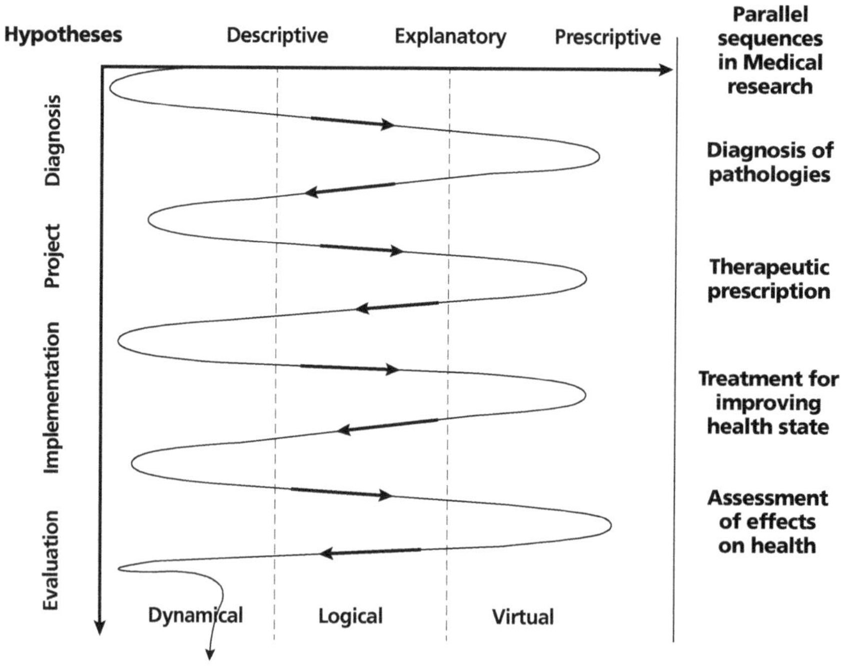

Figure 1.9 Scientific demonstration genesis in order to get robust knowledge.

epistemology is to make a complete horizontal approach to one or more of the four stages, going more or less far, depending on the time available and the organizational context.

The ambition of the scientific project depends on the state of knowledges regarding the studied object. Thus, research on a little studied object can be content to elaborate a scientific contribution only at the stage of what we call here the diagnosis. Thus in medicine, the discovery of a new pathology or a significant variant of an existing pathology can constitute an essential contribution through the simple descriptive analysis of the pathology's features. In this case, modestly, the explanatory analysis will be part of a new research program, carried out by a large number of researchers. The spearhead of the explanatory analysis is constituted by the prescriptive analysis that will consist of defining a care-protocol to improve the patient's health. It is surprising that some academics in the management sciences, in France and in other countries, deny the scientific character of prescription, which is indispensable for any experiment. They rather consider, without discussion, that the research must stop at the explanatory analysis or interpretative stage. In our opinion, this view is obsolete and harmful. Moreover, it constitutes a real obstacle to the progress of management science, as the needs of companies and organizations for innovative models, principles, concepts, methods, and practices are immense. Yet, these needs do not coincide with the major part of the academic research field, as shown by the barometer of the National Foundation for the Teaching of the Management of the Enterprises (FNEGE).

Applied Research Replication

The above analogy also deals with the question of the validity of theoretical statements. In the human, social, economic and management sciences, the fundamental and the abstract are often confused, abstraction being considered as the signal of fundamental knowledge. In contrast, in medical science and in management intervention-research, basic research often follows an inductive approach based on concrete situations. In qualitative intervention-research epistemology, it is in the concrete/abstract bond that the robustness of generic knowledge is tested. Fundamental research and knowledge are then defined in terms of the large number and variety of applications they allow.

An important aspect of the analogy with medical research is that this type of research consists of making diagnoses, prescriptions, and treatment and evaluating their effects. This is the same approach as intervention-research, which consists of describing, explaining, and predicting. Both research methods have a common scientific approach—the human body while respecting its integrity and the social body whose integrity is to be preserved or built. Scientific progress in medicine has been discontinuous: we went from Hippocrates in antiquity to Pasteur and Claude Bernard. A period of obscurantism occurred, especially in Middle Ages, between Hippocrates and Claude Bernard (1865, 1947). During this long period, medicine was only taught by the exegesis of texts.

Hippocrates had stated from antiquity that the patient must be spoken to in order to realize a diagnosis, just as the actors are called to speak in qualitative research. We rediscovered the experimental method in the 19th century. The treatment of pathologies is an integral part of medical science. Physiology is defined by pathologies. Good health is defined in terms of the absence of pathologies. It is the *applied research* that leads to *fundamental research,* using an *inductive* process. Medical instrumentation and publication, both sources of dialogue have made considerable progress, and medical research networks are dynamic and numerous (Landrivon & Delahaye, 1995). Their exchanges make it possible to create tentative consensus on theories and methods. Descriptive study is clearly important, as we always start from a diagnosis, even to introduce a solution that has succeeded in a large number of cases, as well as for intervention-research applied to socio-economic theory.

REFERENCES

Arkhipoff, O. (1985). Un, deux, trois, beaucoup ou comment l'imprécision vient aux comptables [One, two, three, many or how inaccuracy comes to accountants]. Économies et sociétés*: Sciences de gestion, 19*(6), 21–33.

Benghozi, P. J. (1990). La négociation d'une recherche: une étape clé dans la méthodologie d'intervention [Negotiating a research process: A key step of an intervention-research]. *Economies et Sociétés: Revue Sciences de gestion, 15,* 35–47.

Bernard, C. (1855, 1860, 1947). *Principes de médecine expérimentale* [Experimental principles medicine]. Paris: PUF.

Boje, D. M. (2004, 2011). Qualimetrics contributions to research methodology. Preface to H. Savall & V. Zardet, *Recherche en sciences de gestion: approche qualimétrique, observer l'objet complexe.* Paris: Economica. English translation: *The qualimetrics approach: Observing the complex object.* Charlotte, NC: Information Age.

Boje, D. M., & Rosile, G-A. (2003). Comparison of socio-economic and other trans-organizational development methods. *Journal of Organizational Change Management, 16*(1), 10–20.

Buono, A. F., & Savall, H. (Eds.) (2007). *Socio-economic intervention in organizations: The intervener-researcher and the SEAM approach to organizational analysis.* Charlotte, NC: Information Age.

Buono, A., & Savall, H. (Eds) (2015). *The socio-economic approach to management revisited: The evolving nature of SEAM in the 21st century.* Charlotte, NC: Information Age.

Carré, J. J., Dubois & Malinvaud, E. (1972). *Analyse causale de la croissance française* [Causal Analysis of French Gross]. Paris, France: Seuil.

Emery, E. F., & Trist E. L. (1960, 1969). *Socio-technical systems.* New York, NY: Penguin.

Gephart, R. (1988). *Ethnostatistics: Qualitative foundations for qualitative research.* Newbury Park, CA: SAGE.

Gephart, R. (2004). Qualitative research and the Academy of Management Journal. *Academy of Management Journal, 47,* 454–462.

Girin, J. (1982). Le dit et le non dit [The Said and the Unsaid]. *Economies et Sociétés, Revue Sciences de gestion, 3,* 1602–1604.

Hammersley, M. (1992). Deconstructing the qualitative–quantitative divide. In J. Brannen (Ed.), *Mixing methods: Qualitative and quantitative research* (pp. 127–143). Aldershot, England: Avebury.

Kwesiga, E., & Pattie, M. (2005). Is management science built on a shaky foundation? The Case for intersubjective certifiability. *Revue Sciences de gestion-Management sciences-Ciencias de gestión, 50,* 33–68.

Lamarque, E., & Dubois, P.-L. (2014, 2017). *Baromètre FNEGE: les attentes des entreprises en matière de recherche en management* [FNEGE Study: The Weights of organizations as regarding management sciences]. Paris, France: FNEGE.

Landrivon, G., & Delahaye, F. (1995). *La recherche clinique: de l'idée à la publication.* (Clinical research: From Conceptualization to Publication). Paris, France: Masson.

Moisdon, J. C. (1984). Recherche en gestion et intervention [Research in management and intervention]. *Revue Française de Gestion, 47/48,* 61–73.

Moisdon, J. C. (2014). Note de la rédaction (à propos de l'article Savall & Fière) (Editorial Note on Savall, H., & Fière, D.'s article). *Journal de Gestion et d'Économie médicales, 32*(5–6), 353.

Neuendorf, K. A. (2002). *The content analysis guidebook.* Thousand Oaks, CA: SAGE.

Perroux, F. (1970). Les conceptualisations implicitement normatives et les limites de la modélisation en économie [The implicit normative conceptualizations and the limits of modelizing in economy]. *Economies et Sociétés,* revue de l'ISMEA, *IV,* 12.

Perroux, F. (1979). L'entreprise, l'équilibre rénové et les « coûts cachés [The firm, the renewed equilibrium and the hidden Costs]. Préface de l'ouvrage de H. Savall, *Reconstruire l'entreprise, analyse socio-économique des conditions de travail.* Paris, France: Dunod.

Piaget, J. (1988. *L'épistémologie génétique* [Genetical epistemology]. Paris, France: PUF.

Riveline, C. (1984). *Pour une ethnographie des organisations* [For an ethnography of firms]. Paris, France: Document de travail, École des Mines de Paris.

Rynes, S. (2004). Qualitative research and the Academy of Management Journal (editor's note). *Academy of Management Journal, 47*(4), 454.

Savall (1974, 1975, 1981, 2010). *Enrichir le travail humain dans les entreprises et les organisations.* Paris, France: Dunod. 3° édition Paris: Economica, 1989. English translation: *Work and people; An economic evaluation of job enrichment.* New-York: Oxford University Press; 2nd edition, Charlotte, NC: Information Age.

Savall, H. (1979). *Reconstruire l'entreprise, analyse socio-économique des conditions de travail.* Paris, France: Dunod. Nouvelle édition: Savall, H., & Zardet, V.

Reconstruire l'entreprise: les fondements du management socio-économique [Rebuilding companies : The roots of SEAM). Paris, France: Dunod.

Savall, H. (1986a). Contrôle de qualité des informations qualitatives, quantitatives et financières extraites des acteurs au sein des organisations [The uality control of qualitative, quantitative and financial data sets collected from the actors of organizations). In *Qualité des informations scientifiques en gestion, Méthodologies fondamentales en gestion.* Paris, France: FNEGE, ISEOR, CNRS.

Savall, H. (1986b). Un regard sur la recherche en sciences de gestion en France dans les années 80 [An overview of management sciences in France during the 80s]. In *La recherche en sciences économiques et en gestion.* Paris, France: Éditions du CNRS.

Savall, H. (2003). An updated presentation of Socio-Economic Management Model. *Journal of Organizational Change Management, 16*(1), 33–48

Savall, H., Bonnet, M., & Péron, M. (Eds.) (2004). *Crossing frontiers in qualitative and quantitative research methods.* Proceedings of the AOM-RMD/ ISEOR International Conference. Lyon, France: ISEOR.

Savall, H., Bonnet, M., Zardet, V., & Péron, M. (Eds.). (2007). *Innovative research methods to create valid and operational knowledge.* Proceedings of the AOM-RMD/ ISEOR International Conference. Lyon, France: ISEOR.

Savall, H., Zardet, V. (1987, 2016). *Maîtriser les coûts et les performances cachés, Le contrat d'activité périodiquement négociable.* Prix Harvard l'Expansion de Management Stratégique. Economica, 6ème édition 2016. English translation: *Mastering Hidden Costs and Socio-Economic Performances.* Charlotte, NC: Information Age.

Savall, H., & Zardet, V., (1996). La dimension cognitive de la recherche-intervention: La production de connaissances par interactivité cognitive [The cognitive dimension of intervention-research: The production of knowledges thanks to cognitive interactivity. *Revue Internationale de Systémique, 10*(1/2), 157–189.

Savall, H., & Zardet, V. (2003). The contribution of dialectic synthesis to positivist and qualitative methods towards enhanced scientific quality in management research. Milan: *EURAM Congress,*

Savall, H., & Zardet, V. (2004). *Recherche en sciences de gestion : approche qualimétrique, observer l'objet complexe.* Préface David Boje. Paris, France: Economica. English translation: *The qualimetrics approach: Observing the complex object.* Charlotte, NC: Information Age.

Savall, H., & Zardet, V. (2013). How to negotiate explicit scientific consultancy contracts with companies? Advantages and constraints for both: companies & researchers. Paper presented at the Academy of Management Conference, Orlando, FL.

Savall, H., Zardet, V., & Harbi, N. (2004). Analyse transversale de diagnostics économiques: Approche qualimétrique appliquée à des données qualitatives. In *CrossingFfrontiers in qualitative and quantitative research methods.* Proceedings of the AOM-RMD/ ISEOR International Conference (pp. 571–588). Lyon, France: ISEOR.

Schein, H. F. (1994). *Listening from the Field.* Boulder, CO, Westview Press.

Seale, C. (1999). *The Quality of Quantitative Research.* London: SAGE.

Solow, R. M. (1956). A Contribution to the Theory of Economic Growth. *The quarterly journal of economics, 70*(1), 65–94.

Thiébaut-Bertrand, A. (2010). Contribution à l'analyse de reconfiguration d'activité permettant de préserver et d'améliorer le rapport qualité des prestations/maîtrise des coûts à l'hôpital. Cas de la transfusion sanguine dans les hôpitaux publics français (Contribution to a reingeneering process allowing to foster the quality of health services in hospitals). *Thèse de doctorat en sciences de gestion,* Université de Grenoble Joseph Fourier.

Van de Ven, A., & Johnson, P. (2006). Knowledge for theory and practice. *Academy of Management Review, 1*(4), 802–821.

Weick, K. (1989). Theory construction as disciplined imagination. *Academy of Management Review, 14,* 551–561.

Zardet, V., & Krief, N. (2013). Analyse de données qualitative et recherche-intervention [Analysis of qualitative data sets and intervention-research). *Recherches en sciences de gestion-Management sciences-Ciencias de gestión, 95,* 211–237.

CHAPTER 2

NEGOTIATING AND CONDUCTING AN INTERVENTION-RESEARCH PROCESS

The Case of Socioeconomic Intervention-Research

Véronique Zardet

The aim of this chapter is to present and analyze the specificities of intervention-research as a scientific research method, clearly different from the practices of consulting and action-research (Savall, Zardet, Péron, & Bonnet, 2012). The discussion also examines the strengths and limits of this approach, both for companies and researchers. The content for this chapter is based on the personal experience of the author, involving more than 35 years of intervention-research practices with the team at ISEOR—the Socioeconomic Institute for Firms and Organizations. Created in 1975 in Lyon, France, ISEOR focuses on applying the concept of intervention-research to generate scientific knowledge in management and to simultaneously help

Intervention Research, pages 29–45

companies conduct their change processes, improve their performance, and solve their major issues (see Buono & Savall, 2007, 2015).

To date, more than 600 researchers have participated in the work of this team, more than 150 PhD thesis have been defended, and several thousands of research reports, papers and articles have been published. This conception of research is rare—in France and across the world—in the management discipline and has not yet acquired full recognition in academia.

After examining the specificities of negotiating a research-intervention contract with a company, the chapter looks at the characteristics of intervention-research, also referred to as "scientific consultancy," probing the link between the intervention-research activity and publication. The chapter concludes with a discussion of the challenges of intervention-research, explaining the economic model of such a practice, which opens up new horizons at a time when public research budgets are increasingly constrained.

NEGOTIATING A CONTRACT: A KEY PHASE FOR THE SUCCESS OF INTERVENTION-RESEARCH

Like a consultant, an intervener-researcher has different ways of contacting a company: prospecting sometimes, usually through a recommendation from a current or former client, or, especially in the case of ISEOR, spontaneous calls from companies. After initial contact, the negotiation of the intervention-research contract is a long process, which constitutes a key factor in the success of the intervention itself.

One of the challenges of any client engagement is what constitutes a successful intervention—and this becomes even more important in the context of intervention-research. We propose that an intervention-research project is evaluated according to two simultaneous success criteria (David, 2000; Moisdon, 1984; Plane, 2000; Savall, 1986; Savall & Zardet, 1996, 2004). First, the aim is to achieve the objectives of the company in terms of improvements, which are made explicit during the negotiation process. Second, the objective of the researcher is to transform the company in order to produce new knowledge. Thus, there are three main specificities in the process of negotiating an intervention-research: (a) a process of successive iterations, (b) a phase of listening to the company representatives, and (c) the negotiation of methodological specifications.

A Process of Successive Iterations

At least three to four meetings are required first with the introducer and then with the decision-maker, in essence a "commercial relationship," to initiate a genuine dialogue that will lead to an agreement on the progress of an intervention-research, concretized by the drafting and signing of a methodological specification. The negotiation process often lasts 4 to 6 months, regardless of the size of the company, and 6 to 12 months in complex organizations. The quality of the negotiation is a key-factor in intervention-research success, because it is at this stage that the content and methods of the intervention-research are precisely defined in consultation and the principal leaders' willingness to change is tested. In contrast, it happens, admittedly, rarely, that an overly rapid negotiation leads to failure, that is to say, a refusal to sign on the part of the company or an interruption after the start of the intervention-research.

An Essential Listening Phase

The intervention-research negotiations, as we practice them, start with a one-to-two-hour listening session, during which the intervener-researcher listens to the *introducer* who has previously contacted the research team, before any discussion of a service offer, an intervention-research method, or even a budget. Strangely, some leaders express themselves very openly and spontaneously from this first contact, providing information and opinions to the researcher they probably have never expressed before. This listening appointment, besides the fact that the leaders express their issues to an "unknown" third party, also reveals expectations and challenges that will later become the objectives of the intervention-research.

Frequently, all the problems mentioned are challenges, strategic objectives, and goals for the company, expressed in the *natural language* of the interlocutor. For example, the head of a small construction company told us during this first interview that he was in a very precarious economic situation with his associates and that the president did not fully assume his responsibilities. The aim of the intervention-research was therefore to consolidate the managerial role of the firm's managers and redefine the roles of its associate in the company's functioning.

About 15 days after this listening interview, the intervener-researcher came back to the decision maker to propose an intervention-research project to produce a *mirror-effect.* This project was formulated as a tripartite mix of product-objectives, methods and services (Table 2.1; also see Chapters 5 & 6).

The objectives are formulated starting from the problems expressed by the leader during the first listening interview, providing him with the mirror of his own expression. The dialogue focuses on the content of the planned intervention-research, without any indication of price being given at this stage, regardless of the pressure exerted by the interlocutor of the

TABLE 2.1 A Simplified Example of a Tripartite Intervention-Research Mix

Objectives	Methods	Services
Objectives of the company	Methods used by intervener-researchers	Actions and operations realized by the intervener-researchers team
A Recovering the economic situation of the company B Increase cohesion of partners	• Integral dysfunctions diagnosis: Dysfunctions and hidden-costs • Innovating project-group	• Conducting interviews with the executive team, management and 30% of the staff • Treatment of interviews • Presentation of the mirror effect of the diagnosis • Collection of quantified data • Hidden costs calculation • Methodological animation of 5 project sessions conducted by the project manager and integrating supervisors from different departments and services

company at this subject. Indeed, it is essential that a genuine in-depth exchange takes place on the objectives and proceedings of the intervention-research, "cleared" of possible budgetary considerations at this stage.

A third or even a fourth or fifth interview is necessary to reach agreement on the intervention-research mission, validated by both parties and adapted to the specificities of the company with an agreed upon budget. If the latter is too high compared to the company's requirements, complementary iterations make it possible to redefine the contours of the mission or even its parameters until a satisfactory agreement is reached. It is important to allocate sufficient time for this key phase of the project, ensuring sufficient interaction and reciprocal exchanges with different people in the company.

Negotiation of Methodological Specifications

The negotiation phase is aimed at creating an intervention-research project that is defined and agreed to by the company and the team of intervener-researchers. Focus is placed on the objectives of the research, the methodology designed to satisfy those objectives, and the activities or deliverables that will be implemented by the intervener-researchers during the project.

It is therefore understandable that this negotiation, carried out through the iterative process described above, deals with a precise methodological specification, proposed by the researchers, based on the objectives set out by the company and re-formulated in conjunction with the research team.

The issue is to agree, prior to the start of the research, on the working methods and parameters of the intervention-research, the key-actors who will be interviewed and involved in the various stages, and the practical ways of delivering feedback to the company at different steps in the process. The characteristics of the intervention-research are tailored for each company or organization, but are still based on the methodological principles specific to the research team. The basic form used to formalize this specification, focused (a) product-objectives, (b) product-methods, and (c) products-services is illustrated in Table 2.1 (see Savall & Zardet, 2004).

The content of each intervention-research project is thus adapted to each concrete situation, but always include scientific and "nonnegotiable" elements that must be precisely explained and justified with the future partners of the intervention-research. In case of refusal, the negotiation is stopped. This is a fundamental difference between intervention-research and traditional consultancy, in which the consultant usually adapts to the client's demands and expectations in order to secure the engagement and, of course, the associated fees.

Let us take the example of a broken negotiation due to a failure to agree on methodological, scientific, and "nonnegotiable" elements. An industrial company with about 300 employees, a subsidiary of a major international group, contacted ISEOR after implementing a *lean management* approach. The group's headquarters required the subsidiary to increase its productivity and reduce work accidents. During the first 90 minutes of the listening interview, the leader reviewed the organization of the industrial site and his strategic project for the next 2 years. A few days later, he contacted us to explain that he did not want to involve the company's production sector, which he thought was already disturbed by frequent changes over the recent years. He wanted to limit the intervention-research to the support services group. After discussion with the leader, our research team decided not to proceed with the project, considering that the objectives of improving productivity and reducing work accidents could not be achieved without a socioeconomic intervention in the production sector.

Although the signed specifications have contractual and legal scope, it is also a methodological tool to conduct an intervention-research. Thus, it is regularly reviewed and evaluated in meetings of the steering committee of the intervention-research, jointly with the company. The process can involve negotiated adaptations and thus constitutes a real work tool and a reference source to prevent of any project drift.

A Business Relationship

An intervention-research contract is also a business relationship, all the more so when the services provided are invoiced. Contrary to conventional wisdom, the research team is not weakened, quite the opposite, by this business relationship. Conversely, by ensuring that the financial clauses of the contract are respected, the research team establishes a balanced partnership relationship with the company. To guarantee the independence of the researchers, the intervention-research activity only starts when the initial deposit has been paid. Effective regular payment of invoices by the client company is a guarantee of its involvement and respect for the work of the intervention-research team. In case of nonpayment, this question is explicitly discussed in an interview with the leader. If the company encounters financial problems, a new payment schedule can be negotiated. On the other hand, if it appears that the company does not intend to honor its commitments, the intervention-research is suspended. Any delay or interruption of payment proves to be a true indicator of a degraded scientific partnership.

The issue of the financial negotiation of an intervention-research is always a sensitive's one in the academic world. Indeed, while it may be considered in some situations that an intervention-research can be conducted without financial compensation, one must nevertheless ask the question, "Who pays the intervener-researchers?" On the other hand, a work of intervention-research that has value for the company must be legitimately financed by the company, rather than considering, as some companies or organizations do, that the work of researchers, unlike consultants, would "naturally" be free. The free status also sometimes leads to limiting the undertaking of the company, for example, by frequently postponing or canceling work sessions. Is it not said that "what is free has no value"? Thus, how to negotiate in some complex situations some form of compensation financed by the company? This is the issue that interests all academic researchers interested in practicing intervention-research. Moreover, the latter is a modality for bringing resources to public or private research teams and, in particular, to remunerating the intervener-researchers. In this respect, they constitute an alternative or a complement to public funding, under the common name of contract research, in opposition to conventional wisdom that (academic) research should be free because it is financed by one's taxes.

INTERVENTION-RESEARCH: A TEAM-BASED APPROACH

Intervention-research is an *in vivo* research methodology that proposes to produce knowledge by transforming the object studied (Savall & Zardet, 2004, 2011). An analogy can be made with clinical research methods in medicine (Savall & Fière, 2007, 2014), in which medical researchers treat patients and, by observing the effects of therapeutic protocols, formulate conclusions and publish their findings in scientific journals. Medical researchers are *simultaneously* conducting diagnostic-prescription-evaluation processes by providing patient care and research activities that aim to produce replicable results on other patients (Kwesiga & Pattie, 2006).

Longitudinal Research

Intervention-research is a *longitudinal* research method that observes and analyzes a business or organization over a long period of time. Thus, our research-interventions can last from 1 year to 3 decades, as seen in the case of a long-term scientific partnership (Savall & Zardet, 1995, 2005, 2017). Longitudinal intervention-research missions involve conducting actions and accompanying profound changes within companies and organizations. They have two simultaneous objectives, which is a real challenge: (a) helping the company achieve its objectives of improvement or transformation through internal dynamics (Coghlan & Brannick, 2005) and (b) producing new knowledge that can induce new descriptive, explanatory, and prescriptive hypotheses (Savall & Zardet, 1996, 2004). In intervention-research activity, the difficulty is to keep the two objectives at the same level, that is, to ensure that the time spent on research for knowledge acquisition is not disconnected from the time spent caring for patient. From a concrete and cognitive point of view, both activities are simultaneous: a better knowledge and understandings helps to the actors to better define and apply newly adapted protocols. Nevertheless, time representations are sometimes different. Companies typically demand short-term results, while researchers are more inclined to reason and act with a medium-term horizon for their publishing activities, that is to say, formalizing and writing results that emerge throughout the process of an intervention-research in interaction with the actors of the company.

Leading a Team of Researchers

Unlike consultants who often work alone, intervention-research missions are often carried out by teams. There are several arguments in favor of such an organization of research work. First, intervention-research requires learning, especially for young researchers. An intervention-research team is typically composed of members with different skill levels and experiences, who work together while spreading out the different services. For example, the most experienced individuals will be involved in 10% of an intervention-research program, the youngest in 60%, and the other researchers in 30%. Learning is done through teamwork in the field and then by deciphering and conducting common analysis of the situations experienced in the field of scientific observation.

Second, teamwork allows the intervention-research to be carried out at a faster rate, with companies often asking for short-term results. Thus, several researchers can work simultaneously in the same company, in different departments or units, which allows then to reduce the initial stages of diagnosis and then intensify change and its observation during the project phase (Savall & Zardet, 1987, 2015).

Finally, teamwork facilitates comparisons and connections with the different points of view, perspectives, interpretations and analysis, which are extremely useful when researchers, who are at the heart of the company, risk losing the cognitive and emotional distance necessary to interpret and decode the discourses and practices of the actors of the company (Boje & Rosile, 2003). Weekly meetings of the intervention-research team, working in the same company, help the "decontamination," through a process of confronting information and varying points of view with other team members, in order to improve the decoding of the situations observed. *Cognitive interactivity* and *contradictory intersubjectivity* are thus asked and activated (see Chapter 1), as epistemological principles facilitate distance instead of an illusory objectivity of the researcher (Savall & Zardet, 1996, 2005; Krief, 2005). The alternation between activity in the workplace and return to the laboratory is also an essential aspect of research-intervention work, which makes it easier to distance oneself through thoughtful confrontation with third parties.

Creating Knowledge

One of the conditions for the quality of longitudinal research is the ability to trace results. Indeed, in order to generate knowledge that can be later published, intervention-research involves rigorous and homogeneous protocols common to the various researchers, such as the quality and exhaustiveness of note-taking during the many working sessions in the company, the methods of producing documents for the company, and the collection of documents produced by the company itself. Working as a team of researchers involves taking great care in collecting information and archiving it in a structured way, making it accessible to all team members. In addition, if research is cumulative, by following the example of medical researchers who accumulate a large number of observations in different patients before being able to confirm the validation of new knowledge, it is necessary to develop common working methods across different intervention-research programs. For example, the ISEOR team stabilized a replicable methodology in the 1980s to conduct socioeconomic diagnoses of companies and organizations (Savall, 1978, 1979; Savall & Zardet, 1987, 2014, 2015). Currently, the ISEOR database has more than 1,900 diagnoses of companies and organizations produced according to a common methodology. Starting with semi-directive interviews conducted with a common interview guide, this method consists of extracting field-note quotes (verbatim), classifying them in a nomenclature of themes and subthemes, and then formulating generic key-ideas illustrated by these field-note quotes. Key-ideas, classified in themes and subthemes, are capitalized in an expert system software built according to a cumulative methodology since 1988. This work method allows *a posteriori* analyzes, which are cross-disciplinary, thematic and/or sectoral, due to the materials obtained according to homogeneous protocols. Based on this work, we recently published an article on the appearance of the "TFW" virus (Taylor, Fayol, Weber) in 36 medico-welfare establishments, based on a transversal exploitation of 36 diagnoses involving a significant number of actors, conducted in 36 organizations by different researchers of the team for several years (Savall & Zardet, 2015).

Introducing and Coproducing Change

By definition, an intervention-research within a company is a set of activities aimed at helping the company introduce and then consolidate those *changes* through production methods. These activities require skills significantly different from those of traditional *author-researchers*. Indeed, they must deploy an energy of change (Lacey & Tompkins, 2007), translate and convert concepts into action, and, to succeed in this, develop a demanding *trusting relationship* with the various actors in the company, from the leader to the most modest employee.

Researchers immersed in the organization must, for this reason, adapt their language, express themselves simply, in a partnership that is respectful of the people with whom they speak and work. This requires pedagogical skill, a posture of modesty and mutual respect, devoid of any form of contempt on the part of researchers and actors in the organization. It is thus a question of building an equality relationship that is not, however, devoid of requirements. Indeed, knowledge and insight are shared, with the objective to coproduce, avoiding the postures of the condescending researcher who knows everything... as well as the haughty decision maker who pays!

Indeed, the actors of a company exercise their requirement in the realization of the specifications and contract of the intervention-research, in return for which the company pays the research team. The introduction of change also requires firmness from the researchers to ensure that the initial *co-constructed* methodological specifications are respected and, if necessary, adapted. It is about the need to regularly re-explain, during the course of the intervention-research, the methodological principles agreed upon with the general management, such as the rules for the composition of a project group or the methodology used for the interviews of a socioeconomic diagnoses. This step is critical in order to limit inappropriate methodological pseudo-innovations that could have a negative impact on the quality and traceability of intervention-research.

FROM INTERVENTION-RESEARCH TO PUBLICATION

In the academic world, researchers gain visibility and notoriety through their publications. Thus the challenge is to succeed in alternating research-intervention work in the field and writing the results of the research to be published. The transition from one to the other is not easy, for several reasons. First, the rhythm and duration of an intervention-mission are very different from those of a publication. Next, researchers must identify issues that can be addressed in publications. Finally, the company or organization, the field of research and intervention, must be involved and authorize the publication of the results concerning it.

Managing the Rhythm of Intervention-Research and Publication

An intervention-research project consumes a lot of time and human energy over many months, even years. Publication, in contrast, requires deadlines that must be respected, particularly in the case of communications for professional association meetings. For these reasons, the publication of the results of an intervention-research requires rigorous planning and programming of the time specifically dedicated to writing, especially in the case of articles coauthored by two or more researchers, such as it is often the case.

Identification of Issues and Writing as a Team

The great interest of intervention-research for publication comes from the multitude of issues that emerge from the same intervention-research in a company. Indeed, an intervention-research of several months or a few years allows one to write multiple original publications on different topics, both methodological and managerial in nature. Nobre (2006) has highlighted this phenomenon by showing that the issues expressed at the beginning of an intervention-research are only the visible face of an iceberg. After several months of work in a company, a wide variety of new questions emerge that will lead to analyses and interpretations based on multiple longitudinal observations. One of the challenges is to extract generic issues from specific cases. This can be overcome by a method consisting of analyzing the content of materials resulting from an intervention-research and comparing it with the results already existing in the literature. A set of cases of intervention-research in a knowledge base is an inexhaustible resource to validate results from a single case, comparing it with a larger sample.

The members of an intervention-research team can thus produce cross-sectional publications, qualitative or quantitative analyzes and case-studies with high personal added value. However, one of the essential conditions is to define ethical rules for the concerted use of intervention-research materials. It is a matter of avoiding the tendency to have some researchers devote their energy to conducting the intervention-research, while others, more comfortably, write publications based on materials, created and accumulated by the former. *Rules of equity* must be developed, such as the fact that a researcher cannot access the materials of an intervention-research if these have not been inserted into a collective knowledge base. The principle is that of a prior contribution of each one to the feeding of the collective knowledge base, before pretending to publish results using materials available in this base. Time, effort, fatigue, and personal investment in intervention-research are thereby doubly rewarded. In addition to being paid for their intervention-research activities, researchers can access the materials produced by the research team to produce a thesis, a paper, an article or a book, which is a significant advantage in the academic world.

Obtaining Client Authorization Before Publication

Unlike consultants who have a singular and confidential relationship with their customers, the intervener-researcher adopts a mixed position of *consultant-author*, which is clearly explained during the negotiation phase of an intervention-research project. As a result, the company knows that the researchers will publish results based on their own case. Different ways of publishing are then possible. The safest and most respectful way for researchers is to use anonymous indicators for publication, without mentioning the name of the company. This guarantee of anonymity, which we systematically apply to our team, facilitates the extraction by the researcher of more authentic information, which increases *the quality of the information for scientific use* both for the conduct of an intervention-research and for publication (Savall, 1986). Complementary devices allow some form of quality control by the company of relevance and topicality of published results. For example, in PhD thesis juries directed and prepared by the ISEOR team for over 40 years, a manager or company executive who is a witness of the research is systematically invited to sit on the jury and take part in the deliberations that will validate the PhD thesis.

Getting Client Agreement to Publish

The publication of non-anonymous results is possible when the executive of the company agrees to present the results of the intervention-research at public events, such as a professional or mixed academic-practitioner meeting. Oral presentations of results by the executive or managers may be transcribed and then submitted to the authors for validation prior to publication. They thus constitute a non-anonymous public source of results that can be used both by researchers and by the company.

Consulting and Intervention-Research

The intervention-research methodology can also be called *scientific consultancy*. In this respect, it is different from the generally accepted idea that counseling follows the research, in the same way that many think that applied research *follows* fundamental research. The practice of scientific consultancy is an invitation to continually explore new sectors, new activities, new statuses, new contexts, or new issues considered scientifically relevant and credible, in order to produce innovative scientific knowledge.

The Difference From the Company Point of View

A company or an organization can legitimately ask, "What is the difference between a contract with a consultant or an intervener-researcher?" In the academic community, as in the business world, consultants are commonly seen as service providers who must "obey" their clients. One of the challenges for an intervention-research team is to transform the traditional customer-supplier relationship into a *balanced partnership.* The intervention-research team becomes a real partner and transparency is increased between the two parties involved. Sometimes the company solicits the point of view and even advice from the intervention-research team, based on its scientific expertise, before making decisions in the areas of intervention-research. Shared transparency also means that the company transmits *authentic* internal strategic documents to the intervention-research team, thus contributing to the quality of scientific work.

The Difference From the Intervener-researcher Point of View

Scientific consultancy allows one to answer different questions and themes useful for companies and organizations. In this sense, it is socially useful and explicitly engaged research. One of the evaluation criteria is therefore satisfaction, appreciation, and evaluation by observing, scientifically, how companies and organizations succeed in improving their socio-economic practices and performance by applying new knowledge resulting from an intervention-research. One of the main difficulties is for intervener-researchers to regularly *pass from one universe to another*—the academic universe filled by theories and the universe of companies and organizations filled by observable practice. This also means switching from one *language* to another. Indeed, abstract language, which dominates the academic world, is neither well understood nor adopted by companies and organizations. Similarly, concrete and imagined language is depreciated in the academic world, especially in publications, probably more in Europe than in America. Intervener-researchers who present cases of intervention-research are often suspected of being consultants, which tends to exclude them from the academic community and taint their reputation and academic career. Skill and language alternation are thus a key competence for those who wish to jointly develop intervention-research activities and publications.

Remuneration and Intervention-Research

It is entirely possible to practice intervention-research without remuneration of the researchers or their team, for example in the framework of PhD research, which is sometimes financially supported elsewhere. However, beyond these situations, the company's remuneration for an intervention-research contract has several advantages. First of all, this increases the degree of demand on the part of the company and therefore provides a stimulus for researchers to effectively integrate their work in the transformation objectives targeted by the company. The company or organization funding an intervention-research also has a significantly higher degree of commitment than in "free" research, where the company may consider that it "renders service" to researchers by opening their doors, and that is its main contribution. Transformative research requires a high degree of involvement of the company's stakeholders, from managers and senior managers to the most modest jobs.

Another advantage comes from the possibility for a research team to obtain a source of funding, which comes under the *research contract*. The latter is much more developed today in the physical sciences than in the social sciences. These funds make it possible to financially support researchers, technicians, and administrative teams as well as facilitate the publication

TABLE 2.2 Distribution of Time Spent by the Research Team in Various Activities (Example of ISEOR)

Types of Activities	Time (s)	Time %
Intervention-research projects	1,280	22%
Training	400	7%
Contract negotiations	460	8%
Publications	940	16%
Management of the research team	1,160	20%
Internal missions: Preparation of conference proceedings and editing	1,100	19%
Research and development	460	8%
Total	5,800	100%

process and their participation in various professional association programs. Table 2.2 provides an illustration of the apportionment of time spent in these different activities. The first two activities account for roughly 30% of the time, those that generate resources from companies, organizations or institutions. They make it possible to finance all other activities that do not generate own resources. It is thus a new form of economic model of a research center, which allows scientific and financial autonomy, a prerequisite for innovation, in national and international contexts where public funding for research is decreasing. As an illustration, for over 42 years the research center ISEOR has generated budgetary resources of more than 80 million euro, enabling the Center to train and supervise several hundred PhD students and young PhD researchers, to write hundreds of national and international publications, without depending on public or private subsidies.

ISEOR's activities have developed in partnership with many companies and organizations from different countries of the world, as well as with the University. Indeed some members of the team are university professor-researchers, others prepare their PhD thesis by being salaried for 3 years, and others are administrative and technical personnel who develop their career in private and nonprofit organizations. A partnership agreement between the research center, IAE Lyon and Jean Moulin University recognizes the originality of ISEOR's operating model and the mutual contributions of the various partners in terms of logistical resources and mutual promotion.

CONCLUSION

Intervention-research is a way of observing scientifically the actual practices of companies and organizations, as well as a rigorous methodology that is very useful for the development of the management sciences. Often through ignorance, it is equated with consultancy, because it aims to improve professional practices and to obtain financial resources. The main factors that distinguish intervention-research from consultancy are: scientific rigor and progressiveness of the negotiation process; negotiation, on an equal footing, of the methodological specifications signed and rigorously respected throughout the project; team work using "traced" methodologies, which makes it a cumulative research effort; and, finally, the basis for systematic publications, both at doctoral and postdoctoral level.

An intervention-research team works like a company, in the sense that its activities provide it with financing, which it gets through processes of negotiating new resources. These cover the remuneration of the technical, administrative, doctoral and post-doctoral teams, and fund research and development activities as well as original publications. The coming decades are likely to promote a "horizontalization" of research and counseling activities, in favor of the development of intervention-research that is useful to companies *and* capable of generating new knowledge resulting from real issues on the ground. This continued evolution will mitigate the artificial difference between the life and nature sciences and the human and social sciences (Savall & Fiere, 2007, 2014).

REFERENCES

Boje, D., & Rosile, G. A. (2003). Comparison of socio-economic and other transorganizational developments methods. *Journal of Organizational Change Management, 16*(1), 10–20.

Buono, A. F., & Savall, H. (2007). *Socio-economic intervention in organizations.* Charlotte, NC: Information Age.

Buono, A. F., & Savall, H. (2015). *The socio-economic approach to management revisited: The evolving nature of SEAM in the 21st century.* Charlotte, NC: Information Age.

Coghlan, D., & Brannick, T. (2005). *Doing action research in your own organization.* London, England: SAGE.

David, A. (2000). La recherche-intervention, cadre général pour la recherche en management? [Intervention Research, General Structure for Management Research?] In A. David, A. Hatchuel, & R. Laufer (Eds.), *Les nouvelles fondations des sciences de gestion. Eléments d'épistémologie pour les sciences du management* [New foundations of management sciences] (pp. 241–264). Paris, France: Vuibert.

Krief, N. (2005). Le rôle du chercheur en sciences de gestion: éléments pour une 'intersubjectivité contradictoire [The role of the researcher in management sciences: Elements for 'Contradictory Intersubjectivity.' Lille, France: *23ème Université d'Eté de l'Audit Social*, pp. 12–22.

Kwesiga, E., & Pattie, M. (2006). Is management science built on a shaky foundation? The case of intersubjectivitive certifiability. *Revue Sciences de Gestion-Management Sciences, 50,* 33–68.

Lacey, M., & Tompkins, T. (2007). Analysis of best practices of internal consulting. *Organization Development Journal, 25*(3), 123–131.

Moisdon, J.-C. (1984). Recherche en gestion et intervention [Management research and intervention]. *Revue Française de Gestion, 44,* 33–45.

Nobre, T. (2006). Pour une lecture en hypertexte des organisations par la recherche-action: Le cas du changement à l'hôpital [Hypertext comprehension of organizations through action research: Case of hospital change process]. *Finance Controle Stratégie, 9*(4), 143–168.

Plane, J.-M. (2000). *Méthodes de recherche-intervention en management [Intervention research method in management].* Paris, France: L'Harmattan.

Savall, H. (1974–1975). *Enrichir le travail humain: l'évaluation économique,* Paris Dunod; English translation, *Work and People: An economic evaluation of job enrichment* 1st ed. New York, NY: Oxford University Press (1981)

Savall, H., (1986). Contrôle de qualité des informations qualitatives, quantitatives et financières extraites des acteurs au sein des organisations [The quality control of qualitative, quantitative and financial data sets collected from the actors of organizations]. In *Qualité des informations scientifiques en gestion, Méthodologies fondamentales en gestion.* Paris, France: FNEGE, ISEOR, CNRS.

Savall, H., & Zardet, V. (1996). La dimension cognitive de la recherche-intervention: la production de connaissances par interactivité cognitive [The cognitive dimension of intervention research: The production of knowledge through cognitive interactivity]. *Revue internationale de systémique, 10*(1–2), 157–189.

Savall, H., & Fière, D. (2007, 2014). Étude comparative de méthodologies de recherche en médecine et en gestion. Cas de la recherche-intervention socio-économique d'ordre qualimétrique [Comparative Study of Methodologies of Research in Medicine and Management]. *Journal de gestion et d'économie médicales, 32*(5), 354–370.

Savall, H., & Zardet, V. (1987, 2016). *Maîtriser les coûts et les performances cachés, Le contrat d'activité périodiquement négociable.* Prix Harvard l'Expansion de Management Stratégique. Economica, 6ème édition 2016. Translated in English: *Mastering Hidden Costs and Economic Performances.* Charlotte, NC: Information Age.

Savall, H., & Zardet, V. (1995, 2005). *Ingénierie stratégique du roseau [Strategic Engineering].* Paris, France: Economica.

Savall, H., & Zardet, V. (2004). *Recherche en Sciences de Gestion: Approche qualimétrique, Observer l'objet complexe* [Research in Management Sciences: The Qualimetric Approach, Observing the Complex Object]. Paris, France: Economica. Translated in English: *The qualimetrics approach: Observing the complex object.* Charlotte, NC : Information Age.

Savall H., & Zardet V. (2015). Un obstacle à la modernisation des services publics: Le virus TFW (Taylorisme-Fayolisme-Weberisme): Cas d'application [A Barriere for Progress : The TFW Virus]. Lyon, France: Colloque AIRMAP.

Savall, H., Zardet, V., Péron, M., & Bonnet, M. (2012). Possible contributions of qualimetrics intervention-research methodology to action-research. *International Journal of Action-Research, 29,* 102–130.

Voyant, O. (2005). La production de connaissances d'intention scientifique: Le principe de contingence générique appliqué à l'audit social [The creation of scientific knowledge: The generic contingency principle applied to social audit]. *23ème Université d'Audit Social.* Lille, France, pp. 212–222.

CHAPTER 3

FROM INTERVENTION-RESEARCH TO THE PRODUCTION OF KNOWLEDGE

A Summary of Experimentation

Jean-Michel Plane

Our research in management science began in the Information Technology (IT) production department of a large insurance company, situated on the thirteenth floor of a tower at *La Defense.* The starting point of the project was a 5 month immersion in the company, based on an experimental approach, which gave rise to several discussions (e.g., colloquiums, congress) as well as a first publication. The intervention was dedicated to the analysis of the problems of management connected to a restructuring of the company's IT production department representing approximately 150 people. The first intervention-research gave rise to other thorough investigations as well as long-term experiments, leading to an essay on theorization and defense of a doctoral thesis at the University of Lumiere-Lyon 2, within the

Intervention Research, pages 47–70

ISEOR research team (Plane, 1994). Recruited as a university professor, we pursued this type of research in companies and organizations as consultant-researcher in quite varied contexts. The orientation of the initial research was preserved, although we looked to widen the operating methodologies used, in particular concerning research carried out within the framework of calls from public institutions (Plane, 2016).

Drawing on a review of this research, a fundamental element emerges—the analysis of the interactions between guiding change of the intervention-research and the development of the organization. This research was aimed at analyzing the processes of development of the human potential of organizations. In this perspective, we were interested at first in strategies of intervention, relying mainly on human potential as the first lever of possible development. The importance of the organization's development from the activation of human potential appeared to us when we showed that the difficulties of restructuring a large insurance group could be minimized through a strategy of human development. Finally, we advanced our thesis according to the process of intervention-research, based on productive interactivity of knowledge, stimulating the introspective and conceptive capacities of the actors *and* contributing to the development of the organization. This approach led to us to reflect on the question of the production of management science knowledge, which brought us to gradually develop a number of methodological and epistemological contributions. To deal with the measure of the contributions by an analysis of the research results and to clarify our project of knowledge, we chose to articulate, from this introduction, our epistemological and methodological positioning around two axes of reflection.

EPISTEMOLOGICAL POSITIONING AND ASSOCIATED METHODOLOGICAL CHOICES

The adopted position in this work is constructivism[1] in that we know the intervention modifies the behavior of the actors, in essence, transforming their reality. From this perspective, it is advisable not to obscure the question of the scientific nature of our research approach. In this sense, our work joins a logic through which the production of knowledge as well as the conditions of validity and validation cannot be separated. However, we do not join an approach of radical constructivism, which is too relativist in denying any reality of social phenomena. We think rather that it is a more open attitude of research that aims to give meaning to reality and which we can discover "between the social phenomena some justifiable and relatively stable relations" (Huberman & Miles, 1991, p. 31). The researcher is interested in the set of available knowledge and the emergence of the modes of knowledge necessary for modeling this knowledge.

In constructivist research, the production of knowledge and its validation fall under the same logic of explication of the protocol of analysis as described by Huberman and Miles—the observer is an integral part of the observation (Lévi-Strauss, 1950). If, as we have already underlined, constructivism must be envisaged as an open attitude of research rather than as a definitive paradigm, one has to recognize that there seems be a common denominator. Indeed, we would admit that the researcher produces explanations which are not reality, but ones built[2] on a reality likely to explain it. Such an epistemological positioning leans on methodological choices (e.g., intervention research, qualitative methods), which seem adapted to the research project and on a system of analysis (interactive approach, training action and case studies) designed according to the object of research, which can be varied—from a focus on company directors, management and supervision teams, to employees, management training, and involvement as researcher in organizations.

From the point of view of the operating methodology of the research, numerous experiments have been carried out within diverse companies and organizations over more than 20 years. These experiments present an in-depth character illustrated by the diversity of services and amount of time dedicated to these. The elaboration of our base of experimental information was mainly guided by two criteria. First, we always focused on materials that demonstrated the services realized in the organizations. Second, these experiments formalized a strategic diagnosis from which the organizational and managerial dysfunctions were highlighted. Simultaneously, we also typically formalized our tools of analysis of the organization's functioning, such as the analysis of the state of the entity's skills (mapping of skills) or an analysis of performance indicators (e.g., work on dashboards for project steering). The production of the diagnosis and tools of analysis leads to a phase of project improvement, in which innovative solutions for the organization are explored. This approach is part of a comprehensive and prescriptive logic that characterizes in some respects management sciences since we position ourselves in a praxeological perspective (Cappelletti, 2012; Kaplan, 1998). This research process allows us to collect observation and experimentation on the ground, providing contextualized information as researchers and practitioners agree on a number of methods relative to the intervention. The interactions and their management between researchers and practitioners constitute in the end the essential engine of the intervention-research (Plane, 2000).

Areas of Research, the Quest for Knowledge, and Presentation of Results

Two axes structure our research program in management sciences: the methods of intervention-research in management and the dynamics between human resource management and organizational innovations. The first axis of the approach is dedicated to the problem of the relation between intervention-research in management and organizational development. The second area examines the relationship between organizational innovations and human resource management.

On first analysis, we focused on the contributions of our work from the analysis of the progressive convergence of the research towards a question and an object. Our basic question focuses on the extent to which we could sustainably establish new knowledge about the functioning of organizations through the involvement of a researcher in management practice. Questions also emerged about the theoretical foundation and practical implications that were elicited by intervention-research. These concerns lead us to ponder about the collective action of the actors and the nature of their knowledge. It also raised major questions on the nature of the relation between knowledge and intervention in management science. In other words, this research work aimed to analyze the effects of the interactions produced by the involvement of management researchers in implementing change-related actions in an organization. According to this logic of experimentation, researcher drive innovative actions from the point of view of the mode of management within organizations. Then they will observe the effects of these actions. Finally, the researcher accepts the idea of a universe built from the representations of the actors and is interested in all the available knowledge in the company (Shepherd & Luckmann, 1967).

On second analysis, these investigations led us, little by little, to grasp the importance of the skills and tacit knowledge within complex and dynamic companies working from adhocratic structures based on project-oriented logic. Our attention focused on the extent to which organizational innovations elicited transformations in human resource management (HRM). These changes present new stakes for the HRM function, in particular the model of skills and importance of knowledge. This questioning led us to analyze the case of a company producing electronic boards. To deal with the measure of the contributions of the intervention-research in the analysis of managerial innovations, we chose to articulate this chapter around two axes of reflection. The chapter first describes these foundations: our first research endeavors in the field of intervention in management; and the contributions of the intervention of the researcher in the analysis and development of organizations. The second part is dedicated to the analysis of the case of a company producing electronic cards confronted production-related problems in managerial innovations.

Intervention by Management Researchers: Theoretical, Methodological, and Practical Implications

The importance of research dedicated to methods of intervention-research in management and our positioning in the field of the human resources management gave us a double identity as a researcher. The first one is of methodological order, based on our creation of a number of contributions for researchers in management science before carrying out research in the field. The second is thematic, based on the close relationship between our research and the field of human resource management.

Our initial work was dedicated to the analysis of the relationship between the researcher and the field. It began with our thesis work on intervention-research in management, and continued with the study of the results produced in organizations using this approach.

The Study of the Relationship Between Researchers and the Field

In our thesis work, we tried to understand the impacts and effects produced by the process of intervention-research. This approach is a complex management process through which the researcher is simultaneously confronted with two logics, which, at times, can seem contradictory—the challenge of producing knowledge from interactions realized on the ground, while contributing actively to the organizational development of the company, which is the object of the investigation. From our perspective, this complexity leads the researcher to try to open a discussion on the conditions of validity of the knowledge produced from a work based on experimentation.

The synthesis of the work developed here aims at recalling the questioning and quest for knowledge: *To what extent and under what methodological conditions we can produce valid knowledge from a truly interactive process? On the epistemological plan, how can we endeavor to enter a logic of objectification from inevitably subjective information?* For the main part, the study of the relations and interactions between researchers and actors concern a number of key elements.

First, the *relations between the researchers and the field* must be clarified. Within the framework of an intervention-research approach, the researcher is involved in a cognitive process where there is simultaneously the creation of knowledge and change. From this perspective, it seems that the active participation of the actors of organizations in the research itself can take on two forms. In certain cases, the actors engage without knowing it in as far as the researcher uses the action which was created to produce knowledge. In this instance, the actors on the ground are involved but not aware of it. In other cases, the actors contribute actively to the construction of the research process. Through this type of intervention-research, the actors of organizations are also considered as holding a part of the knowledge and having relevant views on the problem to be developed. The intervention-research projects that we have conducted in a certain diversity of organizations reflects this latter perspective—an interactive method with a transformative aim to try to transform the functioning of the organization in order to observe the effects of the change. This method of intervention-research was particularly recommended by the management research centers in which we have worked.

Second, focus must be placed on the *logic of production of knowledge* and the objectification of information. Such an approach joins in the logic of knowledge advocated by Lévi-Strauss (1950, p. iv), which shows that "in a science where the observer is the same nature as his object, the observer is part of the observation." This epistemological option means trying to bring elements of an answer to the following research question: *Can we draw valid knowledge from subjective data collected on the spot?* Considering this problem, our work aimed at extracting knowledge on the ground by objectifying it, that is, by bringing it back to the management situations in which it was produced. As researchers in the management sciences, we do not consider the phenomena of transfer and counter-transfer, that is, the projections made by the actors of the organization about the intervener-researchers and, reciprocally, as disruptive phenomena which are necessary to eliminate or at worse to mask. Indeed, as soon as there is interaction, there are inevitably expectations, preferences, taboos, things unsaid, and so forth—the analysis of which can be rich in teachings with regard to the intimate functioning of the studied organization. The researcher thus must confront his or her own hypotheses with those of the various actors in view of generating progress in knowledge.

The third point refers to a question of the place and the neutrality of the researcher. Within the framework of the investigations conducted within diverse organizations, we repeatedly noticed that if our will in the process of intervention had been to occupy a position of neutrality, it would have been a utopian dream. Indeed, it seems that this position is difficult to keep on the ground, especially since the actors need representation and mental identification with the researchers, which consequently and inevitably places them in the organizational system. However, our work shows that this system of place is contingent because the researchers can try to build them from their behavior. This phenomenon constitutes for a researcher what Devereux (1980) refers to as the *anxiety of the observer* in the face of the wealth and diversity of his observations.

Fourth is the involvement of the researcher and the management of "distant familiarity" (Matheu, 1986). Numerus researchers in management are confronted with the difficulty of determining the appropriate distance to be adopted toward their field of investigation. This complexity is best addressed through introspection, which every researcher has the capacity to undertake. Through our work, we have shown that the interactions between a researcher and the field of observation can be established as an instrument of the elaboration of knowledge. Researchers, however, should be aware of any potential biases toward the actors they are studying. These biases can create disturbances, to the point of becoming an obstacle to the research, rather than helping to increase the quality of the services provided and improve the level of knowledge and related skills of the actors in their environment.

The level of distance also helps researchers avoid overly exposing to the conscious and/or unconscious risks of manipulation of their work by certain actors. Indeed, an outsider to an organization is often considered as an intruder always suspected of trying to question the status quo and wanting to reveal information about which certain actors prefer to keep silent. All in all, the implication and immersion of a management researcher in an organization raises questions of a greater consciousness of the researcher triptych: acts produced in the organization, impacts obtained, and effects obtained and observable.

Methods of Intervention-Research

Finally, the question of the methods used within the framework of an intervention-research project is important. Our work aims to clarify elements of methods of intervention-research tested in organizations and the theoretical foundations on which they lean. In this way, our observations show that it is possible to analyze the progress of the research strategy to detect methods of improvement with their conduct with the actors of organizations. For example, the interviews with the actors constitute a deviation in the "daily life" of the organization because they constitute the opportunity to gather concrete information on the daily, real-life experience in the organization. On the epistemological plan, it seems that this information can take on a valid character if it is brought back to the processes of interaction in which it was produced. From a methodological perspective, it seems possible, by systems of management of intervention-research, to pilot the informative effects of the processes of interactions on the ground. The techniques used are close to those recommended by Schein (1987), who shows that there are guiding questions that have the virtue of stimulating the capacity of an actor to raise a diagnosis of the professional situations in which he evolves. In fact, these techniques are based on a *"Socratic"* questioning (Schein, 1987). The researcher accordingly has to practice the art of "delivering minds," in the sense where he helps his subjects better identify their problems and imagine their own solutions. Furthermore, researchers in management also have an implicit power that we call *interactive power*. Indeed, we think that they possess the capacity to interact with the actors of organizations because of the services that they provide to try to obtain significant information. In this perspective, our work shows the extent to which the intensity of the processes of interactions between researchers and actors stimulates the development of the human potential in an organization.

FROM INTERVENTION-RESEARCH TO THE DEVELOPMENT OF HUMAN POTENTIAL IN ORGANIZATIONS

Working relationships within an intervention-research project, which are established between researchers and the actors of an organization, are characterized by strong interactions that produce transformations, in essence, the sources of development of the human potential of the organization. These dynamics raise a host of questions: Fundamentally, what results can be produced by an intervention-research project? Are they relatively singular? From the point of view of managerial implications, what are the fundamental transformations that will likely be produced by the intervention-research process? This section of the chapter focuses on identifying methodical elements of intervention-research based on the strong interaction between researchers and actors.

Intervention-Research Contribution "On the Ground"

The role of the transformations created by the processes of interactions between researchers and actors-practitioners is essential. In this perspective, researchers transfer a lexicon—all the key words, in a strong concentration of meaning, used and conveyed by the researchers—to the actors of the organization, a process which is done gradually. This language facilitates the emergence of a common semantic base between the researchers and the actors. It also allows us to considerably reduce the semantic ambiguity that affects keywords relative to the management of organizations and which can be sources of misunderstanding. Finally, the quality of communication increases between the researchers and the actors as well as between the actors of the organization. Lastly, the transfer and the acclimatization of tools of management as well as their use by the actors are also carriers of dense keywords.

As our work has illustrated, there is an instrument-concept couple. For example, a mapping of skills, even beyond its functions, contributes strongly to the clarification of keywords such as decision, integrated training, piloting, skills, and so forth. If language is the privileged instrument of communication between researchers and actors, imitation constitutes a form of communication without language (Hall, 1959). The analysis of the processes of interactions between researchers and actors shows the development of such imitation. This imitation corresponds to conscious or unconscious reproductions of behavior by certain actors of the organization. Furthermore, the concept of energy of transformation in an intervention-research project occupies an important place because the researchers transfer some energy to the actors by implementing the techniques of intervention, proper to the process of research. Human energy thus leads to the passage from idea to effective realization. This new energy, propelled by the process of intervention, leads to a stimulation of practice, which has impacts and effects on the state of the organization's economic and social performance.

In this perspective, we proposed tested methods and techniques of activating the energy of the actors of the organization. It seems that the distance of the researchers from the usual practices of an organization constitutes a real vector of energy of transformation. As our research illustrates, researchers have interactive power with management, allowing them to increase the density of the information that we can extract from an organization. Our results also indicate the conditions under which research-actor relations and interactions become more intense, constituting a literal source of efficiency for the intervention. Building on these observations, we proposed a strategy of human development that is useful for practitioners.

Organizational Introspection and the Conceptive Capacities of Actors

Our contribution to the volume is to highlight the existing relationship between the intervention itself and the production of two types of managerial actions: introspective and conceptive acts.

Developing Actor Introspection

In our work, introspection is when an actor wonders about the impact of what he or she is doing, reflecting on their own production and its effects on the performance of the organization. This approach to delving into the introspective acts of management is based on the idea that researchers can act like facilitators and catalysts who are able to make actors increasingly capable of facing and resolving their problems by themselves. Our work indicates that researchers, by the very nature of their intangible services, develop the introspective capabilities of the people involved in the intervention. It seems that the improvement project groups, set up within the framework of investigations, favor the development of what we refer to as *organizational introspection*. Within this context, management instruments (such as the mapping of skills) support a thorough analysis of management situations. All in all, the development of introspection contributes to an increase in the level of visibility and clarity in the organization.

Developing Actor Conceptive Capacities

Through our research, we tried to support the idea that the objective of an intervention-research engagement is the development of the actors' conceptive abilities. These acts of management constitute levers of considerable action because they are based on knowledge that is proven and implemented regularly by the actors. This logic of distribution of knowledge in organizations interests the actors, who are often in search of new knowledge. We can thus define conceptive acts as practices aimed at the detection of more effective functioning drawn from the formalized and structured accumulation of teachings drawn from multiple actor experiences. It can be recognized by principal conceptualizations of actions, likely to be implemented when a given event occurs. Our work indicates that management researchers are in the position of an *agent of change* in the sense that their mission is to help actors become aware of a series of problems (introspection) and to imagine long-lasting transformations (conceptualization). They participate in the evolution of the possible within the organization. Concretely, the various realized experiments contribute to a logic of organizational development in particular on the following axes: the enrichment of work by training initiatives, new management knowledge leading to greater versatility; the development of piloting through the implementation of management instruments; systems of communication aimed at a synchronization of services (logic of cooperation); and the quality of the professional dialogue.

THE PRODUCTION OF ORGANIZATIONAL INNOVATION: THE CASE OF AN INDUSTRIAL COMPANY

The T. Company, situated in the South of France, is specialized in the manufacture of electronic boards as a subcontractor. These products are intended for extremely varied applications (industrial apparatuses, medical and telecommunications sector) and are sold to customers who design and integrate these electronic boards in systems or devices that they market. The company works with big contractors such as Thomson, Alcatel, Gespac, and Orange rooted in France and smaller companies partly based in the Occitanie region. The company also enjoys the position of favored partner with factories from the Gec Alsthom group. This limited company generates revenues of approximately 15 million euros and employs 75 people. Since 2005, it has been a part of the Fidel group, the number one French electronic subcontracting company.

The core mission of the Fidel group is to design and produce industrial projects. It constitutes a holding company with 17 firms and continues to grow by acquiring new companies. The group's structure is broken into divisions, whereby every company is autonomous in its functioning, results, and own profit center. These companies are specialists in their fields and have to insure their own development both in terms of technology and clientele. Over recent years, the group has been introduced in the secondary market of the stock exchange in Paris with the aim of strengthening its financial capacity.

The T. Company knows how to take advantage of its position within the group. Besides its financial weight, it showcases a brand that reassures the customer and supports the subcontractor's strategy. Furthermore, the company benefits from the sharing of experience—including the transfer of a new, more successful IT tool in production follow-up. Finally, membership in the group allows it to receive customer orders from big contractors in order to restart business. This synergy helped to restore the company's dynamism.

The company, however, has experienced difficulties in terms of its organizational politics and financial results. A key objective of the firm's management is to increase its global net worth by more than 5% net and its revenues, which will allow it to insure the renewal of investments. The objective is to self-finance growth and investments by reducing its operating values (stocks and in production) to a satisfactory level, which is not still the case today. At present, the global net accounting result is of the order of 4%, which is considered as borderline by the manager of the company.

Situation of the Company

The basic business of the T. Company is the assembly and cabling of electronic components on a printed circuit. Endowed with flexible means, this company concentrates its skills and services on the industrialization, purchasing, and supply of components, the cabling of cards, automatic tests or assembly, and product integration. As a production company, its plan is to continue to develop its organizational flexibility and control a set of technologies that will allow it to realize launch series for electronic boards. A challenge is to balance small and average production series, which can vary from a prototype to a series of 5 to 200 products per month, encompassing technologies. The company attempts to produce and control all parameters production in order to offer to its customers the service they expect. Its competitiveness is based on comparable pricing with a high level of quality and respect for deadlines.

Quality management is considered strategic and can be seen concretely by the commitment to a certification procedure, which resulted in the attainment of the ISO standard 9002. Since its founding, the company has maintained an image of quality symbolized by its logo—a bee, which reflects the company's commitment to industrial effort. What, a few years ago could seem secondary, has today become a condition of survival for this type of company as the large contractors they work with have become more and more demanding. The second watchword of production is the deadline.

Faced with greater competition in the electronic subcontracting market, the company made a commitment to minimum deadlines through a system of dynamic scheduling that allows all employees to vary their schedules to meet deadlines. The company has tried to adapt its staff, in essence attempting to transform of the firm's professional environment through new technical trainings (new processes, new machines).

The company is classified among the top 150 French subcontractors and its revenues, since its creation have continued to grow even with more than 1,000 companies in the market. The company's strategy is to position itself as widely as possible in the industrial cycle and to develop high value-added services such as industrialization and design (an activity currently representing 10 to 20% of the firm's activity) in order to handle demand requirements. The company positions itself in the professional electronics market and deals with roughly forty contractors.

Within this context, it is necessary to distinguish between the customers of the Fidel group (Gec Alsthom, Cegelec, etc.) that represent approximately 20% of the orders and the customers outside of this group. Customers have strong bargaining power because they fix rules of the game most of the time. The company has to adapt itself to customer demands and tries to satisfy them to the maximum. Its marketing strategy is to try to be as upstream as possible in the industrial project as a way of being proactive. Its focus is to work with customers specialized in the industrial and medical sector in the southeast of France. The sales force of the company particularly supports products that are well known by the company and for which it has a know-how that allows it to be more successful in terms meeting of deadlines, flexibility, and quality. Furthermore, the company ensures that no customer represents more than 20% of its total revenues in order to avoid problems of dependence, which subcontracting companies are often confronted with. Its marketing strategy is to create real partnership agreements with customers because the objective is to favor long-lasting relations, working hard to develop relational marketing with its customers.

Competitive Positioning

Faced with fierce competition, the T. Company cannot withstand competition through cost. It has attempted to develop its competitive advantage through reactivity and organizational flexibility based on logistical advantages. Precisely, the firm has worked to create first-class service in terms of reactivity, quality, and respect for deadlines with the objective of relativizing the inconvenience of high labor costs through by quality of service, strong reactivity, and impeccable technicality. The company is committed to a permanent process of improvement with respect to procurement costs, which reflects not only the price of the product but also everything associated with it (e.g., quality, capacity of evolution, quality of the information system, delivery) for which the company tries to meet the challenge of world competition. This policy is guided by the firm's strategic intent to generalize partnerships with suppliers as well as customers.

Organizational Innovations

The T. Company relies on the most flexible organization possible so as to limit structure costs and facilitate direct communication between hierarchical levels. The desired level of flexibility depends on the autonomy of the company's staff and sense of responsibility to increase its reactivity. We can thus say that the firm has an entrepreneurial structure because power is held by its manager who have a strategic vision for the company based on the development of its human potential. In this perspective, the company's plan is to set up a new production organization, organized by modules which will allow it to group skills in order to achieve a larger mission. These modules would be of three types:

- Production modules that manage operations from initial estimate through the delivery of the goods. These modules would consist of a buyer, a salesperson, an office person, and the production operators.
- Shared resource modules, which would appear as service providers guided by a customer and supplier logic, being responsible for the management of certain resources of the company (machines, inventory management) for economic reasons. According to this project of organization, every module would be placed under the responsibility of a coordinator.
- Finally, service modules that ensure logistical and administrative support for the entire company. Although the production modules have the autonomy to intervene in the hazards of the short term, the coordination of the group, in particular in the medium and

long term would become a vital dimension. This coordination could be entrusted to a set of service modules each having a transversal mission.

All in all, the purpose of this new, more transversal organization would be to give greater autonomy to the working collectives, develop horizontal co-operation, and create greater versatility by a dissemination of skills inside the modules.

The Management of Human Resources

Even if a human resource (HR) department does not exist as such in the company, T. Company has a voluntarist strategy and an HR policy. Indeed, the function of human resources is fragmented and shared de facto throughout the company. The managing director fixes main themes regarding HR management (e.g., employment, recruitment, remuneration, training, evaluation). This individual also promulgates the rules of the company's social policy in consultation with the members of the staff and, especially, the company works council. The works council consists of 6 members and has a heavy responsibility regarding human resources. It intervenes in all social decisions and plays a large role in remuneration and qualification. According to the managing director, this aspect of the organization presents a cost-saving advantage over having an HR department. The administrative and accounting department takes care of all administrative tasks regarding staff management, from the management of temporary employees and pay decisions, to declaration and leave. The quality department takes care of everything that concerns training (in particular the training plan) and also plays an important role in the management of qualifications and skills. In this way, it is important to highlight the generally low level of qualifications in the company in as far as most of the operators learn "on the job," while we could believe from the outside that electronics requires a high level of qualification. Staff representatives recently sought a more important role in HR management, with their main mission to defend the interests of the employees.

Regarding evaluation, an annual interview was set up to regularly review the skills of every employee and their prospects for promotion, in order to help manage their career. The evaluation system was based on self-assessment and all employees were responsible for the evaluation of their performance according to an index tool. This self-assessment is then commented on by the department head during an annual interview and then validated by the manager. In terms of training, the company committed over one million francs in a training plan, the main objective of which is to develop autonomy and empower the staff. For that purpose, priority was given to training programs that allowed the company to develop a qualifying organization based on the resolution of relational and technical problems. Finally, the company also commitment to the development of internal information and communication through the implementation of concrete tools such as a monthly newsletter, a welcome booklet, and regularly scheduled meetings as well as a corporate development plan drafted by the manager. This synthesis document presented the company mission, its strategic objectives, and its action plan. This project was particularly ambitious and will pose numerous challenges moving forward to ensure the successful transformation of the company.

From the Organizational Project to the Production of Managerial Innovations

The will of the company, in terms of the organizational project and strategic plan, was to pursue its growth policy from the implementation of four axes of priority actions:

- The *reorganization of production* into modules and into autonomous working groups. It was an ambitious project aimed at questioning the manner of working within the production workshop, focused on determining the skills to be gathered in the autonomous working groups. The works council was strongly involved in this project.
- The *grouping of departments*, bringing together groups of people from all departments in a windowed space to favor de-compartmentalization and active communication between the departments as well as the transfer of the functions as planned.
- *Dynamic scheduling*, creating a system of flexible hours to allow employees to vary their schedules (even to being absent from the company) as long as deadlines were respected. A software program was implemented to facilitate the process.
- *Training and staff autonomy* of the staff centered on the development of self-sufficiency and accountability across the entire staff. For that purpose, priority is given to training allowing the company to be self-learning and leading to a qualification in order to improve its global performance: principles of management and interpersonal communication, methods for resolution of problems, and trainers' training. All in all, global performance was redefined in the company as the capacity to face the six challenges previously mentioned (deadlines, costs, flexibility, quality, innovation, variety) from a

vision of the human skills based on the autonomy and the accountability of the actors.

In the end, the T. Company case shows that companies seem to worry more and more about the management of their competitiveness (see Pérez, 2003) in a constant concern about ways to enhance performance. It is in such a logic that they look for new forms of organization, which involve organizational actors to rethink their work and autonomy. In the face of this challenge, the case shows how a company tries to introduce a logic of skills with the development of a qualifying approach to human resource management as its main watchword. This approach is a possible answer to the complexity of the performance to be reached because it is a question of simultaneously achieving results in terms of deadlines, costs, varieties of production, innovation, and organizational flexibility. In this way and in a perspective of increasing competitiveness, companies can develop their intangible investments to develop, in particular, knowledge in management engineering (that is a set of methods and animation tools), redefining the place of autonomy and control of the actor in the work situation.

Management of Skills and Knowledge

In certain a way, this case study shows that the competence model corresponds to a new social attitude, which relies on interactive skills that are acquired and develop in a cognitive logic based on a new mode of learning and a logic of cooperation between the actors. Such a conception of human resource management involves the possibility of improving the competitiveness of firms by the development of organizational flexibility (internal capacities of reaction in relation to the world market). This relies on a qualifying dynamic and interactive principles of functioning, which are sources of renewal of the skills of the actors. In this sense, the case shows that individual and collective learning is based on the control of the regulations of flow and complex events. The change thus takes place in the autonomy of the actors and their capacity to intelligently take responsibility. Finally, the analysis of the case shows rather clearly the fundamental role played by intangible investments within a company, drawing out a strategy of human development while in search of improved competitiveness. For example, it is also the case of the French group Lafarge within which the style of management looks to favor the taking of responsibility, interest, and initiative. In such a perspective, it seems important to wonder about the nature of the production of the human resources function in companies—and it seems we are gradually witnessing a transformation in the role of this function in its contribution to the process of creation of value (see Caby & Hirigoyen, 2001).

The Managerial Implications of Organizational Innovations

Within the framework of previous research work, our contribution was to highlight the existing relation between the intervention of a researcher in management in an organization and the production of innovative acts of management in the organization. From the preceding case, it seems to us important to underscore that intervention-research can favor the development of the autonomy of the actors from two fundamental acts of management: introspection and the conception of methods. Indeed, a change in structure and new principles of actions based on increased autonomy and the search for innovation have to favor this evolution. Furthermore, the positioning of the company in its environment is probably going to evolve in the coming months. The T. Company cannot continue to keep centering competitiveness on its costs—and it is looking for new bases of competitiveness founded on innovation, logistics, and service. With the aim of suggesting avenues of actions inspired by the T. Company case, we shall now turn to the contribution of organizational introspection. Next, we will show the extent to which the conceptive capacities of autonomous actors can contribute to the organizational development of the company.

Numerous publications show that the development of new forms of organization rely on a large learning effort. Through the analysis of the case, it seems that the T. Company focused on developing the introspective abilities of organizational members and conceptive acts of management. These introspective acts are actions leading the actors to wonder about the acts which they produce and on their effects on the economic and social performance of the company. In the same vein, several specialists in the management of small- and medium-sized enterprises underline that the managers spend much time on performance diagnosis and the dysfunctions which would allow them to define possible improvements. More precisely, the acts of management to which we make reference correspond to those management practices repeated periodically when a given event occurs.

This approach to the introspective acts of management is based on the idea that a researcher can act like a facilitator and a catalyst to make numerus actors increasingly capable of facing and resolving their problems on their own. The solutions brought by the actors to the problems with which they are confronted have to contribute in a way to the development of the company's performance. In this way, the researchers, by the nature of their intangible services, develop introspective acts of supervisory management. The groups of the improvement project also favor the development of organizational introspection. The instruments of management (such as the dashboard of piloting or the analysis of skills) lead simultaneously to a thorough analysis of the use of working time within various departments, as well as to a rigorous study of the distribution of skill availability. After all, the development of introspection contributes to the autonomy of the actor because it leads to an increase of the level of visibility and clarity.

The theory of power proposed by Crozier and Friedberg (1980) shows that people at work cannot be simply considered as mere extensions of the machine, as supposed implicitly by the Taylor model, nor either only as a "hand and a heart" as demanded by the proponents of the human relations movement. Crozier and Friedberg show, from their model of strategic analysis, that the actor in the system is above all "a head," or in more concrete terms, an agent capable of calculation and manipulation who adapts himself and invents according to his partners. This conception of the actor is close to the observations developed here in as far as we insist on the idea that the individual is capable of showing creativity once this is activated by the management of the organization. One of the fundamental objectives of training in management is the development of the actors' conceptive acts. It is about acts that are integrated into professional practices, which can constitute considerable levers of action because they are based on tested knowledge and are implemented regularly by the actors.

It is essential that researchers, by the nature of their approach, bring new management knowledge to the actors with whom they are in a working relationship. This logic of distribution of knowledge in organizations is of interest to the actors, who are often in search of new knowledge. The educational character of the mission of the researchers is an essential element in the approach. The conceptive acts are practices aimed at the detection of more effective invariables of functioning from the formalized and structured accumulation of insights drawn from the multiple experiences of the actors. These models show themselves by principal conceptualizations of action, which are effective and likely to be implemented when a given event occurs. For example, managers must be better able to clarify representations, for example, the way they perceive the environment, their position, or their distinct advantages. In such an approach, the decision maker becomes aware of strategic problems and may be capable of leading major strategic axes. Furthermore, the effort for knowledge achieved by a workgroup can appreciably improve the productive and commercial efficiency of a factory. So, the knowledge acquired by the various actors allows one to envisage new practices, whose main effect is to make the strategic orientations held by the workgroup more relevant.

Finally, we can say that researchers, within the framework of an intervention-research, is an agent of change in the sense where their main mission is to help the actors to become aware of a series of strategic problems (introspection) and to imagine long-lasting transformations (conceptualization) leading to an improvement in economic and social performance. All in all, they participate in the evolution of the possible within the organization that is the object of investigations. Concretely, the various experiments carried out in a logic of organizational development can be seen in the following axes:

- The enrichment of human work and the development of human potential by training initiatives, new knowledge in management.
- The development of piloting by the implementation of dashboards and instruments of skill management.
- The implementation of communication systems aimed at the synchronization of services (logic of cooperation) and the improvement in the quality of professional dialogue.

In the face of the economic and social situation and the increasing challenges faced by organizations, the idea of formalizing elements of theory and method in management becomes increasingly important. Indeed, the end of the 1990s was characterized in particular by the development of an informational society based on a knowledge economy where intangible investments became fundamental for a number of organizations. This new legitimacy connected to the dematerialization of the economy and the work is particularly stimulating for researchers in the management sciences, the abstract, methodological and practical contributions of which can be significant for the practitioners.

Perspectives for a Development Strategy for T. Company

The case analysis of the T. Company shows that we can identify the elements that should be considered in order to carry out an organizational innovation facilitated by the development of autonomy in the company. Nevertheless, the strategic and organizational project of this growing company poses a number of questions that researchers can bring to the foreground in the company to contribute successfully to the realization of such a project. What are the difficulties to foresee when implementing this type of project? What are the chances of success? How can the process of change evolve favorably and under which conditions?

The Strategic and Organizational Project of the Company

On first analysis, we can consider that the T. Company, considering its size and its situation, had an ambitious corporate development plan that focuses on its development while contributing to the imperative improvement of its global net income. This project is thus highly strategic because it irrevocably commits the company to the long term. The manager has a real ambition for his company and tries to effect change in a structured way, from the use of methods and instruments of management. Nevertheless, the chances of success of the project are closely linked to its capacity to mobilize all the actors of the company. The role of the manager and his team is thus to create the conditions for success for the organizational project. From this perspective, it is important to take into account the opinions of all the department heads thorough interviews. Secondly, they can set up working systems on the project based on their dialogue. Through this approach is based on active listening and dialogue, the management of the company can further contribute to a better acceptance of the project by establishing more confidence and by reducing, in particular, its slightly brutal character. This conception of the conduct of the project involves giving the main actors the appropriate methods and piloting tools, the efficiency of which will depend, nevertheless, on the way the staff are mobilized around the project. All in all, the role of the manager is one of a facilitator but also as a catalyst where the development of autonomy will constitute a key factor in the success of the project.

Management Training

On further analysis, it is important to delve into the interactive character of the approach of transformation of the company implemented. This way, intangible investments will favor the process of change based on the introduction of new methods, tools, and instruments of management. The T. Company set up training programs in project management, thorough interviews, an analysis grid of the time management of the manager, and mappings the skills of the departments or dashboards of piloting intended for the people in charge of the autonomous working units. These tools, which were coproduced with the manager, were relatively structuring and allowed the company to build professional labor relations. Furthermore, the improvement of interdepartmental cooperation and more generally horizontal communication constitute one of the strategic stakes in the change project. With the aim of developing the effectiveness and efficiency of the project, the manager attempted involve all employees in the approach within the framework of project groups.

These working groups presented the advantage of actively linking the set of actors, encouraging them to confide in each other and creating a number of stimulating missions for everyone involved. As an example, one or two employees could think about the implementation of rules and procedures of functioning or about indicators aimed at enriching the piloting dashboards of the company. This type of consultative approach ultimately allowed the manager to delegate, in an arranged way, certain internal activities in order to dedicate himself to business development.

Organizational Solutions

Looking back on the intervention in T. Company, there were four key variables associated with operational, interactive, and voluntary actions. First, in terms of the manager, this organizational change allowed him to become more aware of personal interests, which he found in the effective implementation of a number of change-related actions. As an example, a reasonable management of time and relying on more joint delegation allowed him to dedicate more attention to strategic long-term actions.

Second, in terms of strategy, it is advisable to envisage a clearer differentiation with the main competitors by ensuring more distinctive elements (e.g., logistics, innovation produced, quality). This approach to strategy involves a logic of development of human potential envisaged as much as a prospect for the increase of the company's competitiveness.

Third, in terms of sales management, there is good reason to implement a more ambitious marketing policy piloted by one salaried salesman of the company who is vested in the results. This approach also supported the company in developing its export strategy.

Finally, from the point of view of human resources management, the current policy was soon going to reach its limits. Eventually, the question of the recruitment of a specialist in HR management was going to raised, focusing on bringing in an expert capable of demonstrating the interest and the legitimacy of its function in the company by promoting its own production (of methods, tools, and so forth). Ultimately, it will be a question of rigorously preparing the introduction of the HR function by a new employee of the company as the company turned to a qualitative management approach centred on the acquisition and development of new skills.

In summary, this company case shows how the implementation of qualitative development of the company is possible, based on creating more autonomy for the actors as well as the improvement of the professionalism in management that will facilitate the restructuring of the company and control of its growth.

CONCLUSION

The international constraints of competitiveness and financial profitability force companies to continually look for more productivity and flexibility. This quest for competitiveness cannot be discussed without taking into account the profound changes that organizations and their management are subjected to. The globalization of companies can constitute a real opportunity to develop the skills of employees and their level of qualification. It is in such a perspective that the management systems of skills and knowledge develop. Indeed, the international context characterized by the rise in complexity and uncertainty makes the control of a broad range of key skills, such as capacities of discernment of the international managers, the organization of relational networks, management of emergent projects, synergising different activities, intercultural dynamics, and so forth. Contemporary approaches to management are often based on enhancing production of skills in the context of a knowledge economy and a dematerialization of the company. The development of collective work, the management of teams, and new forms of cooperation in companies result in organizational innovations that can lead to a renewed approach to human resource management.

NOTES

1. The term constructivism is used here in the singular as a paradigm of reference even if we admit that there are several forms of constructivism. F. Wacheux (1996) argues that several constuctivist attitudes are possible (p. 43), all the while insisting notably (p. 27) that the approach belongs to a process of "enactment" (Weick, 1979) whereby scientific production is a form of social construction (Morgan, 1990).
2. This epistemological positioning has significant theoretical and methodological implications for the research. We talked in detail about this in an article published in the *Journal of Business Ethics*, "The Ethnomethodological Approach of Management: A New Perspective on Constructivist Research" (2000). The latest work joins in this perspective. For example, research on leadership (Noguera & Plane, 2016; Plane, 2015) shows that the questions of high potential is a contingent social construct.

REFERENCES

Argyris, C. (1983). Action science and intervention. *Journal of Behavioral Science, 19,* 115–140.

Berger, P., & Luckmann, T. (1986). *La construction sociale de la réalité* [The social building of reality]. Paris, France: Méridiens Klincksieck.

Bournois, F., & Roussillon, S. (1998). *Préparer les dirigeants de demain* [Preparing the leaders of the future]. Paris, France: Les éditions d'Organisation.

Caby, J., & Hirigoyen, G. (2001). *La création de valeur* [The creation of value]. Paris, France: Economica.

Cappelletti, L. (2012). *Le contrôle de gestion de l'immatériel: Une nouvelle approche du capital humain* [The management control of intangibles: A new approach for human capital]. Paris, France: Dunod.

Crozier, M., & Friedberg, E. (1980). *Actors and systems. The politics of collective action.* Chicago, IL: The University of Chicago Press.

Devereux, G. (1980). *De l'angoisse à la méthode dans les sciences du comportement* [From anxiety to methodology in behavioral Sciences]. Paris, France: Flammarion.

Drucker, P. F. (1999). Knowledge-worker productivity: The biggest challenge. *California Management Review, 41*(2), 79–98.

Dumazert, J.P & Plane, J.-M. (2012). Negative deviant behaviors in the workplace: Cause s and impacts to co-workers and human relations. *Revue de Gestion des Ressources Humaines, 86,* 52–63.

Dumez, H. (2013). *Méthodologie de la recherche qualitative* [Methodology for qualitative research]. Paris, France: Vuibert.

Gaarfinkel, H. *Studies in ethnomethodology.* Englewoods Cliffs, NJ: Prentice Hall.

Girin, J. (1990). Analyse empirique des situations de gestion: éléments de théorie et de méthode [Empirical Analyses in Management: Elements of Theory and Method]. In *Epistémologies et Sciences de Gestion* (pp. 141–181). Paris, France: Economica.

Hatchuel, A. (1992). L'intervention des chercheurs en entreprise [The Intervention of Researchers within Companies]. *Education Permanente, 113,* 73–88.

Huberman, M. A., & Miles, M. B. (1991). *Analyse des données qualitative: Recueil de nouvelles méthodes [Analyses of qualitative data: New methods].* Bruxelles: De Boeck Université.

Hubert, G., & Van de Ven, A. (1990). Longitudinal field research methods for studying processes of organizational change. *Organizational Science, 1*(3), 213–219.

Galens, J., & Roussel, P. (1998). *Méthodes de recherche en gestion des ressources humaines* [Research methods in human resources managemen]. Paris, France: Economica, Collection. Recherche en Gestion.

Kaplan, R. S. (1998). Innovation action research: Creating new management theory and practice. *Journal of Management Accounting Research, 10,* 89–117.

Koenig, G. (1993). Production de la connaissance et constitution des pratiques organisationnelles [Knowledge and organizational practice building]. *Revue de Gestion des Ressources Humaines, 9,* 4–17.

Matteu, M. (1986). La familiarité distante [The distant familiarity]. *Gérer et Comprendre–Annales des Mines* (March), 81–94.

Mevellec, P. (1990). *Outils de gestion: La pertinence retrouvée* [Tools of Management: Towards a new pertinence]. Paris, France: Comptables Malesherbes.

Miller, D., & Friesen, (1984): *Organizations: A quantum view.* Englewood Cliffs, NJ: Prentice Hall.

Morgan, G. (1990). Paradigm diversity in organizational research. In J. Haasrd & D. Oym (Eds.), *Theory and philosophy in organizational research* (pp. 13–29). New York, NY: Routledge.

Nonaka, I. (1994). A dynamic theory of organizational knowledge creation. *Organization Science, 5*(1), 14–37.

Pérez, R. (Ed.) (2003). *Management de la compétitivité et emploi* [Managing competitivity and employment]. Paris, France: L'Harmattan.

Pettigrew, A. M. (1990). Longitudinal field research on change: Theory and practice. *Organization Science, 1*(3), 267–292.

Plane, J. M. (2016)., *Management des organisations* [The management of organizations]. Paris, France: Dunod.

Plane, J.-M. (2001). *Action science, intervention on company management and development.* Paper presented at the EGOS meeting, Lyon, France, July.

Plane, J.-M. (2000). *Méthodes de recherche-intervention en management* [Methods of intervention-research in management]. Paris, France: L'Harmattan.

Reix, R. (1995). Savoir tacite et savoir formalisé dans l'entreprise [Tacite and formalized knowledge in businesses]. *Revue Française de Gestion, 105,* 17–28.

Sanchez, R., & Heene, A. (Ed.) (1997). *Strategic learning and knowledge management.* Chichester, England: Wiley.

Sanchez, R., Heene, A., & Thomas, H. (Ed.) (1996). *Dynamics of competence-based competition: Theory and practice in the new strategic management.* London, England: Elsevier Science.

Savall, (1986). Le contrôle de qualité des informations émises par les acteurs des organisations [The quality control of the data collected from actors]. In *Colloque Méthodologies Fondamentales de la Recherche en Gestion* (pp. 206–280). Paris, France: Actes FNEGE-ISEOR.

Savall, H., & Zardet V. (2004). *Recherche en sciences de gestion approche qualimétrique: Observer l'objet complexe* [The qualimetrics approach: Observing the complex object]. Paris, France: Economica.

Schein, E.H. (1987). *Process consultation, volume II: Lessons for managers and consultants.* New York, NY: Addison Wesley.

Senge, P. (1992). *The first discipline.* London, England: Century Business.

Tabatoni, P., & Jarniou, P. (1975). *Les systèmes de gestion: Politiques et structures* [The systems of management: Politics and structures]. Paris, France: PUF.

Tchankam, J. P & Feudjo, J. R. (2013). Une expérience africaine de coaching: Le coaching des PME par les experts-comptables dans le processus de changement OCAM-OHADA en Afrique [An African experience of coaching: A case study research]. *Recherches en Sciences de Gestion, 3*(96), 47–65.

Teece, D. J., Pisano, G., & Shuen, A. (1997). Dynamic capabilities and strategic management. *Strategic Management Journal, 18*(7), 509–533.

Thietarta, R. A. (1999). *Méthodes de recherche en management* [Research in management]. Paris, France: Dunod.

Thompson, J. D. (1967). *Organizations in action.* New York, NY: Mc Graw-Hill.

Wacheux, M. (1996). *Méthodes qualitatives et recherche en gestion* [Qualitative methods and research in management]. Paris, France: Economica.

Weick, K. E. (1989). Theory construction as disciplined imagination. *Academy of Management Review, 14*(4), 516–531.

Weick, K. E. (1979). *The social psychology of organizing.* Reading, MA: Addison Wesley.

Whitley, R. (1984). *The intellectual and social organization of the Science.* Oxford, England: Clarendon Press.

Zarifian, P. (1994). Compétence et organisation qualifiante en milieu industriel [Skills and competencies in the industry sector]. In F. Minet, M. Parlier, & S. DeWitte (Eds.), *La compétence : mythe, construction ou réalité?* [Skills: Myth, construction or reality?] (pp. 111–134). Paris, France: L'Harmattan.

CHAPTER 4

TOOLS AND DEVICES FOR INTERVENTION RESEARCH

The Case of Intervention in Human Resource Management

Florence Noguera

Research in the social sciences and particularly in human resource management is often confronted with ethical, scientific, and methodological problems. These challenges range from cognitive dissonance related to the acceptability of the problems to be solved, and the reconciliation of the values borne by each of the actors in the organization, to the possible divergence between scientific intention, the initial project, and operational actions. The objective of this chapter is to present the tools of intervention-research within a specific field of management sciences—human resources management (HRM). Moving beyond the characteristics of intervention research in the HRM area and the peculiarity of the epistemological devices of the intervener-researcher discussed earlier in the volume (see Chapter 1 & 3), the methods and specific techniques of an intervention-research in HRM is examined, tools that will be illustrated by an intervention-research project carried out within a tax authority of 1,040 agents.

Intervention Research, pages 71–91

THE INSTRUMENTAL CHARACTERISTICS OF INTERVENTION RESEARCH IN HUMAN RESOURCE MANAGEMENT

Intervention research is a method favored as a way of coming close to reality and the situation of management—as they arise in companies and organizations—due to its specific methodological characteristics. The major interest of intervention research is the production of theoretical knowledge stemming from actions carried out on the ground. Intervention research in an HRM context contains several methodological characteristics. One of its fundamental characteristics is that intervention research is research based on *action* as it favors a phenomenological conception of research by studying the phenomena observed from actions of change on observed objects (David, 2000; Plane, 2000). This clinical research methodology attempts to observe companies and organizations "over time to follow the natural evolution or the provoked changes" (Wacheux, 1996, p. 85). It allows us to study the behavior of the actors and to observe the evolution of management practices (Argyris & Schön, 1978), building on the elaboration and validation of hypotheses of knowledge from the observation of field data (Savall & Zardet, 2008). Intervention research thus allows us to transform—to change a situation—and to study the effects of these changes on individual, collective, and organizational levels and generate results, which in this case, reflect the impact of the implementation of a new HRM policy on systems of remuneration.

A second fundamental characteristic is that intervention-research is research *in action*, which joins in the lineage of the constructivist trend (Moigne, 1990) in that simple observation on the ground modifies the behavior of the actors and transforms their reality (Lawrence & Lorsch, 1967). The transformation process of a studied object is not a problem for the researcher but rather a research opportunity. The interaction between the observer and the observed is by definition, within the framework of intervention research, a prerequisite of knowledge. This method is an interactive method whose aim is "transformative," in contrast to so called "contemplative" approaches (Avenier & Thomas, 2013) between researchers and their field. Its objective is both to describe and understand management situations, as well as the methods of animation of HR policy.

A third fundamental characteristic is that intervention research is research *for action*. It consists of producing knowledge and concepts that allow us "to think of trajectories" to which companies and organizations could commit (Hatchuel, 1994). As practice is one of the two ends of intervention research, the communication of created knowledge is also done for practitioners and thus in a language usable by them and translatable in the practices. Intervention research thus draws its characteristics from its rapport on the ground and its vocation to innovate. Within this context, the researcher is much more than an expert applying techniques, tools, and HRM models. One's observation and reflection also produce knowledge, scientific knowledge from an analysis of reality. As these characteristics of intervention research are not as explicit in other sciences, the sciences of management can so be qualified as "science of action" (Argyris, 1995), based on the qualification of researcher-actor or intervenor-researcher. When we speak of intervention research, the researcher is indeed also an actor, that is, in the company of and a participant in change with the actors of the organization.

The Positioning of the Intervener Researcher in HRM

Similar to other disciplines in the social sciences, the role of the researcher—in terms of place, timing, and impact—on the observed object of research raises crucial questions in HRM interventions. Indeed, HRM researchers can be confronted with a range of problems (Arnaud, 1996)—for example, the collected data can be a "mutual parasite" and differences can exist between the act of observation and its reality—due to the researchers' past experience, motivation, and intellectual and ideological choices. Researchers can see only what they want to see by forgetting what they don't like or because of their closeness with the actors on ground. To overcome these difficulties, the researcher has to constantly compromise between the project (guided by its research problem) and the problems on the ground identified by the key decision-makers of the company. It is thus a compromise between a logic of knowledge and a logic of action (Girin, 1986), a compromise which occurs essentially through the definition of the epistemological position of the researcher in the company.

Epistemological Positioning: Alternating Immersion and Distancing

The modus operandi of intervention research in HRM requires the alternation between immersion in a company and distancing in order to conceptualize the research problem and test the defined hypotheses ex ante (see Chapter 1). It alternates phases of formalization and contextualization of duration and of variable intensity with the objective of simultaneously developing the models and tools of HRM for action and the hypotheses and research results for knowledge. This approach is why intervention research constitutes a model of design and piloting of particular change, in which design and implementation of innovation are managed "simultaneously" (David, 2000).

The alternation between conceptualization and experimentation means that certain stages of field work consist of testing, in the sense of experimenting, concept development, tools in a situation of observable management, and then evaluating the results of this experimentation to refine the modelling and concepts, potentially proposing new concepts that result from knowledge acquired from the experimentation. This reasoning joins the model of the recursive loop "abduction-deduction-induction" described by David (1999) on the generation of ideas, the order in which they appear, and the data needed to validate them. *Deduction* is a means of demonstration. This reasoning consists of putting forward a hypothesis, then collecting data to validate it, and finally deducting from it logically its degree of validation. Deduction is characterized by the fact that, if the hypotheses initially formulated are true, then the conclusion must inevitably be true (Charreire & Durieux, 1 999). At the outcome of certain inferences (deduction), the researcher is then able to put forward an explanatory and/or predictive conclusion.

Induction is a process of generalization by which we extend what was observed on an individual basis to a class of objects. This reasoning corresponds to a logical inference that confers a constancy on discovery. Induction is thus the reasoning by which we cross from the specific to the general, from facts to laws, from effect to cause, and from consequences to principles.

Finally, *abductive* reasoning consists of developing an empirical observation that connects a general rule to a consequence, that is to say, which allows us to find the consequence if the general rule is true (David et al., 2000). Abduction confers an explanatory or comprehensive status on the discovery which, in order to create the rule, needs then to be tested.

Within the framework of the process of alternation between immersion and distancing, deduction allows us to generate consequences, induction to establish the main rules, and abduction to build hypotheses. Everyone has their own manner, thus these logics play a role in the construction and validation of hypotheses and thus knowledge. In intervention research, the analysis of materials is carried out gradually, by alternating different logics of reasoning, and thus it is only after a certain time that invariants, constants appear. As an example, the use and importance given by the intervenor-researcher in HRM to the alternation between phases of immersion and distancing with regard to the field of study is the construction of hypotheses. The work of the researcher is indeed based on the formulation of hypotheses comprised of three types: descriptive, explanatory, and prescriptive. *Descriptive* hypotheses (the what) are the ones stemming from the field, from the case evaluation of experiments or from bibliographical materials. The researcher makes, in the case of the formulation of descriptive hypotheses, a selection of relevant signs in the field of research, which one has to verify by observation. The *explanatory* hypotheses (the why) stem from an interpretation or from an explanation of previous reports. The researcher makes a selection of the causes of the relevant signs observed. *Prescriptive* hypotheses (the how) represent the real added value brought by the researcher to the answer of his research. They stem from a proposal of possible solutions, from possible scenarios stemming from the experiment that it will be a question of demonstrating and validating during the process of research.

The construction of hypotheses is done gradually, depending on the accumulation of new bibliographical and experimental materials. The main difficulty lies in analyzing, ordering, and structuring these materials in relation to the research problem and to the main thread of the work. The formulation of hypotheses should allow researchers to structure their thinking and direct their research work. The formulation of hypotheses allows us to capitalize on all the ideas of qualitative or quantitative nature, which will allow the researcher to do a demonstration. The hypotheses grow richer and are constantly modified throughout the research process and, in particular, during the exploitation of the bibliographical or field materials (Miles & Huberman, 2003). Permanent comings and goings between the literature, the research laboratory, and a set of fields allows the alternation between immersion and distancing, in the sense that the researcher joins in a process that alternates between empirical observation, induction, formulation of logico-deductive hypotheses, and real-life confrontation by empirical observation, and so on. For illustrative purposes, Figure 4.1 presents an extract from the body of the hypotheses of an intervention research carried in a tax authority.

Explanatory hypotheses are built by abduction, their effects are analyzed by deduction, the asserted theories are highlighted by induction, and,

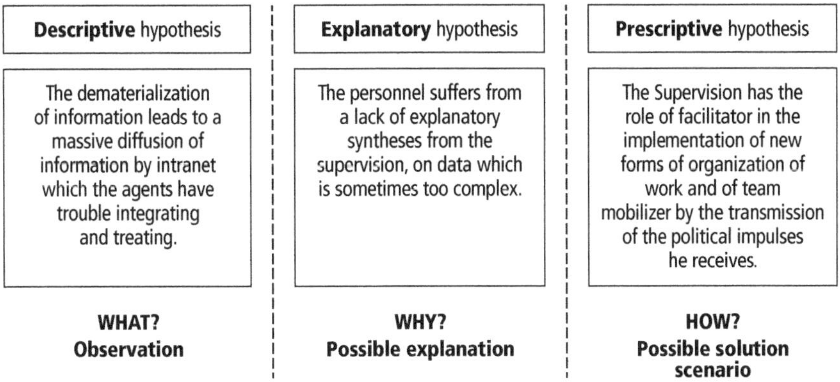

Figure 4.1 Extract from the body of the hypotheses of an intervention-research project within a tax authority.

when they are countered, the process restarts on the principle of abduction by new explanatory hypotheses to be tested.

The Co-Production of Knowledge for Action

Intervention-research in HRM does not limit itself to a simple "collection" of data, but to a "production," even a "co-production," of data with the actors on the ground. Indeed, intervention-research can have as its origin a request for help on behalf of the management of a company or an organization. The co-production of knowledge places the intervention-research in the constructivist paradigm because the change and the transformation process of the studied object are not problems for the researcher but opportunities for research.

Intervention-research is a cognitive and complex process of interactions between the actors of an organization and the researcher, charged, from the point of view of the actors, with teaching HRM methods and tools as well as the stimulation of long-lasting transformations in the mode of management and the functioning of an organization. In the case of intervention- research, we speak about the principle of *cognitive interactivity* between the researchers and actors of the company (Savall & Zardet, 2011), with a permanent aim of increasing the value of the significance of the information handled in the scientific work. Knowledge is co-produced by the actors and the researcher, via their respective social representations, confronted between them by successive iterations (Buono & Savall, 2007), which correspond to permanent comings and goings, as much physical as intellectual, between the laboratory, the place of conceptualization, and the ground, that is, the place of experimentation.

Indeed, this process allows us to gradually build a relationship, a link of "consensus-confidence" between the actors of the organization and the researcher. This is important for several reasons: from listening to what the actors have to say and ensuring the scrupulous respect of ethical rules by the researcher on the use and the presentation of the data collected, to the distance of analysis that the research must keep in the relationship with the company and the will to see the researcher use the data transmitted to bring changes to the organization.

This relationship of trust is widely strengthened during the presentation of the results because this phase allows each of the actors to verify that their words were heard, noted, transcribed, respected, and made anonymous (Matheu, 1986). Work systems, allowed by interviews through the presentation of the results allows the actors of the company to constantly confront and clarify their respective subjective representations and to create a dialogue with the researcher. These interactions of speech, behavior, and representation in this way generate for each of the actors a new refined representation source of the production of knowledge.

INTERVENTION-RESEARCH AND THE PRODUCTION OF KNOWLEDGE: IN WHAT WAYS ARE THEY COMPATIBLE?

Within the framework of intervention-research, the researcher is confronted with a risk connected to political pressure and the mental structures of the studied organization. Indeed, researchers can be subjected to political pressure from the object of the study, which can take them away from their objective to create knowledge. This risk is strong in HRM where the subjects covered (restructuring, remuneration, implication) are sensitive. This political pressure can be explained by the contractual links uniting the researcher and the studied company.

Furthermore, the methodology of intervention-research is a field research method whose border with consultation is sometimes tenuous. Intervention research in HRM uses advice and its tools as a research technology (Cappelletti & Noguera, 2007; Peretti, 2008). The risk for the intervener-researcher is to favor the practical dimension of the work and neglect the scientific dimension, because of political and cultural constraints, or even constraints of time and career.

To describe these phenomena, numerous authors, such as Schein (1984, 1985), prefer to speak about corporate culture. According to Schein, culture is an interconnected group of hypotheses, invented, discovered, or developed by a given group as it learns to face and handle its problems of external adaptation and internal integration. Culture corresponds where this interconnected ensemble works well enough to be considered as valid, and thus deserving to be taught to new members of the group. Cultural pressure can deviate researchers—more or less consciously—from their problem and initial hypotheses. The development of phases of distancing from the studied company, and regular exchanges with people outside the field (e.g., researchers from connected laboratories), allow us to limit these influences. Also, tools and devices of intervention-research are used to collect data which, by turning to the principles of *generic contingency*, *cognitive interactivity*, and *contradictory inter-subjectivity*, will be transformed into knowledge.

Intervention-research aims to transform its research object drawing on observations of the actors' concrete practices. In order to achieve this, intervention-research mobilizes specific and rigorous methods and techniques.

The Negotiation of an Intervention-Research in HRM

The negotiation of an intervention-research project in HRM assumes a prior identification of its economic, social, organizational, and management stakes for the various stakeholders: management, supervisors, employees of the company or the organization, and the team of the researchers. Within this context, the economic stakes require a thorough examination of the strategic perspectives of the economic development of the company. The economic stakes certainly affect the evolution of company's payroll and other induced charges, but also and especially the evolution of products (in the accounting sense revenues) of the company, the improvement of quality, and the development of human resources and the activities of creation of potential.

The social stakes can be found in the plan of the professional and extra-professional quality of life of internal actors connected to the possibility of stabilizing previously precarious jobs, ensuring appropriate remuneration for employees, and organizing schedules. Social stakes also affect external customers through the improvement of the quality of service, in particular the increase of the hourly amplitude devoted to client service.

The organizational stakes concern the satisfaction of the clientele, the versatility of the staff (security and flexibility of functioning), the training of the employees, and communication and coordination, which facilitates synchronization between people as well as the completion deadline of work and activities.

Finally, the management stakes concern the role of supervision and the strengthening of its function of stimulation and control of people and activities, the management of the autonomy of the people and delegation, and finally the implications for employees. The intervener-researcher has to define the main axes, objectives, and contents of the intervention beforehand with the management of the company within a requirement specification (see Chapters 2, 5, & 6). Indeed, before the launch of an intervention-research project, it is necessary to define the objectives, the methods to be used, and the actions to be realized. This decomposition between objectives, methods, and services constitutes a complete display of intervention-research (Savall & Zardet, 1987):

- The *objectives* are the formalization of the results to be achieved with regard to the analysis of the request by the company. It is the representation of the research problem to be solved.
- The *methods* specify the methodology through which the objectives will be reached, which includes the methods and tools that will be mobilized by the intervener-researcher during the investigation.

- Finally, the services are the actions and activities realized by the intervener-researcher according to the chosen methods.

CONTEXT OF THE RESEARCH

As an example of the approach discussed above, an intervention-research was introduced by the department management of a tax authority of 1,040 agents in the form of an intervention-research contract. The contract encompassed: (a) the introduction of quality within tax authority, (b) organization of contracts of objectives and means (Organic and Finance Law),(c) organization of performance contracts for 2003–2005 (the quality of service was a strategic objective), (d) a translation of quality commitments and a regular measure of quality standards (e.g., the "commitment to facilitate your taxes"), (e) preparation of the merger of the French Tax authority and the public treasury, and (f) the dematerialization of tax returns.

The scientific objective of this intervention-research was to understand why agents who often express a strong attachment to public service do not get involved spontaneously in changes aimed at the quality of service to the user. The more operational objectives of the intervention-research were negotiated through a collection of expectations, followed by a document presenting the objectives, methods, and proposed services (see Figure 4.2).

Defining the Scope of an Intervention-Research Project in HRM

The scope of an intervention-research project must be specified in the requirement specifications, that is, the limits of the field, the points excluded from the research, the method and techniques for data collection, and the detailed nature of the investigation. The intervener-researcher defines the field in connection with the company's management and the HR unit, in essence the micro-space within which the research work will be carried out—which encompasses the people to interviewed, the company's material and operational conditions, documents to be used, and a detailed chronology of the intervention with a time budget. The scope of the intervention-research can concern all the employees of the company or only one or several categories of actors.

As suggested by Figure 4.3, it is essential to carry out interviews with all categories of staff working in the scope of the intervention-research (blue-collar staff and/or employees, agents, supervisors, the people in charge of the service, the department or the unit). The staff of the company outside the field of the intervention-research can be involved, the choice made

INTERNAL COMMUNICATIONS ACTION AND QUALITY OF SERVICE

1 SUCCEEDING TOGETHER IN A PROJECT OF SUSTAINABLE IMPROVEMENT OF THE QUALITY OF SERVICE

- Connecting the quality of public service to the improvement of the human, social and economic performance of the agents
- Identifying the problems encountered since the implementation of the "Helping you with your taxes" program (Quality of service program)
- Mobilizing the various categories of agents towards quality, activate all the zones of dialogue and agree to handle all the problems

2 CONTRIBUTING TO THE ADHERENCE OF THE AGENTS TO THE QUALITY OF SERVICE TO THE USERS PROJECT

- Forge the acceptance of the quality program
- Build and maintain the cohesion of all the agents around the quality of service program
- Strengthen the consideration of the agents of the ground

3 PRODUCE ACTIONS FOR IMPROVEMENT

- Build reference tables of functioning in a participative and transverse way
- Develop solutions and actions of progress
- Forge the acceptance of the solutions, negotiate and develop a transversal approach

4 ORGANIZE THE FOLLOW-UP AND EVALUATION OF THE ACTIONS

- Build a system of piloting
- Conceive the processes, the indicators of piloting and an evaluation
- Build a communications action

Figure 4.2 Requirement specifications of intervention-research—Tax authority of 1,040 agents. *Source:* Noguera (2009, 2010) intervention research within a tax authority.

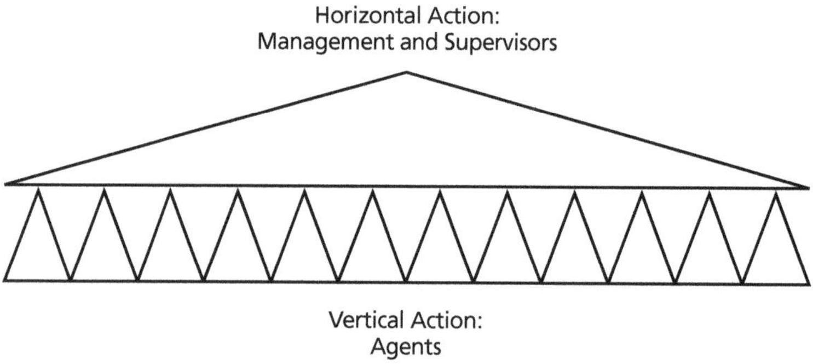

Figure 4.3 Architecture of an intervention-research: The HORIVERT[1] process within a tax authority. *Source:* Noguera (2009, 2010) intervention research within a tax authority.

according to hierarchical and functional connections. However, it is necessary to meet with the manager, HR manager, financial and administrative manager, managing director of the company, and staff representatives (e.g., union representatives, members of the works council, hygiene and safety committee). The field of intervention-research in HRM is characterized by the variety of the levels, domains, and the activities to be observed (mobilizable human resources, social risks threatening the company, the dysfunctions which are the source; Plane, 2000).

For illustrative purposes, within the departmental direction of a tax authority, intervention- research was carried out with 1,040 agents. The experiment within this organization concerned twelve sites (6 urban sites, 3 outer-urban sites, 3 sites situated in rural areas). The intervention was carried out within the tax authority, including the management team, supervisors, the staff, and union representatives (see Figure 4.4). The duration of the research–experiment was 9 months, from January to September 2006. The intervention-research project was built according to a double approach, horizontal and vertical. This tax authority was organized in 7 divisions: an HR division; a logistics, IT, and domain division; an organizational studies and prospective division; a tax audit division, a private individuals division; a contentious division; and a professional division.

We can distinguish two poles of activity, one composed of services with departmental competence and the other composed of services with local competence. The intervention-research focused on services with local competence, that is, tax offices, the tax departments of companies, land registries, property tax offices, and tax revenue offices. The objective of this research was to identify and understand the resistance of the agents in the implementation of a change program aimed at improving the quality of

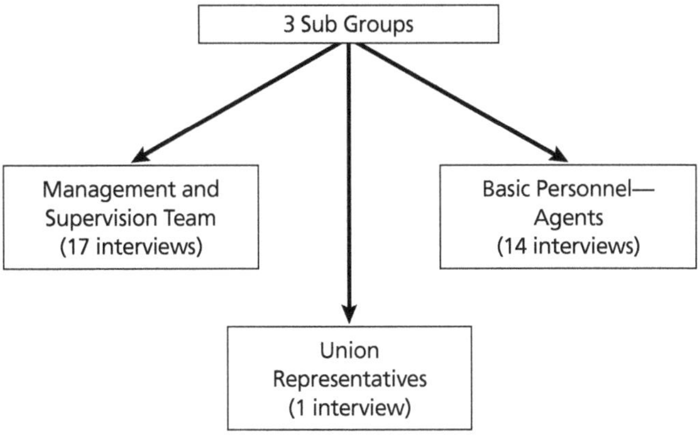

Figure 4.4 Segmentation of the sample

TABLE 4.1 Recap of Number of Interviews Carried Out

Segmentation of the Sample		
Sub-Population	**Number of Interviews**	**Number of People**
Management and supervision team	17	17
Basic personnel—agents	14	69
Union representatives	1	6
Total Interviews	32	92

Source: Noguera (2009, 2010) intervention research within a tax authority

service. An in-depth diagnosis was carried out within the twelve sites according to socioeconomic methodology (Savall, 1975).

The sample (see Table 4.1) represented approximately 10% of the total staff of the general tax office. The sample consisted of 40% men and 60% women. The study favored agents of the services dealing directly with the public: the direct tax base sector in tax offices, the delivery of cadastral extracts service, property sectors in the land tax offices, and tax departments of companies.

Data Collection

Following the example of Girin (1986) and Singly (1993), the construction of field data was not objective, objectification being impossible to achieve because "reality is inexhaustible and can only be described by the mediation of categories of perception." The collection of materials within the framework of a HRM intervention-research project depends on a thorough evaluation of the management situations met in each of the companies and organizations studied. Field work, because it observes reality in all of its complexity and the event in what is short-lived, needs techniques that are simultaneously rigorous, so as not to be overwhelmed by information, and open-ended, so as not to miss interesting and unplanned observations (Grawitz, 1993).

Researcher have several tools of investigation allowing them to collect field data. Among these techniques are: in-depth interviews, direct observation of the situations, and the analysis of internal and external documents of the studied company (e.g., social audit, social dashboard, annual report, training plan, quality charter).

In-Depth Interviews

The interviews constitute the favored technique for collecting a detailed description of the situations experienced by the actors. The interviews also allow the research to explore and examine the dysfunctions and regulations that were implemented.

Exploratory Interviews

The conduct of exploratory interviews is a preliminary step in any intervention- research. This phase allows us to define, with the actors of the studied organization, the themes and subthemes of work. The exploratory interviews conducted with the people in charge of the micro-space consist of collecting significant figures, historical data (e.g., dates of creation, significant stages), and information on the structure of responsibilities. They also highlight the technical, social, economic, and commercial constraints that weigh on the organization of the work, the physical working conditions, the adopted forms of working time, the levels of qualifications, dysfunctions, and, more generally, all the working and living conditions of the employees in the company. These exploratory interviews allow us to obtain a synthetic description of the site, including: the business sector, origin of skills (knowledge, know-how) and their evolution, products, productions, services, company range and volume of activity, relevant market data (e.g., market share, level of export), the type of clientele and the importance of main customers, and the evolution of revenues for the last 3 to 5 years.

The intervener-researcher has to highlight the constraints that weigh on the organization of time and the nature of jobs offered—for example, methods of organization of the work by socio-professional groups, modulation of collective or individualized schedules, compressed work week, overtime, modulation and teams at the end of the week, annualized part-time, time savings account, partial unemployment, temporary work, seasonal workers, and fixed-term contract.

Finally, the exploratory interviews consist of carrying out an analysis of the structures and behavior of the studied company or organization. According to the results of intervention research by Savall and Zardet (1987), an organization is defined as a set of structures and behaviors, the interaction of which produces expected (planned) and real (emergent) functioning. The structures are envisaged as permanent, relatively stable elements, which influence behavior. Five categories of structures can be analyzed by the intervener-researcher: (a) the physical structures (premises, surface, distribution, geographical situation); (b) the technological structures (means of production, level of technology, level of IT integration); (c) the organizational structures (process and flow of production, organization of work teams, the hierarchical and functional organization chart, qualifications, level and number, structures of coordination, committee meetings and working groups, frequency); (d) the demographic structures (staff, ages, seniority, gender, insecure and seasonal jobs, variations over 3 years); and (e) the mental structures (academic level (initial, continuous), training initiative and budget, versatility). The behavior corresponds to observed human actions, having an incidence on the physical and social environment. The latter are characterized by their cyclical nature and their instability. Five logics of behavior can be observed: individual behavior, group behavior, category-specific behavior, behavior of affinity or pressure groups, and collective behavior.

Operating Modalities of the Qualitative Interviews

As a general rule, during an intervention-research in addition to people in the observed field outside people who are at the interface of the studied micro-space are also interviewed. If the size of the micro-space is too big, the researcher with the help of the person in charge of that micro-space, defines a representative sample, generally between 20–30% of the staff of the scope of the intervention-research initiative.

The interviews of management and supervisors are individual and last 1 hour. The interviews are carried out in small groups of three to six people for the blue-collar staff and employees, staff representatives and union representatives, making sure that these groups are homogeneous in relation to the jobs of the participants (people with the same job, the same employment-type or from the same sector). The interviews can also be groups of interfaces, that is, jobs or different sectors. These interviews last approximately 1.5 hours, according to the complexity of the problems that emerge. Other criteria for choosing the people for the group interviews can be considered to ensure the best representativeness of the sample, for example, demographic criteria (senior and new staff in the company, the youngest people to the oldest, men and women) and behavioral criteria (e.g., active people and people less appreciated by the management, introverts, shy people, extroverts). If the studied organization consists of various sites or units, a criterion based on geographical locality will have to be considered, for example, urban, outer-urban, and rural units.

Within the framework of an intervention research two types of interviews can be conducted: semi-directive interviews and directive interviews. *Semi-directive interviews* are carried out based on an interview guide. This approach allow us to collect qualitative and quantitative social and organizational information. The *directive interviews* are generally intended to collect quantitative and financial data from a very precise guide.

The interview guide (see Table 4.2) used within the framework of the semi-directive qualitative interviews is drawn up by the intervener-researcher in interaction with the actors on the ground based on the exploratory interviews undertaken with the people in charge of the studied micro-space. The interview is divided generally into themes, subthemes, and sub-subthemes.

TABLE 4.2 Example of an Interview Guide for Intervention-Research

1 Relations With Users	
1.1 Telephone reception	Hours of telephone reception Material and supplies: phone equipment Management of phone calls Disruptive factors in time management Switchboard
1.2 Mail	Management and processing of mail, e-mails and faxes Sufficient response time to mails Processing of the written complaints of users
1.3 Physical reception	Arrangement and layout of the reception and the premises Hours of physical reception Information and follow up of users Information system Management of Reception
2 Organization and Resources	
2.1 Organization of work	Distribution of tasks, missions and functions Interest of the work Distribution of the workload Autonomy in work
2.2 The Premises	Configuration of the reception Working conditions Safety of premises IT equipment
2.3 Management of Staff	Adequacy training—employment Available skills Training needs System of remuneration
3 Communication and Strategy	
3.1 Communication/ coordination/ concertation	Supervision team Relations with the environment services (private individuals, professionals, corporate services, land registry) Systems of communication–coordination–concertation Transmission of the internal/external information
3.2 Rules and procedures linked to the quality program	Knowledge of the quality program Constraints of the quality program Respect for quality procedures Existence of procedures
3.3 Strategy	Objectives and strategic orientations Communication of the objectives of the quality program Objectives are the object of a regular follow-up The results are communicated . . .
3.4 Management and follow up of quality	Information system (standards/commitments quality of quality program Quantitative, qualitative and financial indicators Mediums of internal/external communication Method of processing and existence of systems of strategic evaluation Human, technical and financial means

Source: Noguera (2009, 2010) intervention research within a tax authority

Conduct of Qualitative Interviews

The researcher who leads the interview has to implement a strategy of intervention following the design of the interview guide. In the sense that researchers who lead an interview is subjected to a muddled flow of information, they have to have an interview strategy in order to maximize the share of useful information. The choice of this mode of data collection can be explained by the desire to collect primary data that is as reliable as possible on the situations experienced by the actors of the organization. It also allows us to collect a large variety of opinions and to propose, afterwards, methods and innovative tools meeting the expectations of the largest number of respondents. During the qualitative interviews, researchers must take exhaustive notes.

As part of the technical plan, during the open qualitative semi-directive interviews the actors met individually express themselves freely on the themes, subthemes, and sub-subthemes of the interview grid. First, they are asked to reflect on what they consider important for them. The duration of expression on the themes can be uneven, so the intervener-researcher might have to refocus the interview, especially if the respondent spends too much time on one theme or sub theme. As a general rule, the themes are handled in their entirety by the actors, while subthemes and sub-subthemes are not systemically handled.

Participative Observation

In-depth analysis of a phenomenon, as specified by Amado (1989), cannot be allowed to be reduced to only what the actors say about it, because they can be ill-informed. Their ideas can also be dependent on capacities of verbalization and translation of real-life or observed situations.

To limit these biases for the relevance of the data collected in the interviews, the intervener-researcher deploys the second technique of data collection—direct observation. Direct observation aims essentially at collecting unbiased information on the studied object. It can be concentrated, diffuse or delegated. It is *concentrated* when the researcher dedicates several hours, even several days to observe the studied object. It can be seen during the participation of the researcher in internal work meetings, during the support of the company in the management of a project of change, or during meetings with at least one of the members of the organization. It can be *diffuse* when any physical presence of the researcher at the work place is an opportunity for direct observation of the object. It concerns the collection, by the researcher, of nonverbal indicators emitted, for example, during interviews (gestures, spatial relation, tone) and the collection of verbal and/or nonverbal indicators when visiting the company. It is *delegated* when the researcher asks the supervision of the micro-space to observe for themselves certain predefined situations and to note what they see over a few days. Whatever the shape, direct observation must be then organized and validated with the actors of the organization to produce relevant and reliable information.

Analysis of Documents

Researchers complete their data by the study of documents such as organization charts, service bills, annual reports, activity sheets, and piloting indicators. These documents provide an additional perspective for understanding certain expressions emitted by the actors during the interviews, by using for example the social information of the company on occupational accidents, absenteeism, and personnel turnover. It also consists of documents realized individually or semi-collectively by members of the supervisory team, such as the dashboard of a micro-space (comprising indicators of activity, work procedures.

The objective of the intervener-researcher, by the diversification of sources of data, is to propose knowledge of generic order, by proposing invariants even if the latter are based on the analysis of particular contexts, in essence, the principle of *generic contingency*.

Data Processing of an Intervention-Research HRM Project

Because numerous data are collected on the ground within the framework of an intervention-research, the treatment and analysis of data in the codification of empirical are critical steps in the process. As such, it is important to select parts of relevant discussion (typical sentences) for the research in a way that the process of analysis is not the result of a random selection.

From the exhaustive notes taken during the interviews, the intervener-researcher should extract 12 to 15 relevant typical sentences per interview, which we also call *verbatim* or *witness sentences.* The witness sentence is a sentence expressed by an actor, short and well formulated so as to correctly capture the evoked problem or the proposed solution. After coding this data, the typical sentences are classified in themes, subthemes, and key ideas. The analysis of the interviews follows a similar pattern, drawing out themes, subthemes and key ideas (see Figure 4.5). The themes and subthemes are considered variables and the key idea is a value of the studied variable.

The interviews are handled by separating the main categories of staff interviewed: management, supervisors, staff, staff representatives, and union representatives. This segmentation allows the researcher to highlight the convergences and specificities of the key ideas between two categories of staff to create a quantitative indicator allowing us to measure the frequencies of the appearance of certain key ideas within the same category of staff (see Figure 4.6). Once the data are treated, the analysis is presented

THEMES	SUB-THEMES	KEY IDEAS	WITNESS SENTENCES
PROCESS AND EFFECTS OF CHANGE	• Working conditions and social climate • Distribution of tasks, responsibilities and autonomy in work • Planning and programming of activities and workload	KI 1 KI 2 KI 3 ...	WS 1 WS 2 WS 3 ...
ORGANIZATIONAL DYNAMIC	• Devices for defining the strategy and strategic orientations • Strategic implementation resources and strategy multiplication • Communication–coordination cooperation • Piloting and evaluating the strategy	KI 1 KI 2 KI 3 KI 4 ...	WS 1 WS 2 WS 3 WS 4 ...
ACTORS' STRATEGY	• Staff management • Involvement of stakeholders and interest in work • Role of internal and external actors • Management methods	KI 1 KI 2 KI 3 KI 4 ...	WS 1 WS 2 WS 3 WS 4 ...

Figure 4.5 Process of extraction from interviews during an intervention research.

Theme: STAFF MANAGEMENT

Sub-theme: System of remuneration

Key Idea: LESS REWARDING SYSTEM OF REMUNERATION
Frequency: (rather often)

We have such a reduced subsidy that it is not easy to motivate the agents on merit, we lack wiggle room.

During the evaluation, even if the objectives have been reached, it does not necessarily mean a better notation for the agent.

We gave the agents a 300-euro bonus as a result of modifications of structure. It is ridiculous! We do not know how to thank them and we do not know how to reward them.

The remuneration is not motivating, the agents say that they have a loss of purchasing power.

Figure 4.6 Illustrative operationalization of themes, sub-themes, and key ideas. *Source* (Spring): Noguera (2009, 2010,) intervention research in a tax authority.

to the respondents during a session of the *mirror effect,* to be validated during a contradictory debate between the respondents and the intervener-researchers. Once validated, materials are used as a working platform for the project group to lead actions of change and improvement. These first results are at the same time a reinforcement of knowledge for the researcher and a platform for change for the actors of the observed company.

Scientific knowledge is built based on a rigorous epistemological system, respecting an adapted methodology and epistemological principles as part of the data gathering and analysis process. First of all, the meta-epistemological principle of an intervention-research is that the research has to be transformative in nature or, at the very least, guided by the intention to transform the organization. By transforming an object of research, one produces knowledge.

There are three other epistemological principles that need to be respected in the conduct of an intervention-research, which we qualify as micro in nature. The first principle is of *cognitive interactivity*, the data are collected by interaction between the researcher and the actor (e.g., in an interview). The second principle is *contradictory inter-subjectivity*, the data collected must be discussed with the actors (e.g., mirror effect). Finally, the principle of *generic contingency*, comparing the results obtained with other cases to validate the data (witness sentences are classified in themes, subthemes, and more generic key ideas built on the basis of hundreds of intervention researches previously carried out by the research unit).

NOTE

1. See H. Savall & ISEOR Team of Research (1974–2017). For training on the Socioeconomic Approach of Management, see http://www.iseor-consulting.com. The HORIVERT approach was developed by ISEOR. It consists of a double globalizing action: a *horizontal action*, of methodological support involving the management and supervisory teams and a *vertical action*, in at least two basic units (service, agency, workshop) which involves people in the execution of the work (blue collar workers, employees) and the supervisor teams for these units. This double horizontal and vertical action allows us to ensure the best integration of socioeconomic intervention in the strategy of the company, and to resolve dysfunctions and strategies which are often interconnected. The HORIVERT approach on intervention is adapted to the biological rhythms of the activity proper to each company or organization and permits total irrigation.

REFERENCES

Argyris, C. (1995). Action science and organizational learning. *Journal of Managerial Psychology, 10*(6), 20–26.

Argyris, C., & Schon, D. (1978). *Organizational learning: A theory of action perspective.* Reading, MA: Addison Wesley.

Arnaud, G. (1996). Quelle stratégie d'observation pour le chercheur en sciences de gestion ? Prolégomènes à toute recherche *in situ* [How to make scientific observations *in situ* in management sciences]. *Economies et Sociétés, 22,* 235–264.

Avenier, M. J., & Thomas, C. (2013). *What kind of qualitative methods are adapted to doing research in which epistemological framework?* Paper presented at the XXIIème Conférence AIMS, Clermond-Ferrand.

Buono, A., & Savall, H. (2007) (Ed). *Socio-economic intervention in organizations: The intervener-researcher and the SEAM approach to organizational analysis.* Charlotte, NC: Information Age.

Cappelletti, L., & Noguera, F. (2007). *Research methods in management consulting.* Paper presented at the Academy of Management Annual Meeting, Doctoral student Consortium, Philadelphia, August.

Charreire, S., & Durieux, F. (1999). *Explorer et teste : Méthodes de recherche en management* [Exploring and testing: Methods of research in management]. Paris, France: Dunod.

David, A. (1999). *Logique, épistémologie et méthodologie en sciences de gestion* [Logic, epistemology and methodology in management sciences]. Paper presented at the 8th Conférence Internationale de Management Stratégique, Ecole Centrale de Paris, May.

David, A. (2000). Logique, épistémologie et méthodologie en sciences de gestion: Trois hypothèses revisitées [Logic, epistemology and methodology in management sciences: Three revisited hypotheses]. *Les nouvelles fondations des sciences de gestion.* Paris, France: Collection FNEGE.

David, A., Hatchuel, A., & Laufer, R. (2000). *Les nouvelles fondations des sciences de gestion* [The new pillars of management sciences]. Paris, France: Vuibert.

De Singly, F. (1993). *L'enquête et ses méthodes: le questionnaire* [The scientific inquiry and its methods: The questionnaire]. Paris, France : Nathan, Coll. Université.

Girin, J. (1986). *L'objectivation des données subjectives: Eléments pour une théorie du dispositif dans la recherche interactive* [The objectication of subjective data: Towards a theory of the framework in interactionist research]. Paris, France: Colloque ISEOR-FNEGE.

Grawitz, M. (1993). *Méthodes des sciences sociales* [Methods in social sciences]. Paris, France: Dalloz.

Hatchuel, A. (1994). Les savoirs de l'intervention en entreprise [The knowledge of the intervention within companies]. *Entreprise et Histoire, 7,* 59–75.

Lawrence, P. R., & Lorsch, J. W. (1967). *Organization and environment: Managing differentiation and integration.* Boston, MA: Harvard Business School Press.

Le Moigne, J.-L. (1995). *Les épistémologies constructives* [Constructiviste epistemologies]. Paris, Fance: PUF.

Matheu, M. (1986). La familiarité distante [The distant familiarity]. *Gérer et comprendre, Annales des Mines,* (March), 81–94.

Miles M., & Huberman A., (2003). *Analyse des données qualitatives: Recueil de nouvelles méthodes* [The analysis of qualitative data: New methods]. Paris, France: De Boeck Université

Noguera, F. (2002). Management stratégique du temps de travail: Instrumentation et impact de l'aménagement—Réduction du temps de travail. Cas d'expérimentation [The strategic management of the working time: Findings

from the case study of the working time reduction]. *Thèse de doctorat soutenue* (January).
Noguera, F., & Coste, F. (2009). Mutations organisationnelles et nouvelles régulations des organisations publiques? Cas d'une Direction des services fiscaux [Organizational changes and public management: The case of a department of the taxes administration]. *Les nouveaux défis du manager public.* Paris, France: L'Harmattan Collection RECEMAP.
Noguera, F. (2010). Les défis posés par la nouvelle gestion publique à la GRH: cas de la Direction Générale des impôts [The challenges of new public management dealing with HRM: The case study of the taxes administration]. *Revue de Gestion de Ressources Humaines, ESKA, 78,* 32–58.
Peretti, J.-M. (Ed.) (2008). *Tous talentueux* [We are all talents]. Paris, France: Editions d'Organisation.
Plane, J.M. (2000). *Méthodes de recherche-intervention en management* [Methods of intervention-research in management]. Paris, France: L'Harmattan.
Savall, H. (1975). *Enrichir le travail humain: l'évaluation économique* [Job enrichment: The economic evaluation]. Paris, France: Dunod,
Savall, H., & Zardet, V. (2011). *The qualimetrics approach. Observing the complex object.* Charlotte, NC: Information Age.
Savall, H., & ISEOR Team of Researchers. (1974–2017). Trainings on the Socio-Economic Approach of Management. See http://www.iseor-consulting.com
Savall, H., & Zardet, V. (2008). *Mastering hidden costs and socio-economic performance,* Charlotte, NC: Information Age.
Schein, E. (1984). Coming to a new awareness of organizational culture. *Sloan Management Review* (Winter), 3–16.
Schein, E. (1985). *Organizational culture and leadership.* San Francisco, CA: Jossey Bass.
Wacheux, F. (1996). *Méthodes qualitatives et recherche en gestion* [Qualitative methods en management sciences]. Paris, France: Economica.

CHAPTER 5

NEGOTIATING AND SELLING AN INTERVENTION-RESEARCH PROJECT THROUGH A STRUCTURED AND RIGOROUS METHOD

Laurent Cappelletti

The objective of intervention-research is to transform organizations to develop their practical performance and to collect data of scientific quality. In this sense, since intervention-research is intended to contribute to the value creation of an organization, ideally it needs to be sold, with the price of its sale corresponding to a fraction of the value created for the organization. Furthermore, the sale of an intervention-research project may motivate the researcher and his team, becoming a source of resources and establish relations between the researcher and the organization which, in addition to its status as a field of observation, acquires the commitment of the client. Nevertheless, to sell an intervention-research requires a methodology of negotiation and sale adapted to the immaterial products-services of which

Intervention Research, pages 93–109

it is a particular form. The chapter presents the key tools and features of an intervention-research negotiation and sales process (see also Chapter 2), illustrating them by studying the case of a sale of an intervention-research with a professional union in the recruitment sector.

CONVERGENCE AND DIVERGENCE BETWEEN CONSULTING AND RESEARCH-INTERVENTION

In order to successfully sell an intervention-research engagement, the salesperson must be fully aware of the similarities and differences between this methodology and the one typically used by consultants.

Intervention-Research as Scientific Consultancy

On the surface, intervention-research takes the form of a consultancy mission. In essence, unlike a traditional consultancy mission, its methodology must integrate epistemological mechanisms for data collection that must be explained in scientific publications. Should we reveal to the client these epistemological devices, which can remain entirely unknown to him? If the researcher wishes to quote the company observed in his scientific publications and thus obtain agreement for it, there is an ethical obligation to reveal the material to the client. If the researcher produces publications that respect the anonymity of the organizations observed, which is in principle our case and that of our research team, there is no obligation to reveal to the client this epistemological "cooking." Indeed what interests the client organization most is the consultancy through which the intervention-research is intended to help it to develop its performance; from the client side, there is clearly less interest in the intervention's scientific background or desire produce scientific publication. In summary, we recommend that researchers who wish to sell their research remain discreet about their scientific aspects and value their performance aspects in the eyes of the client (Savall & ISEOR Research Team, 1974–2017).

The convergence between a consulting mission and intervention-research resides in the fact that both will mobilize advisory tools to transform the organization and help it to develop its performance, for example, through surveys, analyzes, diagnostics, project groups, steering committees, training courses, and management tools. This implies that, as in a consulting firm, the researcher will develop a portfolio of salable consulting methods and services that will be applied for remuneration. The specificity between a consultancy engagement and an intervention-research project is that the treated company is not only a customer but also a scientific observation area (SOA). Consequently, the methods and the services of the intervener-researcher must make it possible to mobilize epistemological devices guaranteeing the quality and validity of the observations made to produce the scientific knowledge—and not only the practical knowledge reserved for the client. For this reason, we refer to intervention-research as a process of scientific consultancy, in other words, a methodology that uses consultancy as a research technology. The non-researcher consultant who works in the office does not worry about the epistemological devices integrated into his methods and consulting services (Buono & Savall, 2007, 2015; Savall & Zardet, 2008).

A question for the researcher, which can often be disruptive to the intervention and its conceptualization and writing process, emerges when the object observed in an intervention-research depends on the client's objectives. For example, if a client company purchases a mission to improve the decision-making processes of its executive committee, the intervener-researcher, who is committed to focus on that object, will not be able to comment on other facets of the organization, for instance, on the working conditions of the company's employees. In this sense, at first glance, the objects observed by an intervener-researcher depend on the objectives of the client and not on the scientific objectives of the researcher. But that is both true and false. It is true that an intervention-research is an inductive process whose data collection is centered above all on the problems that the client wants to treat. But it is also true that, by methodological opportunism, in responding to the client's request the intervener-researcher may be led to make peripheral observations on objects related to the central one being observed. For example, observing the decision-making process of a steering committee to seek out ways to improve it may lead the researcher to observe the workers in the organization under study to evaluate their perceptions of the management decision-making process, and by the way their working conditions. Consequently, and this is one of the strengths of an intervention-research sale, is that it allows one to make observations and (as well as publications) on the central object of the client's request as well as making observations on related and peripheral objects (with additional publication possibilities).

In a way, while econometric empirical research by database may be easier and quicker to implement for a researcher, this approach only allows publications centered on the observed object. In contrast, an intervention-research on a SOA is certainly longer and more complicated to implement, but it allows a greater number of publications not only on the central object observed wanted by the client but also on related objects and peripherals observed during the research. As another example, based on an intervention-research carried out to foster the socioeconomic performance of a large company in the surveillance and security sector, we wrote dozens of publications (communications, articles and books) not only focused on the socioeconomic performance aspects of this organization, but also on its management control system, enterprise risk management, commercial constraints, quality management, conflicts management in its governance, and so forth (see Cappelletti, 2005, 2009; Cappelletti & Baker, 2010). Similarly, whereas it is not possible to do so from an empirical research that forms a block, it is possible to make different publications on the same object using the various tools mobilized through an intervention-research—a publication stemming from diagnosis, another one from project groups, and so forth. To a certain extent, intervention-research is similar to an astronomer observing a galaxy: the researcher can describe this galaxy but can also more finely target planets within this galaxy to describe them elsewhere. That said, what are the key epistemological mechanisms of intervention-research that researchers must integrate into the methods and consulting services that they will sell to a client?

Integrated Epistemology of Intervention-Research

The integrated epistemology of intervention-research is based on three key principles that the methods and services it engages must incorporate (see also Chapter 1): cognitive interactivity, contradictory intersubjectivity, and generic contingency. *Cognitive interactivity* implies that the collection of data and observations result from relational interactions between the researcher and the actors, for example, through interviews, diagnoses, or training-action sessions. *Contradictory intersubjectivity* means that the collected data will also be the subject of mirror-effect sessions between the researcher and the actors within the observed organization to validate the data through consensus, for example, through steering committees or interactive diagnostic presentation sessions. This epistemological principle provides that the researcher also gives his opinion on the validity of the data collected through his expert-opinion. Thus, intervention-research is not a quest for an illusory objectivity arising from the separation between the researcher and the observed object. On the contrary, it refutes the quest for "objectivity" in human sciences, which recognizes its congenitally subjective aspects. Its quest is, if one accepts the term, for "objectifying the subjective data collected" through the contradictory intersubjectivity principle. *Generic contingency* implies that during the phase of distancing the SOA the data collected will be positioned with regard to the existing literature as well as the results of previous intervention-researches to assess findings between those with a degree of regularity (generic character) and those with a degree of specificity (contingent character).

To summarize, the scientific intention of intervention-research consists of a rigorous epistemology based on methods to characterize the knowledge created according to their generic or contingent character (Savall & Zardet, 2008, 2011). One, of course, could question the level of client interest in such epistemological "cooking" and the extent to which it is simply easier for the researcher to focus solely on the consulting dimension of intervention-research. As we have written before, we recommend caution and discretion when discussing these epistemological dimensions. In some cases, the revelation of this integrated epistemology, which can perfectly remain concealed from the client, risks scaring away the client company by its complexity—thereby missing the sale. In other cases, the willingness to purchase intervention-research from a client may result, apart from a desire to improve performance through rigorous consulting methodologies, from a desire to contribute to research in human sciences in a societal perspective. It is then possible, with humility, to approach these scientific questions with the client. A fortiori, the case may occur, that the client himself wishes to become a researcher-actor (Savall, 1974–2017).

TOWARDS A STRUCTURED AND RIGOROUS METHOD OF SELLING INTERVENTION-RESEARCH

Selling an intervention-research engagement means making the client pay a fair price for the intervention, that is, the price corresponds to a fraction of the value brought to the client, in a way that allows the researcher to release the resources which he expects and is acceptable to the client. To succeed in this challenge, it is necessary to adopt relevant behavior generating respect from the client as well as a rigorous method.

Pay as a Reflection of Client Respect

A first behavioral observation on the sale of an intervention-research is that it causes joy and happiness that brighten the routine of the engaged-scholar. We are happy when we sell, and this creates a cohesive effect on the research team. It is often said that the commercial sense and ability to sell is innate and many intervener-scholars have doubts about their role of seller, despise the commercial dimension of their trade. However, even from a young age, we are in a logic of charm and sale with our parents or teachers to get what we want. So everyone has a potential to sell that is going to be more or less stimulated over time, but no one is irretrievably condemned not to be able to sell.

Another important behavioral observation is that in order to sell an intangible object such as intervention-research, the researcher will have to adopt an appropriate attitude, in addition to a sales method that will be discussed, during the sales process as well as the production phase of the intervention-research. This attitude consists of being respected by the client and in maintaining an ascendant position (i.e., the intervener must maintain a higher level of expertise in intervention than that of the client during the entire project). Obviously, you may lose a client if he feels better than you to run the intervention. Unlike the sale of a physical object, such as a car or a house that closes upon delivery to the customer, an intangible object acquires its visible form during its implementation phase. Nothing prevents a client from stopping an intervention-research mission in progress because it does not suit him. In order to successfully sell an intervention-research and then to produce it to its end, the intervener must from the very first contact with the client be respected by the latter. In other words, the goal is to make the client understand that the intervener-researcher is not a service provider but instead a manufacturer of high-value products. The intervener-researcher must not accept anything less from the client, letting him or her know with subtlety and firmness in some cases. To summarize on this point, the intervener-researcher must be pleasant without being complacent with his client.

Secondly, the intervener must retain an initial influence on his techniques from the first contact with his client and then during the negotiation and production phases of the intervention-research project. It is the intervener-researcher who is the expert and not the client. To do this, the speaker-researcher must be very clear about what he sells: methods and services in the space of the organization as an expert in response to a request from the client. The client is in charge of this demand, but not the methods and services to meet them. This is why the sale after negotiation should be formalized in a precise intervention agreement that is up to the intervener-researcher to protect permanently. Consequently, during the negotiation phase, if the intervener-researcher does not have the skills (i.e., control of methods and services necessary for the processing of the client's request), he must not attempt to sell this intervention-research. Similarly, during the production of intervention-research, one must keep regular appointments with the client—the paying decision-maker of the mission—explaining and demonstrating how the methods and services put in place will meet the demand over time. But the intervener-researcher should never have to accept that the client refutes the methods and services or seeks to restructure them in his own way. Imagine patients explaining to a doctor how to make a medical diagnosis or prescription. If this scenario every happened, it would be the professional death of any doctor through the loss of their ascendancy over their patients. But this, of course, presupposes good mastery by the intervener-researcher of the methods and services proposed and then sold (Cappelletti, 2012; Savall, 1974–2017; Savall & Zardet, 2008, 2011).

The Three Stages of the Intervention-Research Sales Process

In addition to these behavioral qualities that are indispensable for selling intervention-research, the intervener-researcher must rely on a sales technique specific to intangible objects such as intervention-research. This technique is based on a three-step process: (a) a first listening meeting with the client, (b) a second appointment to present the methods and services offered to meet the client's demand, and (c) a third appointment to sell the price of the intervention-research engagement. During these appointments, ideally, the intervener-researcher will have to act in concert with a colleague to take exhaustive notes and capture the information exchange. Otherwise, intervention alone is possible, of course. The intervener should always act with humility in mastering this three-step process, skillfully presenting it to the client.

The first appointment is used to make an inventory of the client's objectives. It should consist of 90% listening to the client on the part of the intervener-researcher: what does the client want and what are his objectives with regard to performance improvement wishes? At this point, the question of who is physically the client emerges. In this context, the client is the decision-maker of the intervention-research mission. In most cases, the decision-maker is fairly easy to detect—typically the head of the targeted organization, possibly accompanied by its chief financial officer. But in some cases, the decision-maker is actually a more complex human group. For example, in a negotiation with a town hall, the decision-maker may be the mayor with his director of services and the financial director of the mayor's office. It is therefore these three people who will have to be gathered by the intervener-researcher in the three appointments. During the first meeting, the researcher asks only questions about the client's demand and objectives, taking complete notes on the objectives expressed by the client. At the end of this first appointment, depending on the objectives expressed, the intervener-researcher is in a position to know if he is competent to respond to the request. If this is not the case, the intervener must terminate the negotiation. It would indeed be suicidal professionally for him to seek to answer a request that he is not competent to deal with. If this is the case, the researcher will schedule a second appointment with his client a few days after the first.

In the second appointment, the researcher presents the methods and services offerer to the client to process his request using a tool called the

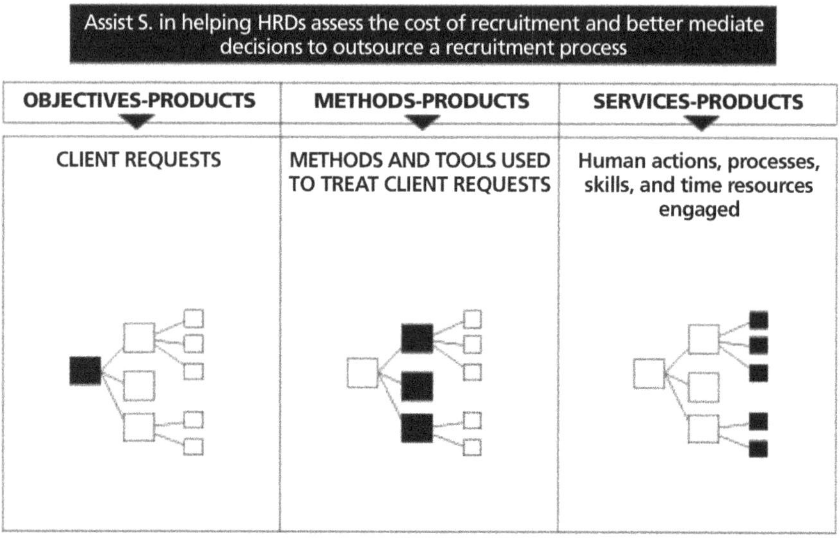

Figure 5.1 Example of OMSP: The case of a request from a professional union in the recruitment sector (S).

OMSP (objective-method-service-product), a synthetic tool summing up objective-products, method-products, and service-products that constitute the specification manual at the center of the intervention agreement (Buono & Savall, 2007, 2015). The matrix of this tool is presented in Figure 5.1, in the case of a request from a professional union in the recruitment sector.

The OMSP's first column uses the client's own words to describe the objectives. This column "belongs" to the client. In the second column, the researcher presents the methods (diagnosis, implementation of a project group, etc.), which is detailed in services in the third column (number of diagnostic interviews with persons involved and duration, number of project group sessions with persons involved and duration, etc.). The OMSP materializes the intangible object sold—the methods and services in response to a request. In addition to the OMSP, during the second meeting, the researcher also formalizes the representation of the intervention-research in space through its precise architecture (who are the people and services of the company that will be affected by intervention-research?) as well as its representation in time through its schedule of implementation.

The discussion then begins during this second appointment on the participant-researcher's understanding of the objectives of the client formulated during the first appointment, and the client's understanding of the methods and services proposed as well as the feasibility of the proposed architecture and planning. If there is no agreement between the client and intervener-researcher on this qualitative proposal, there is no third appointment dedicated to the sale of the price of intervention-research. In essence, the proposed intervention stops at this point.

The third appointment is dedicated solely to the sale of the intervention price because qualitative sales and financial sales are based on different factors. The third appointment is therefore financial and concerns the presentation of the sale price and its justification. To determine the selling price, the intervener must first define the upper and lower boundaries of the price, proposing a price located between these two terminals. This price is for the methods and services offered to meet the demand as well as the days of production that they involve for the researcher (and his team if not alone). Indeed, the key to selling the price of an intangible object is to offer a complete price for this object and not a tariff of the days necessary for its realization. As an analogy, the intervener-researcher sells a price for "a car that rolls" and not "days needed to make the car." In essence, the "day rate" must remain a manufacturing secret (except in the case of a response to an invitation to tender or the day rate is formally requested). An underlying goal is not to tempt the client to negotiate a price reduction by seeking to reduce the number of days of production. To determine its price limits, the intervener-researcher must first define the maximum day rate that he wishes to apply. This is based on an analysis of the rates charged by one's competitors, consultants or other researchers. Thus, on the European market for management consulting, the average tariffs considered in the high range are approximately 3,000 euros per day, average tariffs around 1,500 euros, and low tariffs less than 1,000 euros. The intervener-researcher must then, through an internal analysis of his own organization, define the full cost of a day of intervention-research production. This full cost constitutes the lower limit of his day-to-day rate. In order to realize a margin and to generate net own resources, which remain the economic objective of the sale, the researcher will have to sell his work beyond this lower limit. In the end, the day tariff is defined by the consultant between these two upper and lower boundaries according to his marketing and financial positioning strategy.

This tariff then serves to develop the intervention estimate, which is also never communicated to the customer. This estimate makes it possible to define the price of the intervention that is communicated to the client during the third appointment. In this appointment, if the client validates the price and accepts it, the intervention agreement can be signed without any problem. If the client seeks to negotiate the price, it is necessary to argue to justify it not according to the days that the intervention-research calls for but according to the *value* that it is likely to create for the client. This subtle commercial skill consists of demonstrating to the client that the sale price of the intervention will be largely self-financed by the gains it will generate for the client, while being as truthful as possible for obvious ethical reasons.

This demonstration assumes that the researcher-speaker has reflected on this upstream demonstration. It is done orally, on the basis of examples, and it never becomes a formal agreement element. Indeed, the intervener-research, like a doctor, has an obligation of means but no results. He is therefore committed to the intervention agreement on methods, services, architecture, schedule, and a price that must be respected—but the focus is on the means, not the results. Even if carried out exactly as agreed, outcomes still depend in part on factors that the intervener-research cannot not control, such as the behavior of the client during the intervention or variations in the socioeconomic environment of the client organization.

If the customer wishes to lower the price proposed for budgetary reasons, this may be acceptable by reducing the methods and services proposed and hence the number of days necessary for their production. But in this case, the intervener-researcher must know in advance to appropriately narrow the intervention so that it does not threaten the processing of the demand and the objectives of the client. Generally, in the case of price negotiation by the customer, a reduction in the intervention is possible within a limit of 5 to 10% of its perimeter, but rarely more. As a last resort, the researcher must not hesitate to refuse to sell the intervention if the client wishes to reduce prices that exceeded the limits of his own resources and the achievement of the objectives of the mission. It is better not to intervene at a discount price that devalues the mission than to intervene in this case because the resulting loss of ascendancy will inevitably undermine the quality of the research-intervention and hence its final results. In summary, the state of mind appropriate for this third appointment is that of making the company be aware that it is not doing the researcher a favor by offering him a SOA, but that it is the client who is fortunate to have the intervener-researcher develop the program. And this, of course, presupposes that the intervener-researcher is convinced of it him or herself.

Once the sales price is accepted by the client, it remains simply for the intervener-researcher to set out the payment schedule. This schedule spreads over the duration of the intervention with monthly payments and 20% of the sale price to be paid as a down payment upon signature. This deposit is important because it engages the client in the intervention and it is legitimate because there will be an investment of preparation of the intervention-research that should be financed. If we did not receive the 20% down payment, of course, we did not start the intervention-research at the client's company (Cappelletti, 2005, 2012; Savall, 1974–2017; Savall, Zardet, & Bonnet, 2008).

THE ONGOING SALE OF INTERVENTION-RESEARCH

Following the third negotiation meeting in the event of agreement on the qualitative and financial proposal, the intervention-research process begins subject to the payment of the deposit on signature. The sale, however, does not stop at this point. In reality, it is permanent concern throughout the implementation phase because even a signed intervention is a fragile process that can be easily suspended by the decision-maker if he loses confidence. Therefore, it is imperative to have an intervention agreement signed to ensure at least the continuity of the production. But, in addition, the intervention agreement will be used by the intervener-researcher during the production phase to show the client that the methods and services implemented correspond to what was agreed upon and its application is in process. Let us not forget that, as an intangible object, intervention-research remains invisible despite the meetings and tools that help to materialize it. It must therefore be given maximum visibility to maintain the client's confidence and his engagement in the intervention (Savall, 1974–2017).

The Intervention Agreement: A Tool for Steering the Intervention-Research Process

In order to formalize the process, the intervention agreement must cover the key elements discussed during the negotiation process in three appointments: (a) the OMSP, (b) the architecture and schedule, and (c) the financial annex and payment schedule. To illustrate a convention, we will take the case of the sale of a 2011 intervention-research by a team of three ISEOR researchers to a professional union of recruitment firms, referred to as "S." This syndicate regrouped several thousand recruitment consultants aimed at providing members with a rationale to help them convince human resource directors (HRD; the clients of recruitment consultants) that the full cost of recruiting was lower by hiring a good external consultant rather than trying to recruit themselves. Given our work on the issue, S represented by its president and vice-president (S's pay decision-makers) decided to interview us. The first meeting made it possible to detect the objectives of S beyond its general demand: (a) deepen and generalize the work carried out on the full cost of recruitment through a survey of HRDs that was statistically representative, (b) propose to the HR managers a tool to diagnose a recruitment process to better balance internalization and outsourcing recruitment, and (c) develop S's notoriety with HRDs of SMEs through effective and creative communication (see Figure 5.2).

Assist S. in helping HRDs assess the cost of recruitment and better mediate decisions to outsource a recruitment process

1. Deepen and generalize the work carried out on the full cost of recruitment through a survey of HRDs that is statistically representative.
2. Propose to the HR managers a tool to diagnose a recruitment process to better balance internalization and outsourcing recruitment.
3. Develop S.'s notoriety with HRDs of SMEs through effective and creative communication.

Figure 5.2 Example of a client demand: The case of a professional union in the recruitment sector (S).

The second negotiation meeting with S was to explain (through an OMSP; see Figures 5.3 & 5.4) the methods and services proposed to meet the objectives: (a) conduct a quantitative survey with HRD to determine the full cost of recruitment; (b) facilitate a project group to design a diagnostic tool enabling HRD to better reflect their recruitment decision; (c) animate a steering group with S to define appropriate communication to

Assist S. in helping HRDs assess the cost of recruitment and better mediate decisions to outsource a recruitment process

OBJECTIVES-PRODUCTS	METHODS-PRODUCTS	SERVICES-PRODUCTS
Number 1 Deepen and generalize the work carried out on the full cost of recruitment through a survey of HRDs that is statistically representative.	**Quantitative Survey** • Generalize the dysfunctions and the hidden costs observed during an internal recruitment thanks to a representative sample of HRDs	**Leading a statistically representative survey draws upon a sample of hundred HRDs of SMEs:** • Questionary design • Questionary process • Results analyses
Number 2 Propose to the HR managers a tool to diagnose a recruitment process to better balance internalization and outsourcing recruitment.	**Project Group** • Designing a recruiting diagnosis tool adapted for HRDs • Building the action and communication plan to set up the recruiting diagnosis tool	**4 sessions of project group (2.5h each) with the prospective commission of S.** Each session is divided into two phases: a focus phase with the president and the deputy president of the commission and a plenary phase with the whole commission.

Figure 5.3 Example of an OMSP (page 1 of 2): The case of a professional union in the recruitment sector (S).

Assist S. in helping HRDs assess the cost of recruitment and better mediate decisions to outsource a recruitment process

OBJECTIVES-PRODUCTS	METHODS-PRODUCTS	SERVICES-PRODUCTS
Number 3 Develop S.'s notoriety with HRDs of SMEs through effective and creative communication	**Steering Committee** • Be informed of the works in progress and shake their conformity to the S's policy and strategy • Use the results of the work mode to promote S. branding and that of the recruitment sector	**3 sessions (1h each) with the member of the prospective commission of S.:** • Discussion about the survey • Presentation of ISEOR expert opinion • Validation of the solutions proposed by the project group and definition of a strategy of communication • Each session begins with a head-to-head between the president of the commission and ISEOR
	Option: Training on the Hidden Costs Methodology • Give to a manager of S the basis of the hidden costs methodology	Training session **Performance +**: 4 sessions (2 days each) over a 5-month period of time

Figure 5.4 Example of an OMSP (page 2 of 2): The case of a professional union in the recruitment sector (S).

promote S's image; and (d) conduct training sessions with S's managers on the hidden-cost performance method, an appropriate method for evaluating the full cost of recruitment (optional).

During this second meeting, the architecture of the proposed intervention-research and its planning were presented and explained to S (see Figures 5.5 & 5.6). After discussion and understanding, S validated this qualitative proposal, and a third appointment was the next step, focused on selling the price of the intervention. Taking into account the estimate made, which of course was not communicated to S, the intervention price was fixed at "XYZ" thousand euros (the actual price is coded in this chapter by confidentiality) to be paid according to a monthly schedule with a 20% deposit to be paid upon signing the agreement (see Figure 5.7 & 5.8).

An advance payment when the intervention agreement is signed is an indispensable phase of the negotiation process to finance the preparatory work of the intervener-researcher necessary to start the intervention and to engage the client firmly within the intervention-research. Once agreed on the price and timetable, the OMSP, the architecture, the schedule, and

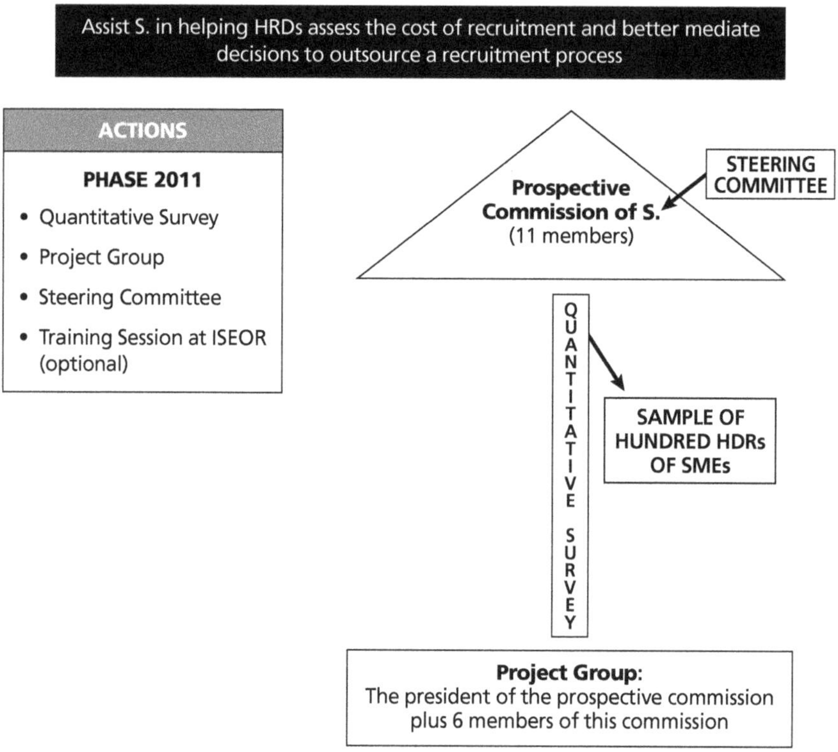

Figure 5.5 Example of an intervention architecture: The case of a professional union in the recruitment sector (S).

Assist S. in helping HRDs assess the cost of recruitment and better mediate decisions to outsource a recruitment process

ACTIONS	MONTH						
	Mar	Apr	May	Jun	Jul	Sep	Oct
STEERING COMMITTEE (3 sessions of 1 hour each)	1			2			3
QUANTITATIVE SURVEY							
PROJECT GROUP (4 sessions of 2.5 hours each)	1			2		3	4
TRAINING SESSION at ISEOR (optional) (4 sessions)	1		2		3		4

Figure 5.6 Example of a schedule: The case of a professional union in the recruitment sector (S).

INTERVENTION IN A PROFESSIONAL UNION IN THE RECRUITMENT SECTOR (S.)

Budget (in €)

Actions

• Steering committee	X K€
• Quantitative survey	Y K€
• Project group	Z K€
TOTAL	XYZ K€

Figure 5.7 Example of the pricing of an intervention: The case of a professional union in the recruitment sector (S).

INTERVENTION IN A PROFESSIONAL UNION IN THE RECRUITMENT SECTOR (S.)

Payment Schedule

Deadline	**Amount**
Deposit payment upon signature	a €
March 20	b €
April 20	b €
May 20	b €
June 20	b €
Total	**XYZ K€**

Figure 5.8 Example of the payment schedule of an intervention: The case of a professional union in the recruitment sector (S).

the financial annex became the documents of the agreement signed with S. The management of this agreement in terms of respect for the means used (methods, services, planning, architecture, schedule of regulations) becomes a permanent agenda item for the intervention-research steering committees between researchers and the president and vice president of S.

The Search for Accomplices During the Intervention

The researcher's respect for the intervention agreement is a central element in maintaining both the client's respect for the researcher and his or her ascendancy over the client. Any attempt to disregard the intervention agreement by the intervener-researcher must therefore be formally prohibited. Just as any attempt by the client to depart from the intervention agreement, for example by refusing certain agreed services during the course of the assignment or by failing to pay the invoices at the scheduled deadlines, must be avoided by the researcher through courtly but firm discussions that may require courage. This courage could go as far as threatening to stop the intervention if the client deviates too much from the agreement, for example by not paying bills or blatantly lacking respect and elementary courtesy. A rigorous control of the intervention agreement by the intervener-researcher should attempt to prevent such extremes which, on analysis, prove to be extremely rare if the rigorous and structured method of selling the intangible process has been respected. The scrupulous steering of the intervention agreement also helps to maintain the complicity of the decision-makers. Indeed, in particular in a large-scale intervention, it is important that the intervener-researcher to develop internal accomplices, that is to say, people of importance in the studied organization who are ready to support the researcher in the event of attacks and criticism. An intervention-research process, and this is part of its charm, is that the process is rarely "a long quiet river" because, by the changes that it causes and subsequent questions that it creates, often induces "resisters" to implementation and opposition can emerge. This opposition and resistance can sometimes come from internal competitors of the intervention-research, for example, members of the organization who wanted to carry out the intervention by themselves or those who have it refused similar interventions in the past.

CONCLUSION

Once the intervention is sold during the implementation phase is it is useful to continue to maintain a specific dashboard of the intervention-research that includes the intervention agreement as well as the gallery of key actors of the intervention, including accomplices, resisters, internal competitors, the decision-maker, and so forth. This dashboard serves as a guide in helping to make decisions and plan appropriate actions. It is important to remember that only once the intervention-research has been completed and fully paid that it can be considered that its negotiation and sale have been fully successful (see Buono & Savall, 2007, 2015; Savall, 1974–2017).

REFERENCES

Buono, A. F., & Savall, H. (Eds.) (2007). *Socio-economic intervention in organizations: The intervener-researcher and the SEAM approach to organizational analysis.* Charlotte, NC: Information Age.

Buono, A. F., & Savall, H. (Eds.) (2015). *The socio-economic approach to management revisited: The evolving nature of SEAM in the 21st century.* Charlotte, NC: Information Age.

Cappelletti, L. (2005). Designing and processing a socio-economic management control. In K. M. Weaver (Ed.), *Academy of Management Best Paper Proceedings* (pp. A1–A6). Pace, NY: Academy of Management.

Cappelletti, L. (2009). Performing an internal control function to sustain SOX 404 and improve risk management: Evidence from Europe. *Management Accounting Quarterly, 10*(4), 17–27.

Cappelletti, L. (2012). *Le contrôle de gestion de l'immatériel. Une nouvelle approche du capital humain* [The management control of intangibles: A new approach to human capital]. Paris, France: Dunod.

Cappelletti, L., & Baker, R. C. (2010). Measuring and developing human capital through a pragmatic action research: A French case study. *Action Research, 8*(2), 211–232.

Savall, H., & ISEOR Research Team. (1974–2017). *Trainings on the socio-economic approach to management.* Ecully, France: www.iseor-consulting.com.

Savall, H., & Zardet, V. (2008). *Mastering hidden costs and socio-economic performance.* Charlotte, NC: Information Age.

Savall, H., & Zardet, V. (2011). *The qualimetrics approach* : Observing the complex *object.* Charlotte, NC: Information Age.

Savall, H., Zardet, V., & Bonnet, M. (2008). *Releasing the untapped potential of enterprises through socio-economic management.* Geneva, Switzerland: ILO-BIT.

CHAPTER 6

NEGOTIATING AND SELLING AN INTERVENTION-RESEARCH PROJECT WITHOUT THE SUPPORT OF A WELL-STRUCTURED RESEARCH LABORATORY

Thierry Nobre

Negotiation is a fundamental phase of an intervention-research (IR) project (see Chapters 2, 4, & 5). As in many other human activities, the first contact and exchange with the client firm leave an imprint that strongly influences latter stages. Thus, the researcher in the negotiating phase of an intervention-research project must be fully aware of the stakes of this phase of reciprocal discovery. It requires researchers to clearly define the objectives of the intervention as well as communicate the difficulties and pitfalls that are likely to be encountered, which can undermine a primary purpose—the production of knowledge. The objective of this chapter is to reflect on the lessons of IR negotiations in various contexts ranging from

Intervention Research, pages 111–128

small- and medium-sized enterprises (SMEs) to international organizations—from the perspective of a lone researcher without the support of a strong research team as discussed in Chapter 5.

These lessons favor a praxeological perspective on negotiating this type of research as well as reflect critical issues that any intervener-researcher has to face during the negotiation phase. In a complementary approach to Chapter 5, the discussion proposes lines of actions and devices devoted to an individual researcher who is not in a position to apply the normative process of negotiation as followed by a well-established center such as ISEOR. Indeed, many interveners who want to undertake this type of research are not members of an experimented team and have to build up the selling as well as implementation of their research process on a more adhoc basis. In other words, drawing on a military strategy metaphor, this chapter focuses on the IR negotiation process carried out in a more restricted configuration of the "commando" or "light cavalry" rather than a project conducted with well-organized troops dedicated to this type of approach.

To reach these goals, the chapter illustrates the various questions, findings, and proposals raised by case studies clarify the context and different stakes involved in the negotiating processes selected. This teleological posture explains both the systematic use of negotiation case studies and the focus on the academic process to shed light on the link between the intervention itself and publication. In particular, the chapter examines such questions as: "What constitutes an adhoc negotiation process?"; "What parameters should be taken into account in this context?"; "What is the appropriate behavior of the researcher to successfully negotiate an IR process, focused on reaching managerial *and* scientific and managerial objectives that characterize intervention-research?"

To answer these questions, this chapter is organized in three parts. First, since negotiation is the initiating phase of every IR engagement, it is necessary to reconsider the articulation between research, knowledge, and publication. Clarifying and identifying the stakes of this initial phase—the negotiation with the scientific observation area (SOA)—are crucial since this primary stage constitutes the launching pad that defines the future trajectory of the project and creates the foundations for cooperation and coproduction between the researchers and actors.

Second, the dynamic dimensions of the negotiation process itself is examined in detail. It is necessary to identify and deepen the various key mechanisms and evolutions at work during this stage, emphasizing the interactions between the different categories of actors involved. Finally, the content of the negotiation is discussed in detail, focusing on the elements that are negotiated and the formalized agreements that emerge.

ISSUES AND CONTEXT IN THE NEGOTIATION OF AN INTERVENTION-RESEARCH PROJECT

To describe the negotiation stage of an IR project, it is necessary to insist on a basic finality of any intervention-research—the production of knowledge. To preserve this outcome, there are a number of actions the researcher must undertake—within the context of the different forms of knowledge that an IR project seeks to create as a way of appropriately diversity during the negotiation process.

Second, IR negotiation involves interactions between the researcher and the actors from the SOA that are neither spontaneous nor frequent. Thus there are a number of actions that must be taken into account by the researcher to define a negotiation strategy. Third, intervention-research has a specific chronobiological dimension and the issue of time management has to be taken into account so the researcher can reconcile scientific production objectives with the constraints of agreement in the project.

An Intervention-Research Project as a Source of Multifaceted and Complementary Knowledge

The creation of knowledge is typically the primary goal of the researcher. Thus it is important to highlight the different forms that knowledge that can be developed in an IR project as a way of clarifying the modalities for creating knowledge that the researcher should keep in mind during the negotiation phase.

Publication Is Not Research

A basic clarification concerns the link between research and publication. In an academic context where the pressure to publish is often intense, it is necessary to remember that publication is not research. The publication process is an academic exercise of formalizing and communicating research for peer review. In other words, research is not reducible to publication, but the latter is indispensable to the former. As a matter of fact, prior to a good publication, methodologies have been developed that involve data collection, analysis, and processing activities to address issues that contribute to the creation of knowledge.

Because researchers have different channels to disseminate their knowledge, they should clarify a strategy to create a portfolio of publications. This range of contributions is now institutionalized at the international level—for example, the U.S.-based Association to Advance Collegiate Schools of Business International (AACSB) accredits the best business schools by capturing three types of intellectual contributions: theoretical, practice, and pedagogical. Thus, researchers have different avenues of expression they are encouraged to utilize, enabling them to choose the most appropriate modality and audience for the knowledge they have generated.

In this chapter, we will mainly focus on academic journals, books, and pedagogical case studies. We have excluded papers for congresses and conferences from our field of analysis, although they are an important part of the process to prepare a journal submission, being a well-suited preliminary stage to these latter methods of dissemination.

Analysis using a sports metaphor would classify academic journals in the universe of stringent tests imposed within a detailed codification of the rules of the game, while books might be characterized as "free agents." As a matter of fact, provided book authors have the support of their publisher, they have considerable freedom to present their research as they see fit. Pedagogical publications such as case studies also make it possible to develop research to ensure the link between scientific and educational activities.

Intervention-research, through the privileged link it develops between researchers and SOAs, allows interveners to play with these different types of outlet, enabling them to take advantage of a broad range of publication possibilities. This diversity of possible publication options should be kept in mind throughout the research process and especially during the negotiation phase. Indeed, the nature of the publications targeted by the researcher at the beginning of an IR project is decisive for the subsequent production of knowledge. Consequently, the preliminary, negotiation stage of an IR project is very important to define the effective conditions for mobilization, use, valorization, and communication of the different elements of this intervention (e.g., observations, documentation, interviews.). It ultimately constitutes a "GO/NO GO" filter, which justifies treating this phase with all the seriousness and attention it requires.

Negotiation Context

Basically, the negotiation phase of an IR project is based on a series of meetings with the actors who, at best, do not know each other and, at worst, may initially denigrate each other. As a matter of fact, the negotiation phase of an IR engagement involves, in general, actors who are not accustomed to meet each other on a regular basis—academics and practitioners. The perception of the latter is largely conditioned by the traditional branding of academics whose research is often considered as being too theoretical and too far removed from the concerns of practitioners in the field.

This context may generate a lack of reliance over academics on behalf of practitioners, who might have difficulties taking academics too seriously. Thus the credibility of the researcher is not typically acquired *a priori* during an IR project, and often depends on the researcher's professionalism during initial stages of negotiation. The behavior of the intervener during this phase (e.g., punctuality/delay, listening/talking, opening/self-centering) is crucial to build confidence with the SOA. Consequently, while remaining self-confidant about one's method and expertise, researcher should be humble—even with an impressive publication record

It is important that researchers are clear and transparent with the client, ensuring that they plans, requests, and expectations are fully understood. For researchers working on their own, without the benefit and support of a well-structured research team, this interaction is that much more important as the researcher can count only on him or herself as the focal point of the questions and doubts from the client firm.

Various authors interested in intervention-research particularly emphasize the concept of "coproduction," which they regard as one of the fundamental mechanisms in progress during an IR project (Argyris et al, 1985; Buono & Savall, 2015; Cappelletti & Baker, 2010; Chanal, 1997; David, 2000; Hatchuel, 1994; Moisdon, 1984,). Nevertheless, some of these authors are mainly concerned with carrying out an IR project without necessarily taking into account its initial negotiation phase that leads to the agreement. Drawing on our experience with intervention-research, it is important to stress that coproduction should be agreed upon early on, from very beginning of an IR project. Indeed, coproduction between the researcher and client practitioner helps to build, through incremental interactions, actions that help to guarantee both the implementation of the means of investigation wanted by the researcher and the treatment of the problem expressed by the client.

As IR projects often induce a peak confrontation with reality, it may be fused with sudden surprises for the intervener due to the unpredictable nature of the ground. Thus, a significant objective of the negotiation is, among other things, to master, as best as possible, this unpredictability through rigor and methodological clarity (as explained in Chapter 5, particularly the role of the OMSP tool—objectives methods services products). Consequently, the researcher may be confronted with evolutions that could challenge and even rock the sustainability of the IR project. One of the causes of this unpredictability is the gap between the representation of the functioning of their organization that the actors involved in the negotiation process have in mind and the actual functioning that the intervener will ultimately face. Another cause may stem from the turnover during the IR project that at times involves some of the actors in the negotiation phase. In fact, given the longitudinal nature of many IR engagements, it is not uncommon that those who have played a leading role during the negotiation of the IR project and its agreement (e.g., CEO, CFO, CHRO, project manager, department head) may have changed position or even left the organization. Therefore, during the negotiation phase, the researcher should address the possibility of turnover among key actors, attempting to forecast

IR devices that may ensure, as far as possible, the continuity and sustainability of the project.

There are two major consequences for the researcher that stem from the unpredictable nature of the ground. First, researchers must be aware of and accept this risk; second, they have to realize that this risk may lead to the failure of that particular intervention, factoring that possibility in arbitrations in different projects that are being carried out at the same time. It means that the researcher must be able both to adapt solutions allowing the project to be carried out and to design an appropriate solution of retreat if things would turn wrong to pursue his other research activities.

The Intervener's Time Management From Negotiation to Publication

Intervention-research requires a significant presence on the ground, making it a time-consuming endeavor. Therefore the researcher has to deal with an issue that may seem paradoxical—as an academic, researchers are subject to strong pressures to publish rapidly, but intervention-research requires substantial presence in the field. To cope with this dilemma, researchers do have some levers of action they can draw on.

The first tactic is to rigorously schedule the three steps of the IR process—illustrated by the acronym IREV:

- *Identification* of potential projects and plans for their negotiation. In this stage, the researcher searches for opportunities (or may be solicited to take on a client), converting potential interventions into formalized and agreed upon projects.
- *Realization* of the IR project, implementing the IR tools and devices that have been agreed upon during the negotiation, cooperating with the actors on the ground.
- *Valorization*—the researcher creates a publication in a form that appears to be the most appropriate according to one's own portfolio of knowledge products, professional career goals, and the nature of the results obtained.

Thus researchers should lay out a global vision of their activity to manage the three IREV steps of the IR. Obviously, in order to ensure a steady publication stream, researchers will have to simultaneously conduct these three stages in different projects to generate an ongoing flow of intellectual contribution.

A second lever is that of *collective actions.* Given the energy to be deployed and the time spent, it is difficult for researchers to carry out these tasks by themselves. Beyond methodological and epistemological requirements, a critical aspect of empirical feasibility requires an individual to work with colleagues. Even if a researcher may be isolated from others, that individual should still seek out collaborative relationships when possible that will facilitate project development. Different approaches should be considered, ranging from internal cooperation within the academic field, partnerships with colleagues on site or from other institutions, involvement of doctoral students, or even external solutions, including cooperation with external consultants.

NEGOTIATION TACTICS FOR LONE RESEARCHERS

Moving on from the discussion in Chapter 5, which focused on negotiation as part of a well-developed team, there are specific challenges when a lone individual proposes an IR project. This section of the chapter focuses on the genesis of the negotiation, with specific emphasis on the individual intervener-researcher as the center of our attention—reflecting on the challenge of balancing dual outcomes between academics and actors, with the former driven by scientific objectives and the latter with practice-based expectations.

Key Ideas in the Theory of IR Negotiation

Generally, theories of IR negotiation place the negotiation on a continuum ranging from confrontation to cooperation where different actors, through an incremental approach, try to reach an agreement about a future coproduction. The actors aim at reaching a goal coherent with their own sphere of action—or world in the sense of Boltanski and Thevenot (1991). Practitioners seek solutions to resolve the concrete problems they are confronted with, while intervener-researchers help practitioners solve their problem(s) with the added goal of contributing to the development of knowledge in the management sciences. This confrontation/cooperation dialectic spreads out in a sociopolitical context with human actors, complete with their desires, objectives, fears, and contradictions. Although they belong to the same organization, they may have divergence views, confrontations, and even conflicts. Moreover, the internal actors participating in the negotiation can bring only their own representations of the organization by associating their own strategy in relation to a project that is never neutral for the evolution of their organization. As a result, the intervener-researcher who goes through a negotiation phase typically only meets a few actors of the client firm among many others who are not represented, which *de facto* creates allies and internal opponents for the future project.

Thus, negotiation goes beyond the technical and engineering dimensions of management, which consists of changing management practices, tool, and devices. It imposes *ipso facto* negotiating researchers to position themselves between Casanova and Machiavelli, combining seduction and political maneuvering to succeed in overcoming the divergences to which they may be confronted in carrying out an IR project. The complexity of the internal relations within organizations suggests that there is not a sole way of negotiation but different approaches that require the researcher to scan these internal characteristics. On this condition, the researcher can not only propose the appropriate content but also adopt the adapted behavior allowing one to transform opportunities into feasible projects. It should also be stressed that these preliminary steps, which are full of negotiating maneuvers, create interesting opportunities for collecting information that enable the researcher to be in step with the concerns of client companies and organizations. Thus, they constitute a real outcome derived from the IR project. Then, even if the intervention-research does not succeed—which sometimes does happen—the researcher will have collected a lot of information enabling him or her to reflect on the experience, drawing out new insights in the process.

Generating Requests and Opportunities for Initiating a Negotiation Process

Intervention-research requires the researcher to be in direct contact with companies and organizations. In order to develop the research, the intervener must initially penetrate the organization and then stay there in order to observe relevant managerial phenomena. When intervener-researchers are unable to rely on a structured approach, they must come up with an approach in line with their own skills and capabilities to initiate contacts with possible client companies and organizations, given that one's academic publications merely offer some visibility.

To get in touch with organizations and stimulate an IR request on their behalf, the researcher has three main possibilities:

- A pro-active approach of prospecting, where the researcher organizes meetings with potential partners.
- Solicitations resulting from the researcher's publications (from articles and conferences, to round tables and internet postings). In this case, the work serves as a harbinger of what the client should expect given the themes that have been addressed.

- Solicitations stemming from the word of mouth of previous IR clients. In this case, prospective clients are attracted by previous IR achievements that they have become aware of and that have been recommended to them by companies that have participated in these projects.

Table 6.1 includes illustrative examples of these approaches. Our observations show that a researcher's visibility is directly related to the power of attraction they have in generating a negotiation process and successfully initiating an IR project.

The diversity of approaches for generating an IR negotiation requires the researcher to be able to identify them and convert them into concrete projects. In this vein, some epistemologists like Feyerabend (1975) consider that because research may take many forms the researcher must always be available and attentive to weak opportunity signals. In other words, for Feyerabend, everything can be good for initiating an IR negotiation. Like Girin (1981), who evoked what he called "methodical opportunism," researchers must develop an opportunistic watch that allows them to elicit different situations, engage with these opportunities, and capture information that will enable them to identify possible collaborative opportunities. The range at the disposal of the researcher is very wide (see Table 6.2), from meetings with representatives of companies during the supervision of thesis, to more institutionalized situations like being chair of a conference, roundtable, or panels with managers.

TABLE 6.1 Examples of Different Ways to Generate a Negotiation Phase
• As a doctoral student, I wanted to apply the socioeconomic intervention method in very small post-creation/pre-development businesses. Finding the first client required intense canvassing and a bit of luck. The second client was due to a recommendation of the first client. The knowledge accumulated during these first two IR projects made it easier to secure negotiations with the other five cases studied in my thesis. Indeed, the lessons learned from the first two experimentations provided decisive and contextualized arguments to trigger the agreement of the leaders for the negotiation of the last five cases. Obviously, the directors were surprised that a junior researcher knew their context, their difficulties, and their managerial needs (Nobre, 1995).
• Presentation of the results of the research during the thesis defense was made with guests of healthcare institutions. It aroused the interest of managers of several companies in the healthcare sector who wished to propose new ways of collaboration through IR projects within their institutions (Nobre & Haouet, 2011).
• The quality manager of a hospital having been informed of a previous IR project conducted in the central pharmacy department of the same establishment contacted the researcher, which led to a new IR project focused on the reorganization of his department (Nobre & Merdinger, 2011).

TABLE 6.2 Examples of Capturing Opportunities

From an informal meeting... • An IR project led in a higher education institution (a school of architecture) was initiated through a discussion during a friendly meeting where the academic director of the institution told a circle of friends about his strategic constraints. The researcher was present by chance at this meeting without belonging to this circle of friends. This discussion was the initiation of a contact that subsequently led to a negotiation process.
...to a proactive diversion. • Interested by the results of a research project in which they had participated by hosting researchers for interviews, the directors of a medium-sized company asked the researchers if they knew any consultants who could carry out a strategic management mission. After analyzing the demand, the researchers wrote a proposal that initiated the negotiation process, which resulted in a successful IR engagement with high publication potential (Granclaude & Nobre, 2017).

Key Points in Leading a Negotiation in a Nonstructured Context

In addition to the contributions of Chapter 5 that addressed the key elements of an IR negotiation in the context of a well-structured researcher center, this discussion will turn to some crucial points for researchers who practice intervention-research in a less structured context.

The first point is related to the scientific objectives of the researcher. Based on our experience, we advise intervener-researchers to keep in mind during a negotiation phase the scientific potential of the discussed project and to think about converting the proposed data collection into research problems. The richness of the ground quickly raises significant concerns for the intervener, especially in terms of defining a problem and choosing among those that emerge, which also means excluding others. This decision is often the most difficult to make for the researcher given the interest of the problems arising from the field. Indeed, our experience shows that the creativity observed within the ground often goes beyond human imagination.

Second, it is essential to consider the temporality of the sequences of the negotiation. There is a wide spectrum of negotiations where the different sequences can be linked quickly, while in other cases a "sown seed" can take a long time before germinating, arising and reappearing without any warning signs, weeks or even months after the first steps. Similarly, given the context, particularly in the public sector and especially in the healthcare sector, there are generally slowdowns and accelerations that can be very brutal. In general, the starting phase of making contact and defining an intervention takes place precipitously, but projects often get stuck in the different strata of decision-making. Yet, when a project reappears it must be executed quickly. This reinforces the need for researchers to have a global view of their activities and rigorous time management tools in order to use downtime for production and to anticipate the ways in which, in particular through collective action, these chronobiology IR hazards can be dealt with in a timely manner.

Considering the diversity of potential problems that may justify the demand for an IR project, researchers must also be clear regarding their own knowledge and capabilities, understanding their own limitations in terms of what they can and cannot successfully accomplish. It is essential for researchers to continually define and redefine their own competency grids to fully understand what they are capable of producing. In other worlds, a good intervener-researcher needs to apply Aristotle's philosophical precept—first, know yourself! One of the key competencies for negotiation is for the researcher to know how to listen to the client. Listening is the fundamental mechanism that allows the researcher to initiate the different stages of a negotiation and successfully conclude it with an agreement.

Obviously, reformulating a request or proposal, which is essential to test the mutual understanding of reciprocal expectations, implies three qualities—listening, listening, and listening. This skill of active listening, which calls for capturing a conversation and testing for understanding, is not necessarily innate for researchers who are generally accustomed to delivering knowledge. It is all the more difficult to adopt such an active approach because it must be accompanied by appropriate behavior limiting nonverbal communication so as not to disturb the transmission of messages. In short, during a negotiation phase, researchers who are accustomed to be in the role of the "knowing person" must reverse this traditional relationship to the other by putting themselves in a receptive position rather than one of emission, which *de facto* imposes a form of humility.

Another key point concerns who should actually participate in the negotiation phase. From an academic point of view, given the need to understand and reformulate the client's initial request, it is clearly preferable not to be alone. Also given the asymmetry of information during this phase, where the external stakeholder typically has ideas on many subjects, from the reality and seriousness of the demand, to the credibility and legitimacy of the actors involved in the negotiation process, to technical concerns and depth of the subjects to be examined. *Contradictory intersubjectivity* is a principle that allows the negotiating researchers to avoid the pitfalls of misunderstanding or missing fundamental elements. It focuses on the exchanges between researchers during and after the phases of interactions with the clients that make this "step back" necessary. We advise the lone researcher to search for partners to carry out a negotiation. That said, because temporal constraints show that negotiation under imperfect conditions is always better than no negotiation at all, if it is not possible, go ahead individually.

TABLE 6.3 Example of a Transition From Substantive to Legal Issues

In the case of the negotiation of an IR project in a Belgian university hospital, after having agreed on the various elements of the research—objectives, methods, benefits, duration and timetable, financial conditions, perimeter, relevant and key actors (project manager, internal relay)—the manager of the university hospital entrusted the project to his legal department, which established the intervention-research agreement according to Belgian legislation. In this instance, the researcher had neither the skills nor the resources for making this legal editing. The confidence created during the negotiation process lead to the formalization of the project, which was then subject to final legal review.

With regard to the actors on the ground, it is necessary to have access to the strategic actors of the targeted company. There is always a risk for intervener-researchers of interacting with actors who give the impression that they have more importance than they actually do and/or do not have the power to make decisions. Therefore, negotiation involves a preliminary step of identifying and validating the key actors that should be formally included in the negotiation process. Otherwise, the negotiation could simply be a waste of time. The production of a proposal is not the beginning of the process but the fruit of different stages. Each of them aims to reveal a set of information that enables progression toward a mutual understanding of the expectations and contributions of each of the parties. In the end, legal concerns tend not to be decisive issues. Once the parties have agreed on what they expect from each other during an IR project, any legal issues can be relatively easily resolved (see Table 6.3 as an example).

The Researcher's Posture During the Negotiation Phase

The IR projects that we have conducted with field actors show that two factors are decisive for activating the virtuous circle between negotiation and IR-based knowledge production. They both concern the ways that researchers should position themselves during the negotiation phase in relation to the actors on the ground.

The first point may seem obvious, but it is important to remember that initiating an IR negotiation imposes some preliminary actions. First of all, it is necessary and indispensable to meet the actors of the field—success in proposing an IR project without any physical meeting with the client seems impossible to us. It is also critical to be empathetic in order to understand their difficulties. Likewise, this means collaborating with them to contribute to the coproduction of effective and actionable solutions. This form of research not only targets the production of knowledge but also aims to transform the organization and its managerial practices. For instance, this awareness took a tangible form in a doctoral workshop when a PhD candidate said, "I do not want to go in the field and meet real people. I prefer to stay in my office to do my research." It is clear that not every researcher has the appropriate appetite to be in the field.

Our second, related point, is that an appetite for the field is a prerequisite but it is not sufficient. When researchers intervene with practitioners they can be quickly confronted with stereotypes about academicians and academic life. While they may be credited with certain recognized qualities of the academic world, they can also be characterized by the supposed traits that go with it. Ethical transparency requires interveners to act "with an open face," presenting their objective of helping them while seeking publication and the production of knowledge (see Table 6.4). The potential confrontation of different representations forces researchers to adopt a posture that simultaneously banishes the arrogance of the "one who knows" while also being aware of everything they know. In particular, researchers must necessarily master the actionable knowledge that can be implemented in an IR project. Of course, the intervener-researcher must adapt their expertise to the environment that they navigates, taking into account the codes and conventions on the ground. Thus, the researcher in this initial stage of negotiation is a "knowing listener" who identifies opportunities and potential compatibility by arbitrating between doubt and confidence, initiating the cooperative behavior that will enable them to achieve their scientific objectives while meeting the managerial expectations of the client.

The presentation of the content of the negotiation makes it possible to detail the various elements that must be explicitly formalized in order to confirm the agreement between the two parties. Transparency is critical here, an openness that constitutes one of the pillars of the confidence necessary for continuation of a project. Finally, transparency facilitates clarification of the following key questions: what, who, when, how, and how much? Within this context, it is necessary to further enrich this analysis of the content formalized by two supplements. The first concerns the relationship

TABLE 6.4 Presenting Oneself During an IR Negotiation
Research in the management sciences is not necessarily identified as a resource by companies and organizations. Intervener-researchers must therefore be diplomatic and earnest in order to position themselves among possible options. For example, the status of an associate professor in a university is not well-known or recognized in a small- and medium-sized enterprise (SME), so it is not a decisive argument for negotiation. On the contrary, in a hospital this status was a decisive factor for the CEO in accepting the researcher. For him, it provided the basis for his argument to make his heads of departments—who were also professors in a university—to accept the intervener-researcher as a peer, an outside stakeholder who would work with them on the change project. Researchers should therefore be aware of the possible discrepancy between signs of recognition one might enjoy in their environment and the permanent questioning to which they are subjected to by intervening on the ground.

between the field project and the goal of knowledge production. The second refers to elements that, although not formalized, must be integrated into the negotiation process.

Managing Field-Based Projects and Knowledge Production Objectives

Intervention-research is based on the dialectic between the production of knowledge and finding solutions to managerial problems. Different types of relationships may exist between the explicit reasons for entering the company or organization that determine the deliverables to be produced for the field and the problem(s) that will be selected, processed, and valued in publication. There is a continuum between these two outcomes. Ideally, there is a perfect alignment between field objectives and academic goals, in essence, when the problems on the ground become the focus of publication. This was the case, for example, for an experimentation of management tools in a hospital through the implementation of the "Balanced Scorecard" (Nobre, 2001) and activity-based costing (Nobre 2004, 2006). At the other extreme, there may be a significant gap between the two. In this case, the researcher has to deploy what might be thought of as a "Trojan horse strategy." In this instance, the intervention allows the researcher to enter the organization by paying the equivalent of an entrance fee based on the mission being performed and the deliverables produced. These services are the means of observing *in situ* and in real time a management problem that is of interest to the intervener but may not be of interest to the client company. For example, we used this tactic to study the relations of power and governance in a group of hospitals (Nobre, 1998), although it was not at all the formal demand of the client group.

Given the richness of the data collected during an IR project and the inherent unpredictability of the phenomena that may emerge on the ground, the researcher can be surprised by problems relevant to emerging management sciences. These "unexpected observations" may occupy an intermediate place between the objectives of the field and that of the researcher. They result from the opportunist strategy of the researcher. Therefore, the researcher during the negotiation of an IR project should be aware of deploying the devices are necessary to reach one's scientific objectives while serving the needs of the client, being transparent and sufficiently vigilant to seize opportunities that may emerge.

Convergence of Negotiation Processes

The constitutive elements of the negotiation process are widely discussed in Chapter 5. The elements presented here are intended to emphasize a few points relating to the context of the lone researcher or with an unstructured team. Even in a position of a lone researcher or acting in a small team of research, the formalization of the OMSP tool—objective products, methods products, and services products—described Chapter 5 can help to ensure a mutual understanding of expectations and reciprocal commitments. It guarantees an explanation of the reformulation of demand in its strategic and operational dimensions. It is all the more necessary because the researcher acting alone or with a limited team does not have the back office capabilities that can be relied on during the execution of an IR project. The visibility of the intervention for the company or the organization requires the intervener-researcher to explicitly specify from the outset the interveners involved and the deadlines in which the project will be carried out. This transparency is the foundation of the trust that is essential to the successful realization of the intervention.

Another point of convergence deals with the rewards from the intervention. Any task that creates value—in this instance, the IR intervention—deserves incentives whatever the size of the team of interveners. The companies and organizations benefiting from this type of service should be aware of the value created and ready to make a financial contribution. The question of price is then raised as part of the negotiation. As it has been explained in Chapter 5, the proposed cost should be between the market price and the cost of the resources consumed, knowing that a main resource is naturally the time of the researchers involved in the project. The financial transaction is decisive because it requires companies not to take the project lightly, credibilizes the researcher, and engages both parties in a reciprocal obligation of effective engagement.

In addition to the price of the intervention, in order to be able to mobilize the data and elements collected during the IR process, the researcher must include the conditions for their subsequent use in the intervention agreement. Intervener-researchers must agree with their partner(s) on the modalities (anonymity or not, type of data, publication process) for future productions. The researcher may be confronted with very different situations ranging from the company that requires complete anonymity to one that wants to spread information about the project as widely as possible, to the point of even using it as an internal and/or external communication tool. The formalization of this point imposes exchanges on this topic and thus avoids any further problems for the researcher, who at worst would be unable to mobilize an intervention-research for publication.

The Non-Formalized Content

Similar to the psychological contract, there is also an informal context for the conduct of intervention-research, which is primarily the ethics of the

TABLE 6.5 Example of the Refusal of an Intervention
At the request of the board of a large European organization, an IR project was aimed at establishing the organizational diagnosis of an entity carrying out support functions and employing around 500 people. The diagnosis showed the need for significant change. The CEO wished to see this entity, and in particular its director, accompanied by interveners to make this change. Given the status in this type of European organization governed by international agreements, the situation of the director, who was a few years from retirement and well-known for his resistance to change, it was obvious that the situation would be essentially frozen until his departure. Thus, the project did not allow the creation of a satisfactory IR plan, even though it would have been easy to accept the engagement. The researchers therefore declined to intervene in a second stage, although the financial proposal was rather favorable because a fundamental principle was not respected for this type of project, namely the support of the management for effective transformation.

researcher. Although researchers aim to produce knowledge, they should refuse an intervention that they believe will not fulfill necessary moral and/or strategic expectations (see Table 6.5 as an example).

CONCLUSION

The objective of the researcher practicing intervention-research is multifaceted, a combination of aspiring to reach the long-term goal of creating scientific knowledge and helping to resolve short-term managerial issues. This is why, for negotiating and then carrying out an IR project, intervener-researchers need robust techniques and principles, especially when they are carrying out the project by themselves. By choosing an approach that involves coproduction with field actors and the transformation of the organization, methodological conditions and postures have to be applied from the initial contacts on the ground throughout all stages of the negotiation phase. The reference to actual cases of negotiation presented in the chapter was used to identify general principles and guidelines to successfully carry out this initial stage of coproduction, foreshadowing and defining the objectives, and the form and background of the cooperation between the researchers and the SOA. Ability to listen, willingness to cooperate, adaptability, methodological rigor, and so forth are among the key factors of success to entering organizations and remain there by creating legitimacy, which is the guarantee of reciprocal satisfaction. Looking at these different cases and principles, it should be clear that there are several ways to lead IR negotiations, drawing on convergent principals and various tools as appropriate. Researchers, either working along or on a large team, who are comfortable with these convergent principals and tools will be able to adapt their expertise and methodology to different contexts and the characteristics of the organization in which they want to develop an IR project.

REFERENCES

Buono, A. F., & Savall, H. (Eds.) (2015). *The socio-economic approach to management revisited: The evolving nature of SEAM in the 21st century.* Charlotte, NC: Information Age.

Boltanski, L., & Thévenot, L. (1991). *De la justification. Les économies de la grandeur.* (From justification. The economies of scale). Paris, France: Gallimard.

Cappelletti, L., & Baker, R. C, (2010). Measuring and developing human capital through a pragmatic action research: A French case study. *Action Research, 8*(2), 211–232.

Chanal, V., Lesca, H., & Martinet, A. C. (1997). Vers une ingénierie de la recherche en gestion (Towards an Engineering of Research in Management Sciences). *Revue Française de Gestion, 116,* 41–51.

David, A. (2000). La recherche-intervention, cadre général pour la recherche en management [Intervention-research, a general framework for research in management sciences). In A. David, A. Hatchuel, & R. Laufer (Eds), *Les nouvelles fondations des sciences de gestion: éléments d'épistémologie de la recherche en management* (pp. 250–268). Paris, France: Vuibert.

Feyerabend, P. (1975). *Contre la méthode: Esquisse d'une théorie anarchiste de la connaissance* [Against the method: Project of an anarchiste theory of knowledge]. Paris, France: Point Sciences.

Girin, J. (1981). *L'opportunisme méthodique dans les recherches sur la gestion des organisations* [Methodic opportunism in research in organizational sciences]. Paris, France: Ecole Polytechnique.

Grandclaude, D., & Nobre, T. (2017). L'innovation participative en stratégie: Innovation, illusion ou révolution managériale ? [The participative innovation in strategy: Innovation, illusion or managerial revolution?]. In *Workshop: Journées de l'innovation Abbé Grégoire,* Paris, France.

Hatchuel, A. (1994). Les savoirs de l'intervention en entreprise [The knowledge of Intervention Within Companies]. *Entreprise et Histoire, 7,* 59–75.

Moisdon, J. C. (2015). Recherche en gestion et intervention [Management sciences and intervention]. *Revue Française de Gestion, 253,* 21–39.

Nobre, T. (1995). Le processus de structuration dans la petite entreprise [The process of structuration within small entreprises]. *Revue internationale des PME, 8*(3), 121–144.

Nobre, T. (2004). L'ABC à l'hôpital: Le cas de la chirurgie infantile [ABC in hospital: A case study in the childhood surgery sector). *Finance Contrôle Stratégie, 5*(2), 85–105.

Nobre, T. (2006). L'introduction de nouveaux outils de contrôle de gestion dans les services cliniques: Le cas de l'expérimentation de l'ABC dans un service de pédiatrie [Introducing new management control tools in the health care sector: Results from the implementation of ABC in a pediatric service]. *Journal de Gestion et d'Economie Médicale, 24*(3–4), 56–71.

Nobre, T. (2001). Management hospitalier: Du contrôle externe au pilotage, apport et adaptabilité du Tableau de Bord Prospectif [Management in hospitals: From external control to internal management control, outcomes provided by the balanced scorecard]. *Comptabilité Contrôle Audit, 2*(7), 125–146.

Nobre, T., & Haouet, I. (2011). Le cas d´un balanced-scorecard en contexte hospitalier: Eluder la carte stratégique pour privilégier la performance organisationnelle [The balanced scorecard at hospital: From strategy mapping to organizational Performance]. *Revue Française de Gestion, 211,* 103–118.
Nobre, T., & Merdinger-Rumpler, C. (2011). Architecture et changement organisationnel: Le cas du déménagement d'un service de consultation externe au sein d'un nouvel hôpital [Architecture and organizational change: The case of a service in a new hospital]. *Journal de Gestion et d'Economie Médicale, 29*(4), 154–169.
Savall, H., & Zardet, V. (2011). *The qualimetrics approach: Observing the complex object.* Charlotte, NC: Information Age.

CHAPTER 7

CARRYING OUT AN INTERVENTION-RESEARCH PROJECT IN ONE'S OWN ORGANIZATION

Challenges and Specificities

Isabelle Barth

For many researchers, empirical questions abound and access to data is a continual constraint. Yet, literally under the feet of virtually every researcher is a huge potential for research—their own company, university, professional association, and so forth. This chapter focuses on the potential of one's own organization as a Scientific Observation Area (SOA). Our emphasis is not on the use of its members as substitutes—for example, the practice of some scholars who solicit their students or executive trainees to respond to surveys, participate in focus groups, or participate in various scenarios and other simulations instead of engaging "real" actors. The focus is undertaking intervention-research (IR) within one's own organization, which is not a common practice. There are, of course, many underlying

Intervention Research, pages 129–149

concerns, from the fear of damaging one's reputation and risk of disturbing one's colleagues, to anxiety about making a mistake. In many instances all of these concerns are probably operating at the same time, because it can be quite challenging to carry out an IR project that engages colleagues and one's place of work, including its procedures, tools, routines, and so forth that constitute the organization's activity an "common good." The risk of being what we refer to as an "internal" researcher may be to become, at best, a stranger in one's own organization and, at worst, the scapegoat of the change to which the company aspires.

Despite these concerns, conducting an IR project in one's own organization has a number of advantages that the chapter will examine, especially in terms of the goal of improving its functioning and enhancing socioeconomic performances. The challenge is therefore large, with significant expectations in the context of the risks involved.

Drawing on case studies, chapter will examine the experience of internal intervention-researchers along four interrelated lines. First, we will shed light on the respective roles of the intervention and the research that create the process of an internal IR project. Second, we discuss the legitimacy of the internal intervener-researcher. The third theme deals with the research process itself. Finally, the concluding focus is on the learning process loops induced by internal IR research for the company, the researcher, the people in the organization, and the dissemination of knowledge in the management sciences.

MISSION, INTERVENTION, AND RESEARCH: AN INFERNAL TRIO

There is a complex relationship between the organization's mission, the intervention itself, and the research that will be managed by the internal intervener-researcher—a triptych that is certainly rich with possibilities but one that can also prove to be difficult to manage as an insider.

The Epistemological Framework of Internal Intervention-Research

Intervention-research, whether internal or external, belongs to the epistemic paradigm of pragmatic or generic constructivism that draws upon a core expectation (see Chapters 1, 2, and 3)—the production of actionable knowledge by extracting data from the transformation of a studied ground, namely a SOA (see Cappelletti & Baker, 2010; David, 1999, 2001; Piaget, 1972; Savall & Zardet, 2004). This central expectation implies that for the intervener-researcher to conduct a change management project in one's own organization, the focus must be in their research field, with an intervention agreement formalizing the objectives, modalities, and planning of the intervention. Initially, the researcher acts more as a stakeholder, negotiating access to the ground and promising specific deliverables that will meet the expectations of the client. Thus, an IR project implies that the researcher assumes some risk for succeeding in the intervention, being committed and full of energy, with the ability to dialogue with "clients" during the intervention process.

Most intervention-research is carried out by an external intervener-researcher, who is viewed as an outsider of the company under study. In this instance, the negotiation process, if it succeeds, ends up with the sale of services, similar to a consulting engagement and is composed of four major steps: defining the demand, reformulating the demand, formulating the proposal, and signing the agreement (Barth, 2001). The researcher then leads the intervention by spending time internally, for example, conducting interviews, attending meetings, and/or providing training. Apart from these phases of immersion, the intervener-researcher is outside the company under study, creating distance from the ongoing intervention and preparing the research project.

Internal intervener-researchers are regarded as an insider of the company under study. In this case, the IR project is seen as belonging to the people in the organization. The internal intervener-researcher is bound by the contract of employment and not a contract of performance. There can, however, between two types of internal researchers: (a) the researcher who is an employee of the studied organization who starts the research project, and (b) a researcher who is hired by the studied organization in a full-time position to carry out the research project. The analysis and discussion in the chapter are based on the case studies of internal intervention-research summarized in Table 7.1.

The Intervention Agreement

There are two types of agreement that can be identified regarding an internal IR project. The first one engenders a change in the employee's professional position when they become an internal researcher. As an example, before launching his internal IR project, one of the individuals studied occupied a professional position—controller and operations manager—but by becoming an internal researcher his role was modified by the organization and his new position was seen as something rather mysterious. His colleagues became suspicious about his role, because they appeared to think that his research project was masking higher intentions. They began

TABLE 7.1 Illustrative Cases on Internal Intervener-Researchers

Case 1: Sabrina conducted an IR project from 2009 to 2015 in a Business School with the objectives of passing a diversity label for this institution. She defended her thesis based on that material on January 2015 (Perugian, 2015).
Case 2: Sarah conducted an IR project in a higher education institution as a handicap mission manager for students. Her mission was to develop quantitatively and qualitatively the number of students with disabilities. She defended her doctoral thesis on that topic on June 2016 (Richard, 2016).
Case 3: Juliane conducted an IR project in a French management school as head of the entrepreneurial center that she created and ran during the 4 years of her doctoral research. Her thesis was defended on December 2016 (Santoni, 2016).
Case 4: Marine conducted her doctoral research based on the obervations she made when being employed by a compagny (Transco) as a doctoral manager. She was responsible for a gender equality mission in the company, with the objective of implementing real professional equality between males and females.
Case 5: Jean-Christophe joined a large IT company as a doctoral manager to work with the head of diversity on problems associated with religion-related issues. He is at the beginning of his doctoral research.
Case 6: Delphine is a teacher-researcher in a school of management and leads a mission of educational innovation to set up a collaborative digital platform for the development of the soft skills of students.
Case 7: Gildas has been recruited by a business school to create and manage a new subsidiary in China. He has accepted this job on the condition that he also had time to carry out his doctoral research on Corporate Social Responsibility in China.

to see him—whether true or not—as the "eyes" of the board of directors, working to restructure the company. The second case captures the arrival of a new colleague in the company, with a dual professional position—an operational role and being a researcher. Conducting IR engagements as an external consultant is something that staff in a company are accustomed to, but when someone is specifically hired by a company to undertake research is viewed differently, with curiosity and even mistrust.

It is important, therefore, that a company that hires a new employee in the position of being a researcher carefully explain and communicate the nature of the role. In our opinion, transparency on that matter is vital to all members of the organization, and communication must come from the highest level of the company to give legitimacy to the internal intervener-researcher. As an example in Case 1 (see Table 7.1), when Sabrina arrived at the business school in question, she was introduced as a doctoral student wishing to work on the theme of diversity management with the support of the board of directors. Once she began her work, she was positioned by the board as the chief of the diversity project, which was essential to avoid any conflict with the head of the business school's quality department. With regard to the field of diversity, Sabrina was noted to be the chief and not the quality manager.

The Internal Negotiation

Similar to the process with external intervener-researchers, when an internal organizational member attempts to obtain an agreement from the organization to conduct an internal IR project it is necessary to undergo negotiation with key people in the hierarchy. Undertaking an internal IR project on a clandestine basis is guaranteed way to ensure failure. The negotiation involves a number of critical steps to avoid questioning and efforts that might undermine the project. The researcher has to pay attention to two main concerns: the "real" need of the company for an intervention and one's capability to carry out that project.

If the intervener is an internal collaborator, as part of the negotiation that individual should be better positioned than an external intervener to identify the dysfunctions to be reduced and the relevant actions that fit the company and its culture. These are often the two main levers that an internal intervener has to convince key decision makers of the advantages of the proposal.

The added value of an internal intervener could also be based on a doctoral project that motivates the adoption of a new professional posture. In our experience, the internal intervener must not hesitate to present this information to key decision makers in the organization's hierarchy. In addition to one's own personal background, the support that the individual will receive from the team of researchers in the doctoral program, especially the person's supervisor, can be quite valuable. These points may be of a great interest for the targeted company—provided they are presented in a clear and straightforward manner.

During an internal negotiation, it is also very important to negotiate the time budget that will be devoted to the research. As an example, it was literally impossible to carry out an internal IR project while keeping up with one's daily tasks and responsibilities. A trade-off has to be worked out between the internal researcher and his or her reporting manager. Similarly, the access to people and documents to collect data should be clearly defined by both parties. Concerning the data, it is necessary to anticipate zones of confidentiality with guarantees of anonymity and potential embargoes on the publication of the results.

Within this context, the negotiation of a doctoral contract constitutes a full-time job. Indeed, it is necessary to convince a company that such a recruitment can be very useful as a way of enhancing its performance. For example, in Case 5 (Table 7.1) Jean-Christophe succeeded in selling "his recruitment" on the theme of the management of the religious fact in a large telecommunication company, a focus that was linked to one of the firm's major strategic goals at the time of the exchanges. Once Jean-Christophe was hired, he had to specify his mission and time management, in particular how he would allocate his time between the company and his research laboratory. His schedule and agenda were defined annually to cope with both the needs of the company and the constraints imposed by doctoral research, in particular the writing of the thesis during the third year and its defense.

If the intervener is an outsider seeking to be hired by the targeted company to undertake the research, the objectives of the negotiation are the same as those for an insider. These individuals and the basis of their research project should be openly acknowledged, without trying to hide their identity as a researcher. Indeed, there is no question of clandestinely conducting an IR project, clearly for ethical and transparency reasons, but also because it undermines the possibility of gathering necessary materials required for an optimal intervention.

As this discussion suggests, there is a fair amount of convergence in the negotiation of an IR project that led by either internal or external interveners. The key steps presented Chapters 5 and 6 are still valid: attracting the attention of key decision makers, being in a listening mode, motivating demands, rephrasing requests, proposing methods and services through the OMSP tool, and identifying the targeted results (Barth, 2001). Of course, the main difference between an external process of negotiation and an internal one is related to the financial aspects. During the negotiation phase of an internal RI project, it is not the price of the intervention that has to be sold but the recruitment of the intervener and his or her salary.

Define the Mission or the Research?

A question that often arises regarding internal-interveners reflects another trade-off that should be emphasized during the negotiation process—should the focus be placed on the company's mission or the research project? Based on our observations, we suggest that both alternatives are possible. When a company has an important mission of change to go through, researchers can seize the opportunity to demonstrate that they are able to successfully conduct this mission based on their IR capabilities. Researchers can also approach a company by suggesting a range of changes that an IR project could successfully meet, trying to capture the interest of the company in the intervention. Obviously, there is set guideline for these two scenarios and a gap between the objectives of the mission and those of the research may create stress for the intervener-researcher. We have identify two situations that can be sources of stress for the internal intervener:

- The internal-intervener has a defined subject of investigation, but does not see how it fits with current tasks and responsibilities.
- The internal-intervener aspires to undertake research without a precise subject of investigation in mind, relying on key decision makers

and the SOA to raise interesting research questions—but nothing happens.

In these situations, it may be useful for the internal intervener to navigate the literature, looking for insights into what has happened in other organizations, working with third parties for whom distance can provide a more objective perspective. All research is very difficult to carry out alone, and confrontations, intersubjective exchanges, and controversies can help the intervener more fully define a quest.

As an example, Marine (Table 7.1, Case 4) had a research project in mind that led her to search for a doctoral contract with a company. She wanted to work on equality between males and females within companies in the field of gender studies. She achieved her goal by working with the Transco Company, which had strategically target this specific issue, with a focus on how to improve equality between males and females—for ethical as well as performance-based concerns.

In another example, Juliane (Table 7.1, Case 3) presented her research project at a business school that was focused on women entrepreneurship. After listening to her presentation, the targeted school proposed that she lead a project with the goal of creating and running an entrepreneurship center. After a few months, Juliane's observations gave her insights that helped her shape a precise topic of research as well as meet the school's goals of creating a research center focused on ways of developing female entrepreneurship.

Beginning an Internal IR Project

Once the intervention agreement has been defined, stressing the objectives of the mission, it can still be difficult for an internal intervener to begin the research due to a number of underlying challenges—from dealing with a new professional identity for the intervener who becomes a researcher, new working conditions for the intervener who has been recruited to undertake the research, workload management, gaining access to information, and so forth.

Early decisions can play an important role here, for example, a major challenge for the internal-intervener is to decide wonder whether to start with the research or company mission. Indeed, the intervention must be framed by theory to serve the research project, and moving too quickly on the ground without sufficient conceptual background may be counterproductive. Therefore, starting with the state of the art and possible conceptual frameworks appear to be a good starting point—but how far this should go and how long it should last are more challenging issues.

At the beginning of the intervention process, the internal intervener-researcher can be seen as treading in "no-man's land," wrestling with the ongoing passages between the literature and the ground as well as the continuous iterative process that is the essence of any IR project. As we will see further in the chapter, in an IR project the ground is studied from a "provisional" theoretical framework and hypotheses that are deductively created from the literature (Savall & Zardet, 2004). Each phase of immersion within the ground becomes a source to come up with additional hypotheses and insights of an inductive nature. The shaping of the object of the research and the findings stem from this permanent confrontation. Thus questions raised during the beginning of the research are all the more important for the internal-intervener, as that individual is probably less entitled to make mistakes than an external researcher. Indeed, the research is not a newcomer in the company and has already developed a certain reputation. In other words, the internal-intervener generally has a history with the company under study, with all the hopes and emotional dimensions that this matter of fact implies.

As an example of these dynamics, Sarah (Table 7.1, Case 2) wanted to conduct a research project focused on disability in the workplace. She was assigned a mission to accompany handicapped students in a school of management, although this assignment was not perfectly in line with her research project. After a few months of reading the literature, leading her mission, and having observed and interviewed many people, Sarah was able to reshape the research object—the "revelation of disability" among students—that was focused on the field and having a number of scientific potentialities.

In another instance, for several months Jean-Christophe (Table 7.1, Case 5) had been working in a large telecommunications company to observe religion-related issues within the company. The company under study expected that he would be able to create proposals to raise issues stemming from dysfunctions in the management of the religious fact. He found it very difficult to match these expectations without knowing the reality and the functioning of the company. Jean-Christophe came to realize that he needed to undertake a deeper diagnostic of the dysfunctions in the company, traced to poor management of the religious fact within the operational units of the company. Because he did not initially reach agreement on such a diagnostic, Jean-Christophe carried out an additional negotiation to obtain permission of the company under study to make such a diagnostic.

Undertaking Simultaneous Research and Intervention

One of the main difficulties for an internal intervener-research is to simultaneously be an insider employee of the company and a type of outsider through the research process. Therefore, internal intervener-researchers both must be aware of and accept this "schizophrenic" position of not being considered as an ordinary colleague but rather as a stranger within the organization. As a result, internal-researchers tend to create a form of distance with their professional environment because they are permanently in a situation of scientific observation with theoretical filters to decode and understand the phenomena around them. One way of preventing oneself from such disturbing scientific schizophrenia is to express one's feelings in a research journal in which all actions and interactions are related. This approach allows the internal-intervener to capture the memory of the research while maintaining distance from the ground.

Another difficulty is related to the management of data flow and particularly to their access. It is imperative that the researcher be able to identify the sources of data useful for the research. These data may be very different from the information that he or she can collect through daily tasks. Their source is often located outside the scope of one's professional status. In short, the internal-intervener has to manage a dual presence, balancing the demands of the company and those of the research. Both rhythms are often far from being the same. When the company wants to go faster to obtain results, the researcher may need to slow down to ensure distance and make analysis, and *vice versa.* This temporal issue should be taken into consideration during the negotiation phase to create a double planning: one for the company that will be a part of the intervention agreement and the other for the unique role of the researcher.

Marine's mission (Table 7.1, Case 4) was to design and deliver training sessions focused on gender equality at Transco Company. To do that, she negotiated a schedule of travelling and meetings with the collaborators to undertake in-depth interviews that enabled her to more fully diagnose expectations and needs without the need for intermediaries. Juliane (Table 7.1, Case 3), who was working on the development of women's entrepreneurship, used the project of the entrepreneurial center to enter local and regional women's networks in order to meet women entrepreneurs for the needs of her research project. A collaborative platform dedicated to soft skills was one of Delphine's IR deliverables (Table 7.1, Case 6). She had to juggle her time between subjects of the subcontracting company and the rhythms of the academic year. In order to achieve her research objectives, it was necessary for her to schedule tests at regular intervals, which was extremely complex to organize due to the schedule of the students. To complicate matters, it appeared that the stakes of the research did not spontaneously motivate many of the people involved.

Initiating Change

Another challenge for internal intervener-research is initiating the change and stimulating the energy of the actors. They will usually have to undertake this challenge without the support of an external consulting party that could be a source of external energy, a reality that amplifies the difficulties. They must just rely on their own energy and that of the people of the organization who can legitimize their actions. It is therefore necessary for the internal intervener-researcher to anticipate the actors' resistance to change that could be stronger than faced in an external IR project. Consequently, the internal intervener-researcher should obtain the necessary support of and arbitration by the head of the company during the negotiation phase. When processing the research, setting up a steering committee that includes the head of the company proves to be very useful. Through the steering committee, the intervener-researcher can regularly give feedback on the results of the project, update progress, any difficulties and problems that have emerged, and stimulate decisions to reduce resistances and project blockage.

Creating proposals for pedagogical innovation (Delphine's research), creating an entrepreneurial center (Juliane's research), influencing equality policies (Marine's research), or creating a desk in China (Gildas' project) are illustrations of the types of actions that provoke change in organizations and, by definition, disturb their established equilibria. Forecasting to restructure a company or announcing that people are going to be disassembled to build another one, although promised as "beautiful" and "solid," will create resistance. Whatever the resistance may be, our experience is that such missions can still be carried out by internal-researchers provided that they have obtained top management support to obtain the legitimacy they need in their actions in a concerted and supervised manner. Without this support, the intervener-researcher is generally blocked by resistance to change. This was the case in Delphine's intervention: the head manager left the institution where she led her project, and the new manager did not show any interest in supporting her educational innovation project. Gradually, the IR project was slowly extinguished by this lack of interest, although it was never officially ended. In such extreme cases, the internal-intervener must look for other possible fields—or modify the research project. Identifying the causes of rejection and failure of an IR project, understanding the evolution of a project from its beginning to its end, may prove to be even richer experience than the analysis of a successful IR project.

Enlarging the Scope of an Internal IR Project

One of the dilemmas faced by internal-researchers is whether they should enlarge the scope of observations to external fields or other companies. Indeed, one often wonders whether it would be more interesting to extend the research to other grounds (e.g., other companies), basing the research on multiple case studies. In our opinion, it is not necessary to enlarge the scope of an internal IR project, although it is a possible option. Indeed, there are two alternatives for the restitution of the deliverables of an IR project: a longitudinal monograph based on a single case study—that of the internal researcher—or a study based on observations within the internal-intervener's company and external data stemming from observations with other firms. These additional observations go beyond benchmarking integrated in monographic research, reflecting an extension of the scope of the research. Obviously, the latter alternative will require the agreement of the key decision makers for such an extension as well as for the additional displacements, meetings, and data that go with it. Moreover, it is up to the researcher and his or her managers to appreciate the risk taken through such an extension in terms of transparency given to other companies, which may be competitors.

As an example, Sabrina's mission (Table 7.1, Case 1) consisted of implementing a diversity management system in a management school. It was the central object of her research: her thesis described the 4-year process she lived as an insider employee, analyzed the phenomena associated with the experience, and analyzed the evolution of the organizational culture by through an application of Reynaud's (1989) theory of social regulation. The results of the research took the form of a longitudinal monography based on a unique case. Sarah (Table 7.1, Case 2), in contrast, worked in an academic institution on the subject of disability, but at the early stages of her research she came to realize that she needed to meet with different institutional stakeholders on the disability question in France. Her thesis exploited sources far beyond the perimeter of her school. The product of her research was a case study with the observations made within her school as the core body of her work with additional data collected outside her school.

The Legitimacy of the Intervener-Researcher

A reality of any IR project—whether it is led by external- or internal-interveners—is that the interveners must simultaneously fulfill the roles of researcher producing scientific knowledge and change agent producing solutions to help the company. Nevertheless, the challenge for the internal intervener-researcher remains to manage the dialectic between research and intervention as an employee of the studied organization. The challenge is to manage this permanent tension between commitment and loyalty toward the company and the necessary distance required by the research process to produce scientific knowledge.

Thus, a critical stake for the intervener-researcher is to build up one's legitimacy regarding professional and scientific activities. As an intervener and project manager, the individual must be sufficiently credible to gain the confidence of the people engaged in the managerial mission. As a researcher, he or she must also be able to implement a robust method as part of a community of academic peers. This legitimacy is not given *a priori*, it has to be constructed based on principles and technics related to five key questions: (a) the positioning of the researcher, (b) the question of neutrality, (c) the language of the researcher, (d) the ethics of the researcher, and finally (e) the ability to resist the "contamination" of the field.

The Positioning of the Researcher

In an academic publication, whether it is a thesis or journal article, it is essential for epistemic reasons that the practitioner-researcher truly explains their position in the studied organization in a dual role as an intervener and a researcher. Based on our experience, there are three major criteria that should be clarified:

- The history of the practitioner-researcher within the organization, with a description of any networks that have been mobilized to be part of the research.
- A detailed description of the mission of the practitioner-researcher, in particular the relationship with the core business of the studied company (e.g., does the intervener-researcher occupy a position in the core of the value chain or in a supporting function?).
- Does the mission underlying the intervention aim to reduce dysfunctions or create potential and which ones?

As an example, Marine's mission (Table 7.1, Case 4) was to revisit Transco's policy that was not viewed favorably by the company's board of directors. This mission was far different from the one faced by Gildas (Table 7.1, Case 7), which consisted of opening a new desk in China that was a promising development for the studied institution. These distinctions should be clarified to ensure complete understanding for those involved.

The Question of Neutrality

IR principles belong to the interactionist paradigm that rejects the concept of objectivity in favor of *intersubjectivity* (see Chapters 1, 2, & 3). An intervener-researcher, all the more so when internal, must be aware of the impossibility of being truly neutral when making observations because their presence in the organization will necessarily disrupt the surrounding ecosystem. Obviously, it is more difficult to manage a research project when you have a long history of working with colleagues and the loss of distance it entails. The new status of researcher, however, does allow one to create a new form of distance with colleagues. The internal-intervener must still be aware that any distance that is established could engender suspicion among colleagues and anxiety for the researcher, who has to capture findings in the quest of the research as well as for the actors who do not know exactly what the researcher may find. The internal intervener-researcher must be aware of this phenomenon and keep two objectives in mind. First, the need to communicate as much as possible about what is being done, both informally and formally allow for open exchanges. The goal is to reassure and gain confidence. Second, it is important to let colleagues know that the lack of neutrality is a bias one must avoid to create scientific knowledge. When leading an IR project contradictory intersubjectivity, cognitive interactivity and generic contingency becomes the epistemic principles to draw on (see Chapter 1).

Reflecting on the intervener-researchers in Table 7.1, Sabrina (Case 1) like Delphine (Case 6) and Marine (Case 4) had to endure many criticisms and reversals in carrying out their missions. They were all faced with powerful inertia and internal games of competition. They had to understand that these uncomfortable manifestations were also materials and data to analyze for their research.

The Language of the Researcher: Translation and Retro-Translation

The question of language is at the heart of creating confidence with actors during an IR project. The goal for the researcher is to ensure an understanding of each other, using appropriate language to avoid misunderstandings. The intervener-researcher, especially as a newcomer in the studied organization, must gradually adopt and adapt the vocabulary of the company (e.g., technical words, acronyms, cultural expressions) to express the research project in a language accessible to the involved actors. However, the vocabulary of research is often esoteric and obscure for those who are not familiar with academic discourse. To use such a language with the actors may be risky by giving the illusion that the researcher is trying to protect himself through esoteric words. At best, the researcher will be seen as exotic and offbeat, at worst they will be marginalized. Therefore, the key point for the researcher is to find a trade-off between academic language and that of the studied company.

The internal intervener-researcher will have to pay attention to regularly translate academic words into understandable ones for the company and *vice versa*. To do this process of translation, setting up a lexicon may be useful to translate academic words into understandable ones for the ground and to avoid so-called "suitcase words" that everyone seems to knows but with very different meanings in mind. Management research can also manipulate numbers as well as words, which can lead to confusion between the researcher and the actors.

Manipulation

By definition, internal intervener-researchers are immersed within the company under study and at the center of the theatrics of actors. They are thus particularly exposed to manipulations in a way that is certainly more intense than faced by external interveners given their status and stakes of the mission. There are a number of instances where an internal-intervener may be manipulated. A key challenge is when the internal-intervener might be used as an alibi for the leaders of the company. If the individual has not been able to understand the underlying intent of the intervention or detect any hidden motives—a meta-goal of the negotiation process (see Chapters 1 & 5)—the internal-intervener may be led to serve a cause they are not completely aware. Similarly, internal-interveners might be instrumentalized by the people who seek to pass on their ideas through them or aspire to discredit their actions. Organizational politics can play a very destructive role here.

As an inherent aspect of human nature, some degree of manipulation can exist in any IR type of research. In our opinion, the more time spent on immersion in a studied organization, the greater the risk of bias, which can lead to questionable findings. Thus, vigilance is required to manage sufficient distance, even withdrawal, from the ground to detect any manipulations to ensure appropriate analysis of the observations made. There are a number of questions the internal-intervener should continually think through. Should I talk with a friendly tone with the observed actors or keep a neutral tone of relationship? Can we afford to participate in informal events with actors? Should we join coffee machine discussions? These questions may seem trivial but they are essential for an internal intervener-researcher. The distance versus proximity issue is often difficult to manage. How should one use confidences that have been obtained? How should they be incorporated into the research? What nuisance power might they have on the intervention? In thinking through such questions, a good rule for internal intervener-researchers to follow when faced with potentially unpleasant situations is to "be ever pleasant without ever being complacent."

The "Decontamination" Device

It is useful to create "decontamination" devices that allow the internal intervener-researcher to maintain necessary distance from the ground (see also Chapters 1 & 2). Based on our experience, it is an absolute necessity to keep time for reflection, viewing the organization as a "research object."

These "devices" can be as simple as allocating time to read the literature, fully examine the data, ensure reflexivity, and so forth. These efforts have to be part of the schedule of the research and should be negotiated at the start of an IR project. Yet, even though these moments are necessary, they are not enough. It is compulsory to arrange devices outside the organization from the beginning of the research process, ensuring that the internal researcher spend time away from the SOA by spending time with research colleagues, reflecting on and delving into the data without the contamination of the actors on the ground. It is mainly the exchanges that internal-interveners should have with their fellow researchers and (as appropriate) director of research that will help to preserve the necessary distance for the serenity of the research. Such points of decontamination may be held on a regularly basis—during laboratory seminars, meetings with research colleagues, and presentations during conferences and or academic meetings—and can be a powerful tool for development of the research.

Ethics

A question of ethics is central in any IR project that intends to change the organization. There is a constant need from the actors to question the change that is being made and its impacts. Indeed, while some of the effects of the research are mastered and well identified, other impacts are less direct and may remain hidden in the short term but with more significant repercussions in the long run. The internal-intervener may be confident in the validity of the work, but is it also easy to drift away from its central mission. A perceived normality during an intervention may sometimes prove to be harmful. The ethical dimension of intervention-research can be captures with such questions as: "Who will be affected?"; How will they be affected?"; "How far should we go in creating change?" It is important to underscore that the search for scientific intention does not justify everything.

As an illustration, Sarah (Table 7.1, Case 2) conducted research on the disclosure of disability. She conducted interviews with many people and gradually came to realize during her doctoral research meetings that she had a hidden hypothesis influencing her work—the he fact she had a disability. Both for scientific and ethical reasons, she was convinced of the need to reveal this realization and to take it into account in her analysis of documents and interviews to limit the impact of this potential bias.

THE RESEARCH PROCESS OF AN INTERNAL IR PROJECT

An IR process has its own chronobiology. It may last a few weeks up to several years. Yet, regardless of the time frame, IR is based on a detailed and specific research process that presents many opportunities and challenges that the researcher has to meet in order to successfully complete the project (see also Chapters 1, 2, & 3).

Epistemology: Transforming to Create Knowledge

Intervention-research is captured by the expression "change to know," in line with of one of the great theorists of constructivism, Jean Piaget (1972): "One knows an object only by acting on it and transforming it." An IR project is distinguished from action research by the contractualized nature of the agreement between the researcher and the studied organization through which they share an "idealized" vision of its future and a contractualized conduct of change to achieve it (David, 1999).

In looking at Sabrina's intervention (Table 7.1, Case 1), for example, her mission was supported by the strong conviction that organizations are responsible for successfully managing diversity. For both parties—the company and the researcher—a more diverse, egalitarian organization that fights against discrimination is an organization with a greater sense of well-being in the workplace, greater commitment to the work, lessened psycho-social risks, and higher levels of motivation—in essence, an idealized form of organization.

Choosing the Object of Research in the Field

A question that often arises in an internal IR project is that of the object of the research. Very often, the internal-researcher confuses the field with the object of research. As a result, often for months, the framework of the research is blurry, the project becomes too large, and the intervener-researcher misses the opportunity to find something new.

It is therefore a question of being on standby to define the object of the research as well as the first formulation of the research question. It can take several months with the anxieties that go with these hesitations. It is only when the research question is stabilized that the researcher really takes precedence over the intervener.

Several situations may arise. For example, the SOA, that is to say the organization itself, may become the object of the research, but very often the object of the research is a part of the field. One of the difficulties is to choose this "part" because, in an IR process—especially with an internal-intervener—the organization can propose a multitude of exciting and worthy subjects. The internal intervener-researcher has to accept the reality that the research question is likely to evolve over time. It is not about adapting *ad hoc* and arranging validation, but to test its robustness through the iterative process that is at work throughout the research. These dynamics can occur well beyond the intervention itself, because internal-interveners must be able to distinguish the research process from the intervention. Internal intervener-researchers are thus led to rework their research question often through the construction of evolutionary hypotheses. Through an IR project, the researcher is in an abductive process of combining induction and deduction to explore the full spectrum of explanations or interpretations of the observed phenomena. See for instance Marine's planning of intervention-research in Table 7.1. We are far from the hypothetical-deductive research that stabilizes its research question, its body of hypotheses, and its model *before* going to the field, based on literature and an exploratory study.

The Construction and Validation of Assumptions

The process of constructing hypotheses for an IR project—especially one by an internal-intervener—is more complex than a hypothetico-deductive method. Indeed, hypotheses stemming from the literature is a classical approach to research, but in an IR project the research question comes from the observation of the phenomena of transformation of the ground. In the IR process, a hypothesis is not the mere formulation of an observation or the explanation of a phenomenon but rather the support of the construction of the object of research.

It is through these iterative processes that the status of hypothesis is gradually acquired through an enriched formulation. In the classical way of doing research, a hypothesis is something static—it is or isn't validated. In an IR process, in contrast, a hypothesis is something dynamic and the evolution of a hypothesis is the result of the interaction between the researcher and research object that can "move" over time. The task of the intervener is then to transcribe in words this variation to shape this complex research object, something that can be quite challenging from an internal perspective. The bodies of successive hypotheses constitute so many provisional reading grids during the research (Barth, 2004).

The final characteristic of intervention-research, whether internal or external, is the process of validating hypotheses. The intervener-researcher mobilizes a process of duplicating hypotheses and their validation, in order to develop a pattern and formulate an organizing model (Hanson, 1958). We are no longer in a binary version of the hypothesis—that it is or isn't validated—but instead understanding that a hypothesis can evolve in its formulation until it describes-explains-prescribes the object observed with exhaustivity, pertinence, and intelligibility. The hypotheses are then framed in a temporal perspective, with each iteration in succession until there is stabilization and saturation of the model. We must admit the anguish that this process may cause as it is the antithesis of mainstream methods, especially for the internal-intervener. In order to facilitate dialogue with the scientific community, some academics find it simpler to avoid the word "hypothesis" even if it is perfectly adequate, but rather to use the word "proposals." That said "hypothesis" is the right terminology.

Theoretical "Suspension" and the Internal-Intervener

Advancing the IR process raises questions about managing the flow of data in terms of their proliferation and heterogeneous nature. In the case of an internal IR process, there is the additional question of intimacy—the internal-intervener may have with certain information collected from close colleagues. Even if employees are comfortable with this disclosure, it can still present a challenge for the internal researcher.

The analysis begins as soon as the first materials are collected, the researcher examines all the promising ways of understanding, explanation, and prescription. The hypotheses are constantly reformulated, compared, grouped, and tested. They are valuable per se but especially by their actions and interactions, and the phases and degrees that they structure. An intermediate zone is thus created between theory and data, while the analysis is concerned with future theoretical elaboration. The internal-researcher is then in a position of "theoretical suspension" (Pagès, 1979) where he accepts uncertainty and must, in order to advance, accept the possibility of rejection. Each concept discovered or built is considered as being temporary. It gradually gains its legitimacy in its confrontation with the facts. Its relevance must be constantly demonstrated. In intervention-research nothing is ever given once and for all and the idea of closure must be abandoned. This raises the question of the "end" of research.

Ending an Internal IR Project

A difficulty posed by an IR project, which is amplified in the case of an internal-intervener, to "finishing" the intervention. In essence, when does it come to an end? Does the research end with the intervention? Is the mission sufficiently successful that research can claim the production of knowledge? Such questions clearly shape the publication process. Internal-interveners often feel that they must wait for the "results" to share them—an illusion and one must, from the start, understand and accept the procedural nature of this type of research. In short, this type of research never stops, even if the intervention itself ends. The flow of activity continues, colleagues keep on working, and change is at work with its benefits and drawbacks.

Within this context, two scenarios can emerge. In one scenario, the internal-intervener leaves the organization because the contract ends up or because the individual aspires to change positions. The internal-intervener may then return to the organization from time to time to evaluate the effects of the intervention and further integrate observations into the research and writing process. In the second scenario, the internal-intervener concludes the research mission as planned and remains in the organization. The individual is then thrust into the position of "captive watcher" of the continuity of change and typically experiences great difficulty in ending the research. This dilemma is quite difficult to resolve and the setbacks described above are essential to accept what might be thought of as a "mourning" period for many internal intervener-researchers. There will always be something to observe, new outcomes to analyze, and new that phenomena emerge—as such, it is important to realize that it is time to move on to writing the thesis or article, and maybe then onto a completely different project.

The Perspective of the Internal-Intervener

Provided the individual doesn't leave the company at the end of the project, the research process is never completely achieved for an internal intervener-researcher. For an external researcher, it is useful to return regularly to the studied field to make evaluations of the intervention carried out. It is not also uncommon that an IR project is extended in the form of another mission. In short, the researcher never completely finishes the research process, even if he or she is no longer physically with the company. Having carried out an internal research-intervention, individuals in that role have some distinct professional advantages. For some the experience can serve as a type of professional development toward a teaching-research position. Others might draw on the experience and the skills developed to go into the consulting profession or take on higher-level positions with the company in question. It is rare that the employee who has lived such an experience returns to their original position. In addition to the doctorate (for those undertaking the project as part of their advanced graduate studies), the individual has evolved, acquiring skills related to the research mission. The internal-intervener is no longer the same, with new professional cravings that could take the person elsewhere if the original company is unable to offer new opportunities.

Following the completion of her research, for example, Marine (Table 7.1, Case 4) was recruited by her company for new responsibilities in the area of diversity and equality. Despite this new opportunity, she left for a position with another company 1 year later.

At the end of his thesis, Gildas (Table 7.1, Case 7) expected career development within his company. When nothing was offered to him, he left for another professional project that more in line with his new ambitions. Sabrina (Table 7.1, Case 1) did not wish to remain in the school of management where she evolved during 4 years. Despite her success, her mission exposed her to relationships she deemed insufficiently positive to want to stay.

CONCLUSION

The IR role navigates numerous dialectics: researchers vs. interveners, intervention vs. research, academic vs. professional deliverables, professional objectives vs. scientific knowledge, and internal- vs. external-interveners. It takes time, courage, energy, and mastery—the ability to realize that these dialectics that are not oppositions but mutual enrichments.

The case of internal researcher-interveners who makes research inside their companies is particularly interesting because it amplifies the complexity of the IR process. Managing the dialectic of the distance versus the proximity regarding the SOA is certainly one of the greatest difficulties for the internal-intervener to resolve. These individuals will have to learn to look at their organization, colleagues, missions, and so forth with a different lens—that of the researcher. They are also faced with the challenge of being both a colleague and someone who can maintain appropriate distance from the field. At the end of the process, the internal intervener-researcher will developed capabilities and talents that will typically lead to new projects and horizons, including teaching, research, and consultancy. Through the new knowledge and insight these individuals bring to light, they further impact other organizations, helping them understand what they are doing and how to enhance their activities. Whatever the outcomes of an internal intervention, the research process is at work, with its dimensions of continuous learning and reflexivity, for the benefit of the researcher, the organization, and the management sciences.

REFERENCES

Barth, I. (2001). *The sale of consulting: Proposal for a structured and structuring negotiation process.* Paper presented at the Academy of Management & ISEOR Conference, Knowledge and Value Development in Management Consulting, Lyon, France (March).

Barth, I. (2004). *La construction de l'objet de recherche dans la recherche-intervention socio-économique: Un processus dialectique à l'œuvre* [Shaping the observed object in a socio-economic intervention-research project: A dialectical process]. Paper presented at the Colloque RMD-ISEOR, Lyon, France (March).

Barth, I. (2007). *Rôle, objectif et processus de formation des hypothèses dans la représentation de l'objet de recherche en sciences de gestion: Cas de la recherche-intervention* [Role, objective and structuration of the body of hypothethese in management sciences: The case of intervention-research]. Paper presented at the Academy of Management & ISEOR Conference, Lyon, France (March).

Cappelletti, L., & Baker, R. C. (2010). Measuring and developing human capital through a pragmatic action research: A French case study. *Action Research, 8*(2), 211–232.

David, A., Hatchuel, A., & Laufer, R. (2001). *Les nouvelles fondations des sciences de gestio : éléments d'épistémologie de la recherche en management* [The new foundations of management sciences: Epistemic principles of research in management]. Paris, France: Vuibert.

Hanson, N., (1958). *Patterns of discovery.* Cambridge, England: Cambridge University Press.

Pagès, M., Bonetti, M., Gaulejac (de), V., & Descendre, D. (1992). *L'emprise de l'organisation* [The power of organizons]. Paris, France: PUF.

Piaget J., (1972). *Epistémologie des sciences de l'homme* [Epistemology of human sciences]. Paris, France: Gallimard.

Perugien, S. (2015). *Pratiques d'égalité des chances, de diversité et de non-discrimination dans l'enseignement supérieur: Cas de la construction d'une culture organisationnelle en faveur de la diversité au sein d'une business school française* [Equality, diversity, and non-discrimination at university: The case of the settlement of a diversity policy in a business school]. Doctoral thesis, EM Strasbourg, France.

Reynaud, J. D. (1989). *Les Règles du jeu : L'action collective et la régulation sociale* [Rules of the game : Collective action and social regulation]. Paris, France: Armand Colin.

Richard, S. (2016). *Pour une compréhension du processus de révélation institutionnelle du handicap: de l'enseignement supérieur à l'intégration du monde professionnel* [Towards an understanding of the process of revealing disability from university to the professional world]. Doctoral thesis, EM Strasbourg, France.

Santoni, J. (2016). *Contribution à la compréhension de l'intention entrepreneuriale des femmes: Etude de l'influence de l'accompagnement entrepreneurial sur le sentiment d'auto-efficacité entrepreneuriale* [Contribution to the understanding of the women entrepreneurship willingness: Evidence from a case study research]. Doctoral thesis, EM Strasbourg, France.

Savall, H., & Zardet, V. (2004). *Recherche en sciences de gestion: approche qualimétrique, observer l'objet complexe.*The Qualimetrics Approach: Observing the complex object]. Paris, France: Economica.

Theurelle-Strein, D. (2017). Comment favoriser l'acquisition de compétences "qui ne s'apprennent pas"? Etude d'un dispositif d'identification et de développement des soft skills managériales [How to favor the acquisition of skills that "cannot be learned"? Evidence from a case study focused on managerial soft skills]. *Doctoral consorsium,* EM Strasbourg, France.

CHAPTER 8

AN EXAMPLE OF CHAPTERS IN BOOKS BASED ON INTERVENTION RESEARCH

Research on the Theme of Functional Illiteracy and Employment

Marc Bonnet

There is increasing demand in the management sciences to not confine themselves to basic research that is deemed publishable in traditional academic journals—there is a clear need for our research to respond to broader social demands. As in medicine, in which a great deal of research is devoted to suffering caused by a pathology that is hardly curable, in the management sciences protocols need to be developed to improve distressing situations in the life of organizations and companies, and to publish these findings in journals read both by practitioners and researcher-teachers.

This situation is comparable to the suffering caused by functional illiteracy in the context of unemployment. Functional illiteracy, defined more broadly than illiteracy per se, affects people who may have gone to school

Intervention Research, pages 151–161

but who lack basic reading, writing, and numerical skills. People with these shortcomings have difficulty finding jobs, even if they only need to write a job application letter and a resume. Furthermore, companies that employ some staff suffering from functional illiteracy have difficulty coping with this handicap, especially in a world in which productive activities increasingly rely on the written word and digital communication. So they hire very few such people, and they may be tempted to sideline or dismiss underqualified staff or staff who cannot adapt to the digital world. As an example of how intervention research can lend insight into this problem, the chapter presents two publications issued in the form of chapters in a book published by the French Ministry of Employment in *Documentation Française* on the theme of remediation of functional illiteracy in the workplace (Bonnet & Moulette, 2000; Savall, Bonnet, & Moulette, 2000).

THE ORIGIN OF THE SOCIAL DEMAND

The demand was stated by an interdepartmental agency that was reflecting on public policies aimed at tackling the thorny problem of job retention or integration into employment for people lacking basic knowledge, even "functionally illiterate" people. This was an important issue for three reasons.

First, more than 10% of school-leavers leave school without basic literacy and numeracy skills. Even in the case of school-leavers who have acquired them, these basic skills may have eroded with the passing years through lack of practice. Such deficiencies make attempts to provide occupational training ineffective, because these basic skills need to be mastered, if only to read a training manual or use a computer.

Second, the increasing complexity of modern urban civilization means that literacy is increasingly necessary in order to avoid becoming a social outcast—we need to be able to read a map, fill in online forms, or accomplish basic formalities, draft letters or write procedures. In employment contexts, skills requirements are also rising faster and faster. One needs to be able to program tools and equipment, assess data in Excel, and even understand a little English when machine operating instructions have not been translated. Even a civil hall caretaker nowadays needs to know how to manage a schedule using appropriate software, whereas such jobs did not require such literacy skills in the past. Therefore the definition of functional illiteracy is relative: a person who does not know how to fill in a tax return form in this day and age can be classified in this category, which was not the case in 2000.

Finally, there is a vicious circle with regard to the prevention of functional illiteracy. Functionally illiterate people have difficulty admitting that fact and adopt avoidance strategies—for instance, they memorize a procedure that they need to carry out on a regular basis, but are at a loss when the procedure changes, and they dare not ask for information as they are ashamed to admit to their deficiency. Moreover, functionally illiterate people have often performed poorly at school, so they are reluctant to ask for training, which they perceive as a return to school and the bad memories they have of their schooling. Such people are therefore no longer "on the radar" of most training systems, missing the opportunity for remedial teaching, a situation that widens the gap between the most and least qualified people.

With regard to public action, functionally illiterate people often form the hard core of people in long-term unemployment, because they are hard to employ in companies that need qualified staff. When they lose their jobs due to economic redundancy or restructuring plans, they have great difficulty retraining and, more often than not, find themselves permanently reliant on welfare benefits, which puts a strain on public accounts and undermines economic development. Faced with this situation, the public policies pursued by each ministry have their limits—for example, the Ministry for Employment considers that it is up to the Ministry of Education to combat functional illiteracy, but in that case what happens to those who left the education system many years ago? The Ministry of Education for its part considers that academic failure results from other factors, in particular poverty and the lack of social diversity in deprived areas. The Ministry for Employment's policies are thus at a deadlock, attempting to fund return-to-work schemes but realizing that such schemes have very low success rates. The Ministry of Finance has the last word, allocating only a small budget to functional illiteracy remediation schemes.

The interdepartmental national mission in charge of functional illiteracy had therefore run out of ideas for an action plan, notwithstanding the interesting insights on the causes of the problems provided by specialists in education sciences, sociology, and economics. The methods they proposed were specialized, but failed to address the problem in a systemic and operational manner. In hindsight, the lack of any contribution from the management sciences, which typically focus on action and decision, left a significant void. At a conference on the subject held in the Senate on the topic of training underqualified people, we presented the case for socioeconomic management, demonstrating the achievements of a training scheme that incorporated a transformation of work organization in a glass-making company. The subsequent debate was heated, as the union and employer representatives blamed each other for the failure of public policies, putting forth their own ideological arguments. The heads of the interdepartmental mission came to meet us at the end of the conference, requesting our help in formally defining solutions and facilitating a constructive debate based on successful experiments.

Following a number of meetings to prepare a proposal, a research contract was signed with ISEOR, which accepted a lower price than the full cost, as the project was part of the research centre's scientific policy, which among other things explores the conditions under which socioeconomic intervention-research conducted in companies can have an impact on public policies. The contract provided for two complementary actions:

- a pilot experiment in a company through-intervention research; and
- identifying the points in common between successful actions carried out by regional and local departments in charge of employment, and assessing what could be improved in terms of the socioeconomic assessment of the actions.

A team was then set up with a time budget at the ISEOR research centre, including the head of the pilot group (about a 10 hour commitment), a confirmed contributor (about 100 hours), a PhD student funded by ISEOR (200 hours), and two management master-level students on a work-study program (300 hours).

Implementation of the Intervention-Research Process in the Pilot Company

The first part of the intervention-research process consisted of conducting an experiment in a chemical plant with which ISEOR had prior dealings. Employees in that company who were over 40 years old had difficulty adapting to technological advances and the degree of literacy required by the computerization of processes and the increasing number of quality management procedures. Some of the employees were also of foreign origin and had schooling in their country of origin, but they had little command of French. Conversely, plant employees who had been hired more recently had a significantly higher basic level of educational attainment.

In view of the number of young job-seekers, the company had in recent years hired graduates who were overqualified for the requirements of their posts, which led to other difficulties, as the company could not promote them quickly to positions of responsibility. Moreover, a rift formed between the underqualified or functionally illiterate workers and the young, better qualified workers. Faced with these difficulties, the plant's management attempted to train the functionally illiterate workers through refresher programs, but most of these workers were reluctant and had the impression of being made to "go back to school." The company's management wondered whether it would be better to its illiterate workers in other companies, or even lay them off, even if that entailed significant redundancy payments.

With the agreement of the plant's management, the socioeconomic intervention-research process proceeded according to the usual rules and protocols: (a) a diagnosis stage, involving interviews with all grades of staff, to compile a list of problems and hidden costs, and (b) then a project stage to work out and implement an action plan based on a socioeconomic assessment of the cost effectiveness of the intangible investment of the actions. The mirror-effect of the socioeconomic diagnosis made management and staff realize that it was not the functionally illiterate workers who cost the company money but rather the lack of appropriate preventive measures. As an example, errors in mixing chemicals were common due to a lack of rigorous monitoring of procedures, which generated hidden non-quality costs (Savall, 1974, 1980). Another example was the time spent by the supervisory staff in doing the work of their subordinates through lack of confidence in the work of the functionally illiterate workers. This time-wasting activity resulted in delays in updating trials of new products and industrial risk prevention plans.

Given this assessment, the socioeconomic action plan consisted of preparing integrated training manuals with the supervisory staff. The manuals explained how to apply the work procedures and instructions in a simple, practical, and illustrative manner. The preparation of these integrated training manuals led the supervisory staff to bring themselves up to date with regard to the technical innovations in the company, by cooperating with the maintenance and research and development departments. This groundwork also made them aware of the benefits and strategic importance of devoting time to innovation rather than to doing other people's jobs. The staff training sessions were then conducted by the supervisory staff themselves, who described them as "work procedure explanatory sessions" to avoid using the term "training," which had created misgivings and mental blocks as the word reminded the functionally illiterate workers of their past failures and humiliation.

During the "explanatory" sessions, a new relationship of trust and delegation formed between the supervisory staff and the employees: the illiterate workers understood the explanations, which drew on their practical experience, not on abstract theory. The workers were also made aware of the importance of learning chemical formulas, which whetted their appetite to request courses on literacy. Above all, their self-confidence was boosted and they saw the supervisory staff in a different light from the usual reproaches for incompetence. The supervisory staff also learned to listen to the functionally illiterate workers' remarks, discovering their very pertinent comments during the explanatory sessions on improvements to be made to procedures and equipment. The assessment of the action (Savall,

Bonnet, & Moulette; 2000, p. 177) showed that the return on investment of the functional illiteracy remediation process was less than 4 months, which was much more effective than the company's other investments.

As a way of illustrating the improvements that were made, there were

- fewer errors and productivity losses;
- time savings for supervisory staff, who were reassigned to trials of new products;
- time savings for maintenance staff, who were reassigned to fine-tuning new equipment; and
- time saving for the quality department, who were reassigned to perfecting products.

The process also helped sustainably improve labor relations in the plant, by showing all categories of staff that management cared not only about the plant's cost effectiveness but also about living conditions at work and the future of the staff. It also evaluated external performance, such as the impact of remobilizing people in the family context, the parents restoring their children's appetite and pride in succeeding at school. Subsequently, this plant showed its parent group how it had mastered its skills development and technological capacity processes. This led to the plant being made the pilot plant for the group worldwide for part of the chemical products, and the plant continued to take on more workers over the years, whereas the group's initial intention had been to relocate the activity. This intervention-research process thus instilled in decision makers counter-intuitive ways of thinking, contrary to what they had learned in their own management training programmes. They discovered that it was not the underqualified employees who cost the company but rather the lack of appropriate socioeconomic management measures—they also realized that industrial decline in a context of international competition was not inevitable.

The Common Points of Experiment in Functional Illiteracy Remediation

To have an impact on public action, it is important to go beyond the dissemination of the results of a single experiment, especially one based on an example of a successful intervention research process in a chemical plant. This is because the mental maps of decision-makers are characterized by an analytical and specialized approach, more often than not of a legal nature as far as public decision makers are concerned, and by predominantly short-term thinking focused on financial returns for private-sector decision makers. Moreover, the well-known effects of mimicry and isomorphism of neo-institutional approaches make decision makers incredulous or blind to the hidden dimensions of rationality. During presentations of the results at national level, they tend to content themselves with saying, by way of an excuse: "the experiment was interesting, but its success is only relative to the specific context, and it is not reproducible for many reasons."

In socioeconomic theory, this line of argument is considered characteristic of mental structures infected by the "virus" of managerial fragmentation (Savall, 2015). So the research had to be supplemented by a wide-ranging analysis beyond one based on a single intervention. To that end, it was proposed to assess other successful actions in a variety of situations and geographical locations to find points in common with regard to their success factors. It was not just a matter of comparing the content and "best practices" of the actions, but also of decoding the underlying theoretical principles that could shed light on the key success factors. This search for a socioeconomic management theory applied to functional illiteracy remediation is based on the "generic contingency" principle underpinning the qualimetrics research method (Savall & Zardet, 2004). Indeed, each intervention-research case produces two types of knowledge: *contingent knowledge*, specific to the company or organization, and *generic knowledge*, which is more science-oriented and reproducible in any context.

In conjunction with the interdepartmental agency and correspondents in different regions of the country, a dozen experiments were assessed in-depth. They reflected a variety of situations: industrial undertakings, service companies, soft services and cleaning services, local crafts, farming undertakings, cooperatives, training organizations, and trade unions. The intervention protocol did not involve supporting the execution of the experiments but rather assessing their outcomes with the parties concerned, to jointly produce monographs that were authoritative in the eyes of the companies' managers, employees, and financiers. This approach was based on the principles of *cognitive interactivity* underpinning the qualimetrics intervention-research method (eliciting tacit knowledge from actors in the field) and *contradictory intersubjectivity* (achieving a partly shared representation of complex actions carried out). The first product of this work, carried out with the help of master's degree students on a work-study programme, was a manual of cases created for the correspondents of the interdepartmental agency. The underlying goal was to enable them to answer the questions of socioeconomic actors such as the following one:

> I am confronted with situations of functional illiteracy in my company, and my training advisers don't know what to suggest. And yet, it acts as a brake on company development and I wish to avoid making layoffs. Can you give me the references of successful actions in an industry similar to mine?

A second, more academic type of work done at ISEOR was a doctoral thesis in management sciences (Moulette, 2002), which set out to identify the common points of all the actions. This analysis led to an update of the five generic principles that were implicit in the case of the intervention research process in the chemicals firm. These five principles were the following:

- *Relying on experience and interaction in instructional processes*: In all the analyzed cases, there was no point reverting to school-type training, but one had to draw on the situations experienced by the functionally illiterate or underqualified. This is because these people had structured their knowledge and intelligence based on their practical experience, which is invaluable when one has to address complex situations. Recognizing this intelligence and building up new knowledge based on the strong points of these people helped unlock the learning of more theoretical knowledge and compensate for the gaps in basic training.
- *Involving managerial staff*: The impact of confidence was confirmed in all cases as a crucial factor for applying the knowledge acquired during the training sessions. Without such coincidence, memorization and recall does not occur and the investment in training is largely lost after a few weeks. One such example is that of a craftsman who entrusted his functionally illiterate employee with the task of billing using Excel after having trained the employee using a simplified sheet of instructions. The employee in question was then able to perform this task on a daily basis, thereby consolidating the learning process, while at the same time enabling his boss to spend more time responding in a timely manner to requests for quotes.
- *Including functional illiteracy remediation in a multidimensional upskilling action plan for organizations*: The most successful actions did not consist of specifically targeting the functionally illiterate but rather in implementing an overall plan while drawing on the tacit knowledge of people in situations of functional illiteracy. As an example, an integrated training course on work procedures and instructions in a furniture company enabled all the staff to acquire expertise, which led to ISO 9000 certification and commendation by the auditors.
- *Assessing actions to accelerate organizational learning*: The assessment of successful actions, even when they had limits, helped change people's mind-set and perceptions of the potential for progress, thereby sending a message of hope that counterbalanced the despair induced by toxic managerial practices (accounting and management audit) centred on cutting visible costs. In a cleaning firm, for instance, after the assessment of the process the manager

stated: "We discovered that we had an extraordinary wellspring of high-potential people."

- *Coordinating actions carried out in employment with a process of empowerment of the functionally illiterate*: Functional illiteracy is often connected to family and social difficulties, and companies and organizations are not solely responsible for personalized action plans that construct a progressive retraining process. This presupposes management at local level, for instance, when a company hires someone coming from economic integration schemes who continues to be supported without any anti-corporate bias by the trainers and social workers.

These five factors formed the beginnings of scientific-oriented rules for recommending actions, by differentiating them from the recipes that practitioners try to apply by merely transposing the content of a single successful experiment without having identified the principles underpinning its success.

Multi-Stakeholder Intervention-Research

Intervention-research can be seen through a socially responsibility lens, as in the case of medicine, where the research benefits patients, families, the faculty and its students, and society as a whole. It is also research that can partially fund itself, as long as one knows how to negotiate relations in the field and one abides by the rules of conduct and epistemological rigor. For qualimetrics-based intervention-research, seven categories of beneficiaries of the research have been identified, as summarized in Table 8.1.

Material Removed for Publication

The publication of two book chapters in *La Documentation Française* by the Ministry of Employment went hand in hand with other forms of dissemination of the research findings: roughly 10 presentations in regional and national symposia and radio-broadcast interviews (BFM). There is also an encyclopedia chapter on the management of human resources in the context of functional illiteracy and management of underqualified personnel.

Two limitations, however, are noted. First, with regard to the publications, the research appeared too applied at the time for publication in an academic journal. Two remarks were made in this respect: "the research is not theoretical enough" and "sample insufficiently representative of the database to be processed by structural equations." Despite such concerns, the past several years have witnessed increased acceptance of intervention-research in academic journals, partly due to growing pressure from

TABLE 8.1 Contributions and Remuneration of Each Stakeholder in the Intervention-Research Process

Research Stakeholders	Inputs to Intervention Eesearch on Functional Illiteracy Remediation	Contribution
Research teachers	Accumulation of high-quality scientific data	Support for data collections and conceptualization
Research centre	Contribution to the dissemination of theories and to reputation	Partial internal financing on research budget
PhD and MA students on work-study programmes	Collection of scientific observation data for the doctoral thesis and dissertations	Time spent (paid) and work on positioning in relation to the literature on the subject
Companies and organizations where the research took place	Better quality management and the long-term survival of the companies	Time spent on taking action, largely self-funded, as attested to by the socioeconomic balance sheets
Society, in particular the illiterate and their family circle.	A change in perception and messages of hope to defy the inevitability of situations of functional illiteracy and social exclusion	Research partially funded by society
Consultants, trainers and correspondents from government departments	Training in scientific functional illiteracy remediation methods, and contribution to the policy of full employment.	Participation in assessment and in experience feedback
State	Contribution to more pertinent and cost-effective public action	Partial funding of the research

management training institutions to conduct research with managerial impact. This naturally presupposes having the collected data translated and presented in a manner acceptable to the research community who have experience in field work or intervention research.

Second, as for the impact on public management, the research program was dropped after a change of government, as the ministries changed. The new staff of the interdepartmental agency wished to prioritize research on prevention of functional illiteracy at the school level, in view of the political debate surrounding accusations levelled at the French state education system for poor performance. It is regrettable that intervention-research has not been carried out on this theme, showing how the French state education system could cooperate with other stakeholders in each region to remedy the multiple causes of academic failure. An underlying goal should be to encourage collaboration rather than seeking to turn key stakeholders against one another—in essence the responsibility of public action.

CONCLUSION

The contributions and limitations of these publications on the basis of intervention-research illustrate the immense social responsibility management sciences have in terms of innovating both in companies and organizations and in the field of public management. It should be noted from Table 8.1, which focuses on the contributions of intervention-research from the perspective of various stakeholders, that the career of the research teacher could be guided by a quest for publication quantity rather than the quality of the research itself. If one were writing publications in the field of medical research on the same topic, the order of the table would be shocking and one would undoubtedly have put in first place the impact of research for the benefit of patients.

REFERENCES

Bonnet, M., & Moulette, P. (2000). Requalifier les salariés en situation d'illettrisme. Enseignements tirés d'une douzaine d'expériences dans des entreprises [Requalifying employees in situations of illiteracy: Lessons learned from a dozen experiences in companies]. In *Illettrisme et monde du travail* (pp. 193–202). Paris, France: La Documentation Française.

Moulette, P. (2002). *Contribution à la gestion de la remédiation aux situations d'illettrisme en entreprise* [Contribution to the management of remediation of situations of illiteracy in companies]. Doctoral thesis in management sciences, under the direction of Marc Bonnet. Lyon, France: ISEOR, University of Lyon.

Savall, H. (1974). *Enrichir le travail humain dans les entreprises et les organisations* [Work and people: An economic evaluation of job enrichment]. Paris, France: Dunod.

Savall, H. (1979). *Reconstruire l'entreprise: Analyse socio-économique des conditions de travail* [Reconstructing the enterprise: Socio-economic analysis of working conditions]. Paris, France: Dunod.

Savall, H. (1981). *Work and people: An economic evaluation of job enrichment.* New York, NY: Oxford University Press.

Savall, H., Bonnet, M., & Moulette, P. (2000). Méthode socio-économique de requalification et d'insertion des personnes illettrées dans l'emploi [Socio-economic method for retraining and integrating the illiterate into work]. In *Illettrisme et monde du travail* (pp. 171–182). Paris, France: La Documentation Française.

Savall, H., & Zardet, V. (2004–2011). *Recherche en sciences de gestion: Approche qualimétrique. Observer l'objet complexe* [Research in management sciences: The qualimetrics approach: Observing the complex object]. Paris, France: Economica.

Savall, H. (2015). TFW virus concept history. In J. Conbere, H. Savall, & A. Heorhiadi (Eds.) *Decoding the socio-economic approach to management* (pp. xvii). Charlotte, NC: Information Age.

PART II

PUBLISHING INTERVENTION-RESEARCH

CHAPTER 9

CONCEPTUALIZING AND PUBLISHING ORGANIZATIONAL INTERVENTION-RESEARCH

Anthony F. Buono

Reflecting on the challenges of capturing the essence of qualitative field work, John Van Maanen (1998, p. xxv) noted that "There are probably rules for writing the persuasive, memorable and publishable qualitative research article, but rest assured, no one knows what they are." Coming from one of the field's preeminent qualitative researchers, his observation can be more than a little daunting for those beginning to work in this realm. Van Maanen's comments underscore the ongoing challenge inherent in conducting and capturing high quality qualitative work—there aren't any clear-cut criteria or procedures that will ultimately lead to a noteworthy publishable paper. In essence, there is no accepted "boilerplate"—no standardized template—for capturing and presenting a qualitative research study (Pratt, 2009). These same sentiments and concerns are readily applicable to intervention research, which typically draws on mixed-method approaches.

Intervention Research, pages 165–181

Within this apparent constraint, the chapter explores the underlying dynamics of conducting and publishing intervention research, focusing on the nature of intervention research and actionable knowledge and conceptualizing the publication process, from initial writing and design, to framing the analysis and article itself, to selecting appropriate outlets/journals. Taking a critical view of the way in which many intervention research papers are presented, the discussion also draws on the most common reasons why editors reject these submissions. The chapter concludes with a final reflection on some of the practical "nuts and bolts" associated with the publication process and ethical considerations in conducting and publishing this type of research.

INTERVENTION RESEARCH AND ACTIONABLE KNOWLEDGE

Part of the mission of the Academy of Management (AoM)—the largest professional association for scholars of management and organization—is to ensure that our science-based knowledge is relevant and responsible, providing insights that make a valuable contribution to our society and its institutions. In other words, a core goal is to produce knowledge that is truly actionable—transcending purely scientific concerns and enabling organizational members to draw on these insights to make informed choices about practical problems and opportunities and to effectively implement solutions to these challenges.[1]

Over the years, the majority of researchers within the Academy have done a credible job of creating knowledge that is scientifically sound and methodologically rigorous. Indeed, AoM scholars have generated an impressive body of management and organization theory and research findings. Critics contend, however, that these scholars have been far less successful in making sure that this knowledge is applied and disseminated to a broad audience—that much of our knowledge fails to cross the gap between research and practice; it stays on the academic side of the chasm, left frequently in esoteric terms. Consequently, few practitioners read this body of academic research or appreciate its practical value, drawing instead on materials published in more readable popular magazines and outlets as well as their own experience to guide their actions.

An underlying goal of intervention research is to meet this challenge, fulfilling a tripartite focus on (a) helping a specific group or organization to effectively deal with current problems and challenges as well as (b) drawing on that experience to contribute to a broader understanding of the underlying dynamics of organizational performance and effectiveness (c) in a way that is clear and understandable to a broad audience. As illustrated in Figure 9.1, in order to contribute to new insights into ways in which we can

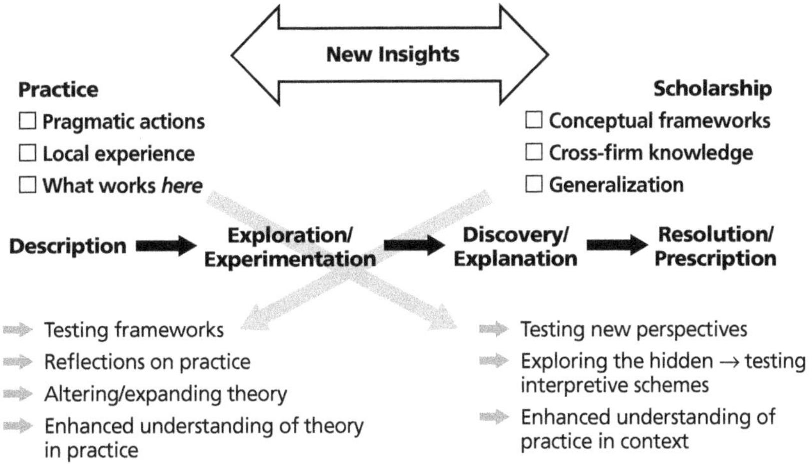

Figure 9.1 Intervention research and actionable knowledge. *Source:* Adapted from Buono (2009, p. xvi).

enhance group and organizational performance, an underlying key is the iterative interaction between practice and concepts, going from what works in the here and now to what is generalizable to a broader cross-section of firms and situations. A basic goal of intervention research is to produce such actionable knowledge, providing an enhanced understanding of theory in practice as well as an enhanced understanding of practice in its larger social context.

As suggested by many scholars, however, the ideal of actionable research remains a rather elusive concept (see, for example, Aldag, 2012; Nielsen, Buono, & Poulfelt, 2017). Summing up the debate on actionable research ignited by Pearce and Huang's (2012) assessment of the "wasted resources" of *non-actionable* research, Bartunek and Egri (2012, p. 245) argue that "an important objective of scholarly research is to inform management and organizational practice," encouraging academics to "find new ways to seek out and identify research questions as well as to improve the translation and communication of their findings to non-academic audiences." The challenge to inform and enlighten both practitioners and scholars—which is the essence of intervention research—raises questions about how we conceptualize and approach the ideal of what constitutes "quality" research.

Quality Research: Traditional Versus "Actionable" Views

The traditional way of conceptualizing quality in research and the research process has evolved around three basic challenges—(a) the extent to which the research provides formal theory about pervasive phenomena (b) using rigorous analytic models that are anchored in the established literature (c) to test hypotheses with valid and reliable (typically quantitative) data. While this approach has produced an impressive body of scientific evidence, it largely focuses on the needs of the academic community itself, providing smaller and smaller incremental contributions to our knowledge with less and less relevance to the world of practice.

The idea of *actionable* knowledge suggests an alternative view of quality research. Departing from the traditional approach to knowledge creation—what has been referred to as Mode 1 research (i.e., producing discipline-based knowledge for its own sake)—actionable knowledge is reflected in what Gibbons and his colleagues (1994) referred to as Mode 2 research, where multidisciplinary insight is applied to specific problems in the real world as a way of producing new knowledge. Within a Mode 2 context, quality research addresses significant issues, problems and/or challenges—from initial description and exploration/ experimentation to discovery/ explanation to potential problem resolution and prescription (see Figure 9.1). A goal is to discover phenomena that make various social entities (from organizations to institutions to the larger society) a "better place," changing the way we think about the phenomena being studied—and capturing that insight in a way that helps to deal with immediate concerns while contributing to our general body of knowledge.

As summarized in Table 9.1, there are a number of tensions across these two perspectives on research quality, captured by the polarizing rigor-relevance debate. An underlying concern is that over time our desire for technical rigor has moved us away from the "soul of relevance" that is the essence of practice (George, 2014). Quality intervention research is intended to be both relevant and rigorous in ways that are useful both to practitioners and academicians.

CAPTURING INTERVENTION RESEARCH

The traditional approach to writing up quantitative research, which can be thought of as latter stage inquiry (see Figure 9.2), typically follows a

TABLE 9.1 Interpretations of Quality Research: Tensions

• Rigor of mathematical models	• Richness of descriptive/multisource data
• Hypothesis testing	• Framework building
• Paradigms	• Modeling
• Statistical significance	• Substantive significance
• Discipline-based	• Multi-/transdisciplinary
• RIGOR	• RELEVANCE

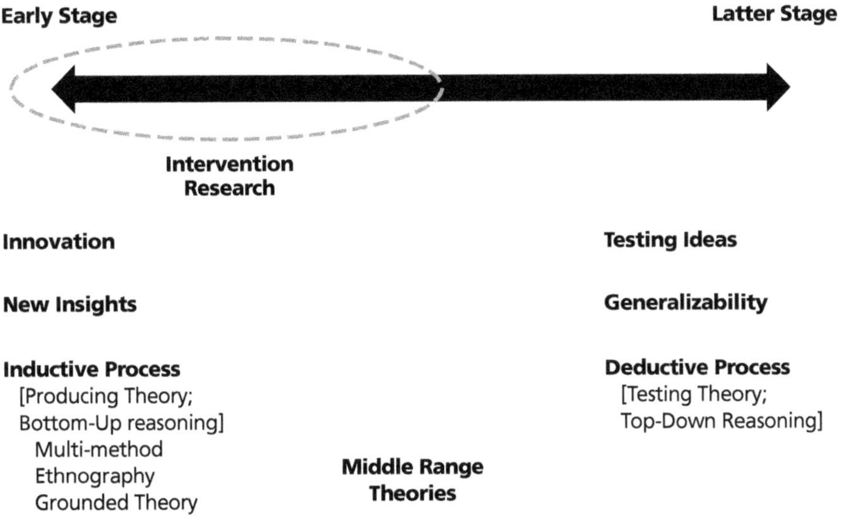

Figure 9.2 Conceptualizing intervention research: Early- versus latter-stage research.

well-defined structure from the introduction and literature review, to hypotheses and research methods/study design, to results, discussion, and conclusion. In essence, this type of research reflects the faithful execution of a carefully crafted plan based on deductive reasoning, a process of reasoning from one or more premises/hypotheses to reach logically certain conclusions. An intervention research paper, in contrast, requires a different approach, presenting more of a structured narrative that emerges from inductive reasoning, moving from specific instances or situations to create generalizable conclusions.

Framing the Paper

The client needs help—but does the underlying problem and the subsequent research have a compelling story to tell? Not every intervention or consulting engagement we carry out will necessarily provide us with the depth or challenge that others will find useful or enlightening. Especially for publication in so-called "A-level" journals, contribution to theory and knowledge is based on the significance, novelty, curiosity, scope, and actionability of the issue being studied (see Colquitt & George, 2011). Often referred to as the "so what" factor (Melnyk & Morrison-Beedy, 2012), an underlying key is to conceptualize the problem or challenge, the potential impact of the intervention, and the possible significance of the results (i.e., the extent to which knowledge in the field of study will be enhanced) in a way that will capture the reader's interest. Within this context, a number of questions emerge when one begins to conceptualize an intervention research paper. For example, what does the client need and to what extent might this lead to an interesting article? Who is the intended audience? What is the significance of the data set? What about its broader social and cultural context? Why should the reader be interested? Is there sufficient data to make the case, moving beyond a few random, arbitrary data points to a more systematic assessment of the situation? How repeatable is the intervention and analysis (transparency)? Although an advantage in intervention research is that data sets typically involve a range of methods and multiple sources of data, a challenge is to capture this richness in a way that the reader can follow your logic and what was done.

When framing the paper, a core challenge is to illustrate to the reader how you are inductively building theory. In capturing the intervention, it is important to create a compelling case—*what* is the story? *why* is the topic important?—using the introduction to situate theory and to explain *why* the setting and/or intervention provides an interesting case that will lead to a better understanding of the phenomena in question. Thus, a typical intervention research paper begins with a provocative question or challenge via a story and theory narrative—the opportunity to grab the reader's attention—providing a framework for the data and information that follows. A goal is to raise questions about our current understanding of a given phenomenon that sets the stage for the creation of new insights—potentially generating the basis for "new ways of seeing" the situation, from the practical steps one could take to improve or build on current practice, to the assumptions we typically make, to the theory underlying conventional lines of inquiry (see Shaw, Bansal, & Gruber, 2017). As Bansal and Corely (2012) note, the introduction should frame the paper, being careful not to reveal too much information—to the point where the theory/insight doesn't appear to emerge from the data—or too little—to the point where the paper seems overly broad and unfocused. The paper's literature narrative should provide a framework to understand/view the textual data, exposing gaps in theory/understanding and setting the background for the intervention.

An underlying challenge with intervention research is that the intervention itself—and its design—may not necessarily begin with an intriguing question per se. It typically commences with a problem or challenge faced by the unit in question. The initial goal—focusing on what might work in the here and now—is usually to facilitate the organization's ability to meet that problem. As the problem is specified, however, the next step is to develop what might be thought of as a program theory in which the core features of the intervention are detailed (see Fraser, Richman, Galinsky, & Day, 2009)—in a way that has broader appeal beyond the group or organization in question.

The introduction is then followed by a descriptive account of the intervention, which lays out the challenge(s) and what was done. Care should be taken to clearly depict why the intervention occurred and what happened during the engagement. Context is important here. Since most interventions are typically iterative as well as generative in nature, any insights must be placed in their larger cultural and social context. The discussion, for example, should capture such considerations as the needs and aspirations of the various actors involved in the situation, if, and why, they changed during the intervention, the various barriers (individual, sociocultural, structural, etc.) that existed, and organizational constraints and broader contextual factors (e.g., norms and taboos, collaboration challenges, regulatory factors, financial limitations) within which the intervention took place (see George, Howard-Grenville, Joshi, & Tihanyi, 2016).

In discussing the intervention—what was actually done during the engagement—it is crucial to be as detailed and transparent as possible. Although pseudonyms are typically used, it is still important to provide a general description of the organization and its broader context and the relevant socio-demographics of the intervention population. This section should also capture the nature of the intervention itself—what took place, how long it lasted, who was involved in what role(s), and so forth. Since a good deal of intervention research involves interaction with and the engagement of practitioners/organizational members, it is also important to be clear as to what roles they played, especially in the gathering and interpretation of the data.

The data narrative should provide a clear story about the data collection process, focusing on the type of information that was collected, how it was accumulated, and the characteristics of the subjects, leading into analysis (methods/interpretation) and outcomes (results/ findings). If a sample of the organization is being studied or utilized for the intervention, it is important to indicate how the respondents were selected, their longevity with the organization or work unit, and other relevant characteristics.

Given the complexity of such field work, there is ample latitude about appropriate methods— from qualitative interviews and observations, to quantitative surveys and questionnaires, to assessments of financial data, to field notes and ethnographies. Again, there is no "boilerplate," no prescribed template to serve as a checklist. As reflected in Figure 9.1, the exploration and discovery phases can often be serendipitous, and, as such, research rigor must be conveyed through authenticity and openness, with rich descriptions of the data that capture a "trail of evidence" that is conveyed throughout the paper (Bansal & Corley, 2011). In comparison to traditional quantitative research, where the author can point to well-known data sets and appropriate statistical tests, a thoughtful intervention research paper provides a detailed account of the engagement's "journey," from initiating the project to finalizing the manuscript (see Bansal & Corley, 2012). The underlying key is to fully convey the "who, what, where, when, and how" of this journey in a way that enables the reader to grasp and understand how the intervener moved from the data through analysis to final insights and theoretical contribution.

As part of a well-constructed story narrative, theory should give meaning to the data while the data provide context for the theory. A core challenge is thus in the presentation of the data and underlying theory. A typical shortcoming is when the data-theory mix is out of balance—in many instances, authors talk about the data, drawing out their interpretations of what is happening but without sufficient detail about the data itself, referred to as "too much 'telling' and not enough 'showing'" (Golden-Biddle & Locke, 2007; Pratt, 2009, p. 857). At the other extreme, authors can slide into overly "thick" descriptions of the data but without sufficient conceptual reflection on what the data mean and how they contribute to new theoretical or conceptual insights. The key is to explore ideas in an iterative process, drawing on inductive and interpretive reasoning, a "middle range" approach (Merton, 1949) to theory construction that integrates empirical phenomena with existing theory, drawing out working hypotheses that evolve during day-to-day research and observations.

The next critical dimension of the paper is the analysis, ensuring a "thick," detailed description that captures the actors' experience and how the results were determined. Depending on the number of respondents involved in the process, a growing trend reflects coding of interview and field note data, being careful to fully describe how the content was analyzed, how categories were determined, and how the responses were allocated across those categories. In these cases, it is useful to include summaries of the primary data in tabular form to provide the reader with a fuller insight into the experience and a clearer basis to understand the analysis and interpretation of the data. When presenting this information, it is important to avoid making intuitive leaps between the data and one's conclusions, using specific examples to illustrate key concepts and showing how these examples represent the broader data set.

The paper then concludes with a focus on how the findings emerged from the data and surfaced from the analysis. Here is where the author should revisit earlier research questions and goals, moving toward an explanation of how those questions were answered and the goals were achieved. This section should draw out the broader implications and unanswered questions from the intervention, delving into how these insights relate to key management or social science research issues.

As reflected in Figure 9.3, the process of writing a meaningful intervention research article is also iterative in nature, where the writing process itself is part of an exploratory journey of identifying gaps, inconsistencies,

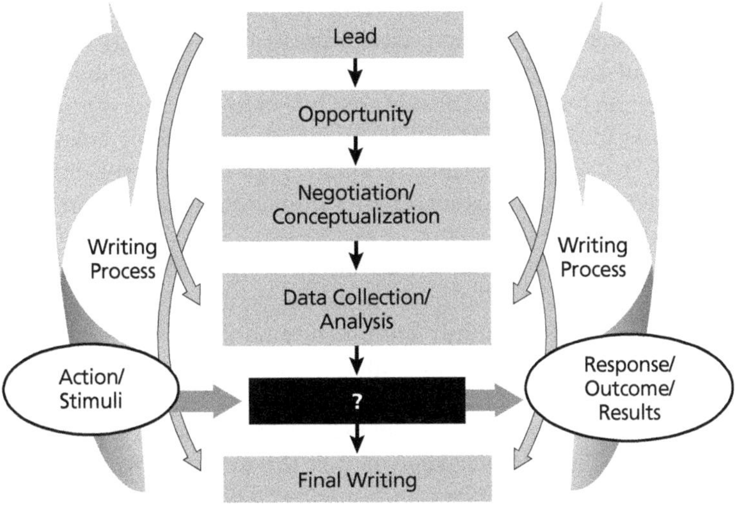

Figure 9.3 Writing and the intervention research process.

and questions that require analysis and discussion (see Bansal & Corley, 2012). Thus the actual writing of the paper doesn't begin when the intervention is finished and the researcher reflects on what has transpired. Thoughtful articles typically reflect a more generative and dynamic process, where the writing process begins in the project's early stages.

Part of the goal is to create a journey that enables the reader to better understand the "black box" of organizational life, exploring the various responses and outcomes that emerge from different actions and stimuli.

Why Editors Reject Intervention Research Articles

When editors reject a particular paper, the author(s) typically receives a detailed explanation of why the paper fell short of the journal's standards or expectations. These reasons reflect the integration of the editor's thoughts about the paper with the comments and critique of the reviewers. Although never pleasant to receive, virtually everyone who has aspired to publish in an academic journal has received a negative decision letter. As Ireland (2009) suggests, learning from that experience and the input of one's peers is a critical part of a successful scholarly career. Most researchers use that feedback to rework and revise the paper and eventually submit the manuscript to another outlet.

There are myriad reasons why editors reject a research paper, from flawed research designs, to measurement and data-related concerns, to an unsound research design where the research question, theory, method, and data analysis are not consistent or clearly presented. To a large extent, rejections occur due to poor operationalization of the issues discussed above—there is a mismatch between the research question and intervention design, the study raises measurement and data concerns (e.g., using cross-sectional data to analyze change/causality, too many measures/perspectives from a single/limited source), the research isn't sufficiently grounded in the literature, and so forth.

Another concern is that the research question itself isn't clearly stated or conceptualized. In far too many instances, central concepts are poorly presented or used inconsistently and the methodology and study design are unclear or vague. As a result, the paper is seen as overly descriptive rather than analytic in nature. In other instances, the data collection is poorly carried out and/or presented and the data are not sufficiently contextualized. The analysis thus suffers as it appears that the paper draws unsound conclusions and/or unfounded generalizations—in essence there are intuitive leaps from the data to the paper's conclusions. Finally, too many papers are poorly written paper or the text is simply too long (e.g., lack of focus, rambling). Drawing on the critical eye of trusted colleagues can be very beneficial here, as we often read what we think we wrote rather than what we have actually committed to paper.

CONCLUDING THOUGHTS

Successfully publishing an intervention research paper is as much an art as it is a science. The discussion above has attempted to lay out the process of conceptualizing and framing the paper and to provide a general sense of the approach one should take with this type of research. In addition to this type of conceptualization, there are also what might be thought of as a number of "nuts and bolts"-type decisions that can influence the editorial and/or peer review process, from selecting the right publication outlet to ethical considerations in the research and publication process.

Early Feedback

In general, most papers are rarely submitted to a journal without initial feedback from professional colleagues. As an early testing ground, drawing on one's professional network—trusted colleagues and researchers in the field—can uncover potential shortcomings or raise issues that might have been overlooked. Another tactic is submission to professional association meetings—for example, the AoM, European Group for Organization

Studies (EGOS), British Academy of Management (BAM), Organization Development Network (ODN), and so forth. While acceptance to these conferences is competitive and submissions go through a review process, the comments from the conference reviewers as well as discussion from participants when accepted papers are presented are usually very useful in further developing the paper.

Gaining Attention

Once the paper has been written it is important to carefully consider the title and abstract, especially since that will be the first feature of the paper the journal editor and reviewers will see. Although it may seem obviously important, many authors rush through the abstract, missing an opportunity to guide the reader.

The paper's *title* should summarize the main theme of the article and, as much as possible, reflect its contribution to the field. The *abstract* should also be carefully crafted, briefly drawing attention to the aim and scope of the intervention, the key problem(s) to be addressed, the methods used and the data set, key findings and limitations, and implications for theory and practice.

Another important, but often overlooked aspect is the submission letter to the journal editor. Many people think that the abstract is sufficient to draw attention to the paper's content, but a cover letter presents an opportunity to convince these readers that the research/intervention is well worth reviewing. A good cover letter, which should short and to the point—roughly half a page—should outline the main theme and focus of the paper, underscoring its novelty, and briefly explaining the paper's relevance to the target journal (see Shaikh, 2016).

Finding the Right Journal

In general, one of the first things to consider when selecting a journal to submit a paper is the type of article that one is writing—is the paper more concept- or data-based or does it have a combined focus. As a starting point, it is useful to scan possible journals, examining the publication's aims/scope and journal metrics (e.g., acceptance rates, impact, geographic reach, peer review speed). Many publication houses have journal finders, where one can submit a paper title, abstract and field of study for suggestions as to appropriate outlets.

Open Access Versus Subscription Journals

The internet is significantly changing the journal landscape. Journals are typically either *subscription-based,* free only to subscribers or members of a particular organization or association or *open access,* with free and permanent access to published research, with clear guidelines for sharing and using the content. While there are some hybrid journals that are a combination of open access and subscription publications, caution should be taken when faced with author-pay systems. Some legitimate publication houses will give an author the choice of paying a fee if they desire open access to the article, which is then only available to subscribers if that option is not taken. However, newcomers to the research and publication process should be wary of the increasing presence of a type of academic vanity press, where journals (as well as conferences) solicit manuscripts, present misleading metrics about the position and readership of the journal (or conference), and require authors to pay a fee to publish (or present) their paper.

Growth of Predatory Publishers

Referred to as predatory publishers, these periodicals charge publication fees in the guise of open access without the type of editorial service associated with legitimate journals. These journals have a bogus review process, with the promise of "timely reviews" (typically within 1 week) but without any content or feedback associated with the peer review process, with questionable editorial board membership with the same names appearing with multiple journals. Young scholars new to the profession, especially those from developing countries, are noted to be particularly vulnerable to such flattering invitations to publish their work and have been referred to as "pawns" of what, in essence, is a new business scam (Straumsheim, 2017).

Referred to as the "seamy side of open-access publishing," many open access journals began with the aspiration to make scientific papers available to everyone. Their proliferation, however, has resulted in thousands of fake open-access journals (Kolata, 2017). Jeff Beall, a scholarly communications librarian at the University of Colorado, initially coined the term predatory publisher, culling a list of these journals that do not meet expected academic standards, which some have referred to as a journal "blacklist" (Butler, 2013; Van Noorden, 2014). Although "Beall's List" was terminated in early 2017, suggested to be in response to threats of legal action, cached versions of the list are still available online (e.g., "waybackmachine" internet archive). Of course, not all open access journals fall into this category of fraudulent publications—but caution is urged. If an author is not familiar with a journal, it is highly recommended to confer with colleagues and explore journal ranking services (see, for example, thinkchecksubmit.org) prior to making a submission decision.

Peer Review

For those just getting started, the peer review process itself can be rather daunting. When a paper is submitted to a journal, the typical process begins with a careful reading and early decision by the editor. In many instances, the manuscript may be rejected right there—referred to as a desk rejection—based on the editor's determination that the paper is not suited for that particular journal. In some instances, the editor, especially if she or he thinks the paper has promise, will suggest alternative submission outlets that appear to be a better fit.

If the paper passes this initial assessment, it is then sent out for review (typically 2–3 people). Although the process varies by journal, the typical approach involves respected people in the field with expertise in the general area of the paper. Reviewers usually focus on the overall quality of the paper, filtering out manuscripts that have been poorly conceived, designed, or executed, and focusing on the merit and validity of the study/intervention. Looking at the overall presentation of the paper, good reviewers also provide recommendations on specific ways to further improve the paper.

This assessment can be quite valuable to the author—papers are rarely accepted during the first round. The author(s) will receive either a rejection or a revise and resubmit determination. In most instances, the editor will also inform the author of the relative risk involved in the resubmission process. When an author receives a "high risk" revision it typically means that although the manuscript has promise there are significant concerns about the study itself that might not be able to overcome in the revision process. In most instances, it is advisable to follow up on a revise and resubmit decision as the paper has already passed initial editorial review. It is not uncommon for a paper to go through two or even three revisions before ultimate acceptance, although papers are usually either accepted or rejected after the first set of revisions.

A revise and resubmit decision should be viewed positively. In reworking the manuscript, it is important to highlight the changes made in response to the reviewers' comments, being very clear as to what was done in response. The paper's author(s) can disagree with the reviewer comments, but if one takes this route he or she needs to be very clear as to why they did not follow the recommendations.

Ethical Considerations in Organizational Intervention Research

There are general ethical principles and guidelines for any research involving human subjects, as reflected in the Belmont Report.[2] This report contains three core principles, which researchers are required to follow: (a) respect for people, which is intended to protect human subject autonomy, treat them with courtesy and respect, and allow for informed consent; (b) beneficence, attempting to minimize any risks, guided by a philosophy of "do no harm" and a commitment to maximize benefits from the research; and (c) justice, ensuring that reasonable, nonexploitative, and well-considered principles guide the research and subject selection. The challenge for intervention research is that the intervention is often not designed with these three factors in mind, focused much more intently on resolving the issue faced by the group or organization. For example, subject selection is typically influenced by the relationship of an individual's or group's role and position with respect to the issue being studied rather than the type of scrutiny that goes in selecting subjects from a broader population. Moreover, since participants are members (employees) of the organization, informed consent is rarely, if ever, sought. Yet, despite these challenges, intervention researchers should still follow the spirit of the Belmont Report, ensuring that the subjects they work with are treated in an ethical and responsible manner.

Publishing Ethics

There are several taboos in the publishing process, from simultaneous submissions of the same article to more than one journal at a time, to plagiarism and research fraud (fabrication & falsification), to a failure to disclose possible conflicts of interest (which might prevent someone from being unbiased). Since peer review is typically a time consuming, laborious process, journal editors expect that the paper they are placing for review has not been simultaneously submitted elsewhere. If a paper is rejected, the author is then free to submit it to another journal.

While plagiarism and fraud are reasonably straightforward concerns, there are grey areas that further complicate the process. For example, authors are often tempted to turn a single paper into several submissions, a process referred to as "salami slicing." While this practice is generally seen as unethical, authors often write up and publish different phases of a longitudinal project—which is an acceptable practice as long as each subsequent publication adds value and new material. A similar practice is when a paper is purposefully written for different audiences, playing up theory and conceptual development in a well-referenced paper for one audience and focusing on practice implications and prescriptions for another. Sometimes referred to as duplicate or redundant publication, the main concern is when authors produce highly similar articles with minimal modifications or attempt to write several articles when one would be sufficient (King, 2001).

Another concern deals with questions of authorship, especially since a good deal of intervention research is done by teams rather than individuals—for example, who should be included as an author, in what order should authors be listed? There are no clear cut answers for many of these questions. In best practice, the integrity of the researcher is the best guide, attempting to be as open and transparent as possible in making such decisions.

CONCLUSION

As this brief chapter has indicated, thoughtful intervention research is difficult and challenging, pushing the researcher to meet the needs of two masters—practitioners and traditional academics, often with differing perspectives on quality and useful research. Although there may not be a specific template one can follow, the broad guidelines suggested here are intended to facilitate the research and writing process. The iterative nature of high quality organizational intervention research—going back and forth between practice and theory, exploring what works in the here and now and drawing out ramifications and insights that can be generalized to the broader population—is also reflected in the process of writing an organization intervention-based article. As the chapters that follow in this section indicate, if one thinks of the underlying process as a journey, one that continuously unfolds as the intervention and its outcomes emerge, researchers can position themselves to capture the empirical and conceptual contributions that materialize in a way that will ultimately fulfill the needs of both audiences.

NOTES

1. This discussion is drawn from the theme of the 2004 meeting of the Academy of Management, which focused on actionable knowledge; see http://aom.org/Meetings/annualmeeting/past-meetings/theme2004.aspx.
2. See *The Belmont report: Ethical principles and guidelines for the protection of human subjects of research,* written by the National Commission for the Protection of Human Subjects of Biomedical and Behavioral Research. https://www.hhs.gov/ohrp/regulations-and-policy/belmont-report/

REFERENCES

Aldag, R. J. (2012). Bump it with a trumpet: On the value of our research to management education. *Academy of Management Learning & Education, 11*(2), 285–292.

Bansal, P., & Corley, K. (2011). The coming of age for qualitative research: Embracing the diversity of qualitative methods. *Academy of Management Journal, 54*(2), 233–237.

Bansal, P., & Corley, K. (2012). What's different about qualitative research? *Academy of Management Journal, 55*(3), 509–513.

Bartunek, J. M., & Egri, C. P. (2012). Can academic research be managerially actionable? What are the requirements for determining this? *Academy of Management Learning & Education, 11*(2), 244–246.

Buono, A. F. (2009). Introduction. In A. F. Buono (Ed.), *Emerging trends and issues in management consulting: Consulting as a Janus-faced reality* (pp. vii–xx). Charlotte, NC: Information Age.

Butler, D. (2013). Investigating journals: The dark side of publishing. *Nature, 495*(7442), 433–435.

Colquitt, J. A., & George, G. (2011). Publishing in AMJ—Part 1: Topic choice. *Academy of Management Journal, 54*, 432–435.

George, G. (2014). Rethinking management scholarship. *Academy of Management Journal, 57*(1), 1–6.

George, G., Howard-Grenville, J., Joshi, A., & Tihanyi, L. (2016). Understanding and tackling societal grand challenges through management research. *Academy of Management Journal, 59*(6), 1880–1895.

Gibbons, M., Limoges, C., Nowotny, H., Schwartzman, S., Scott, P., & Trow, M. (1994). *The new production of knowledge.* Thousand Oaks, CA: SAGE.

Golden-Biddle, K., & Locke, K. (2007). *Composing qualitative research.* Thousand Oaks, CA: SAGE.

Fraser, M. W., Richman, J. M., Galinsky, M. J., & Day, S. H. (2009). *Intervention research: Developing social programs.* New York, NY: Oxford University Press.

Ireland, R. D. (2009). When is a "new" paper really new? *Academy of Management Journal, 52*(1), 9–10.

King, C. R. (2001). Ethical issues in writing and publishing. *Clinical Journal of Oncology Nursing, 5*(3), 19–23.

Kolata, G. (2017, March 22). A scholarly sting operation shines a light on "predatory" journals. *New York Times.* Retrieved from https://www.nytimes.com/2017/03/22/science/open-access-journals.html?hp&action=click&pgtype=Homepage&clickSource=story-heading&module=second-column-region&region=top-news&WT.nav=top-news/&r=0>

Melnyk, B. M., & Morrison-Beedy, D. (2012). Setting the stage for intervention research: The "so what" factor. In B. M. Melnyk & D. Morrison-Beedy (Eds.), *Intervention research: Designing, conducting, analyzing, and funding* (pp. 1–10). New York, NY: Springer.

Merton, R. K. (1949). *Social theory and social structure.* New York, NY: Simon & Schuster.

Nielsen, R. K., Buono, A. F., & Poulfelt, F. (2017). *At the knowledge interface: Developing co-created research competency.* Paper presented at the Academy of Management annual meeting, Atlanta, GA, August.

Pearce, J. L., & Huang, L. (2012). Toward an understanding of what actionable research is. *Academy of Management Learning & Education, 11*(2), 300–301.

Pratt, M. G. (2009). For the lack of a boilerplate: Tips on writing up (and reviewing) qualitative research. *Academy of Management Journal, 52*(5), 856–862.

Shaikh, A. A. (2016, April 4). 7 steps to publishing in a scientific journal. *Elsevier Publishing.* Retrieved from https://www.elsevier.com/connect/7-steps-to-publishing-in-a-scientific-journal

Shaw, J. D., Bansal, P., & Gruber, M. (2017). New ways of seeing: Elaboration on a theme. *Academy of Management Journal, 60*(2), 397–401.

Straumsheim, C. (2017, January 18). No more "Beall's list." *Inside Higher Education.* Retrieved from https://www.insidehighered.com/news/2017/01/18/librarians-list-predatory-journals-reportedly-removed-due-threats-and-politics

Van Maanen, J. (1998). Different strokes: Qualitative Research in the *Administrative Sciences Quarterly* from 1956 to 1996. In J. Van Maanen (Ed.), *Qualitative studies of organizations* (pp. ix–xxxii). Thousand Oaks, CA: SAGE.

Van Noorden, R. (2014). Open-access website gets tough. *Nature, 512*(7512), 17.

CHAPTER 10

PUBLISHING INTERVENTION-RESEARCH RESULTS

Understanding the Peer Reviewer Mind-Set

Henri Savall

The intervention-research process generates *many* and *various* materials that the researcher accumulates over time. An intervention-research is first built on an *initial research object.* This foundation is followed by the researcher's approach in interaction with the "field of scientific observation," producing information that can be placed in a *tree of sub-objects* that emerge from the original object. Thus, starting from a *central theme* of research, the process brings out *multiple subthemes* that are potential opportunities for monothematic publications. The same case of intervention-research can thereby provide a range of publications on various themes. Intervention-research requires a significant *investment of time* from the researcher, but the return on investment is very high based on the opportunities of original publications that it offers.

Intervention Research, pages 183–188

PUBLISHING INTERVENTION-RESEARCH: RISKS AND OPPORTUNITIES

There are two major obstacles to publishing intervention-research that correspond to risks of a different nature. The *first one* results from the temptation of the intervener-researcher to continue to accumulate field materials, postponing writing and article submission. The actual writing of a journal article takes significant time—in essence, the *cost of entry* and a *step backwards* from the convictions that the researcher has acquired during the experimental and learning process. Publication is less a production of knowledge than an exercise of creating *readable communication* of the results of research. It targets readers who have not experienced the process of producing the results and have *no reason to believe a priori* the argument of the researcher. They will be all the more demanding when it comes to demonstrating the scientific validity of the results proposed for publication.

The practice of intervention-research requires an anticipation of the time for scientific work, necessary for the researcher's approach on the field of observation, which implies *precise programming* reflexes in his or her schedule. When the time comes to prepare a publication, the *same requirement* of sufficient time programming for *writing* is a key success factor for publishing.

The second difficulty occurs from alternating between the rigorous exploitation of the collected materials and the analysis of the *relevant literature* with the object of research and the theme of the publication. Underlying this dynamics is the indispensable humility of the researcher author, who will have to convince the reviewers and then the readers through a real *demonstration*. This difficulty is psychological, arising from the contrast between the researcher's conviction in their field work and research results and the *a priori legitimate incredulity* of the reviewers. This chasm requires robust arguments in relation to the extant literature. *Intervener-researcher-authors* must therefore mentally prepare themselves for accepting all the remarks or suggestions of the reviewers appointed by the targeted academic journal or colloquium organizer to evaluate the quality of the paper.

When authors receive legitimately critical reports, their irritation is at first a natural and "universal" reaction. It is advisable to allow a few years to pass and to consider that the reviewer is a *micro-sample* of the readership that the researcher aims to reach and that the reviewer is therefore "*always right.*" Our experience of over 40 years as founder and director of the journal *Recherche en science de gestion–Management Sciences–Ciencias de gestión*, has shown that even a report considered "malicious" by an irritated author can contain valuable and exploitable ideas that will improve the quality of the publication. The probability that any reader, beyond the reviewers, will have the same reactions at a later stage is not a null point.

Ethical Considerations

As intervention-research is often carried out in *teams*, it is important to highlight some ethical rules concerning publication. Researchers may be tempted to specialize, some in the conduct of the intervention-research process itself and others in the analysis of the literature and writing the paper. Experience shows that such *specialization* often produces frictions and even conflicts between the researchers. There is thus a *polemical gap* between the researcher who prefers field work and rarely takes the time to explore the literature and fine-tune the paper and the researcher who prefers writing, a more comfortable exercise that requires less energy expenditure and cultivates an excessive taste for abstraction.

Another important rule to be observed is either the anonymity of the company or organization as a field of scientific observation, or a written authorization on its part, duly negotiated and anticipated. Indeed, the intervener-researcher has a moral obligation not to publish, without organizational consent that the company has revealed of its "intimacy." The intervener-researcher who does not respect this ethical rule is typically "punished," as well as his fellow-members, by the refusal of further access to scientific fields of observation.

REFLECTING ON AN ARTICLE IN AN "A-RATED" U.S. ACADEMIC JOURNAL BASED ON AN INTERVENTION-RESEARCH PROJECT

The development and replication of qualitative intervention-research methodology led us to conceive and develop, with our ISEOR researchers, a rigorous *method of content analysis*, taking into account the phenomenon of *polysemy* of words treated in qualitative analyses (see Savall, Zardet, Bonnet, & Péron, 2008). This polysemy, which makes the same word have a different meaning according to the actors (both transmitters and receivers), makes *lexical* analysis partially ineffective and creates considerable interpretation *biases*. Our method of content analysis allows one to take into account the *diversity* of the *natural languages* of the actors encountered by an intervener-researcher during the research process. It also makes it possible to combine these varied languages with the *scientific vocabulary* codified by the researcher in building scientific-oriented statements.

Drawing on more than 100,000 interviews from socioeconomic diagnosis conducted by ISEOR researchers, it is clear that actors in organizations express themselves in *differentiated language registers*, depending on the organization's functional areas (departments), level of education and training, and degree of literacy. In ISEOR's method of content analysis, these *verbatim* statements are classified under *key ideas* formulated by the intervener-researcher, in standard language useful for the treatment of the object of research. Verbatim statements are *field-note quotes* because the actors who have expressed it are witnesses of the practices that constitute the "raw material" treated by the researcher.

The transition from the verbatim to the key idea in normed language requires a *contextualized translation* of the meaning by the researcher in a way that captures the true expressions of the witness-actors. Lexical analysis is not used in intervention-research applied to socioeconomic theory because it has considerable limits due to of the polysemy of the words and ideas used by the actors in their professional practices. The ISEOR has had to build a *system-expert software* program, referred to as SEGESE, to construct a *tree nomenclature* of themes/sub-themes relevant to the research object, in a language register developed by the researcher.

This nomenclature made it possible to classify the field-note quotes collected by the researchers in interaction with the actors who expressed them. The groups of field-note quotes in each sub-theme are then translated into a synthetic statement in the form of key ideas. This makes it possible to respect the polysemy of the words used by the actors, to restore the researcher's responsibility to fully understand them. Indeed, intervener-researchers witnesses the circumstances and the actors' strategy of speech, which allow them to contextualize and relativize the interpretation of the field-note quotes. The automatism of the expert system brings an added value in the classification of ideas by the intervener-researcher, but it does not replace human intelligence and insight, being careful not to crush the indispensable interpretation of the ideas collected from the actors-witnesses on the practices studied.

The academic journal *Organizational Research Methods* is one of the top 10 management journals, an "A"-ranked journal in the United States, supported by the Academy of Management. It publishes a high proportion of *quantitative* articles, which has made its reputation. In 2008, the journal editors decided to publish a special edition on *qualitative* methods. We had original material based on 474 reports written by 56 reviewers over a period of 28 years of articles using a qualitative method, published in the journal *Recherche en sciences de gestion. Management Sciences—Ciencias de gestión.* This journal, which I cofounded with the great French economist François Perroux in 1978, deliberately included an extremely simple model of report composed of a few broad and open sections. My aim was not to guide the reviewers' evaluation and the journal did not prescribe any explicit quality criteria.

Our original publication project was to apply our method of content analysis based on ISEOR's extensive intervention-researches, to study these 474 reports in order to discover if patterns emerged from their content analysis. The 56 evaluators who authored these reports belong to a wide variety of universities and research centers from different countries and form the scientific committee of the academic journal. It was therefore a question of eliciting *implicit criteria* used by the reviewers of these qualitative research articles, based on the field-note quotes in various languages used by the evaluators in their reports. The content analysis made it possible to define a tree of themes and sub-themes relevant to the object of the research, namely the *quality* of the articles published in this academic journal. In-depth analysis of the specific field-note quotes contained in the reports led to the formulation of generic key ideas, which express either qualities or faults raised by the reviewers.

This research began with the development of a generic software using the same structure as the *system-expert software SEGESE* that was used for socioeconomic diagnosis in nearly 2,000 organizations. The next step was to classify the field-note quotes by entering them in the software. The results analysis identified 19 *critical points* of the items highlighted in the reports, as well as 10 *generic quality criteria.* These elements did not result from an instruction of normative nature, which would have been given a priori to the reviewers by the journal's editor. They emerged spontaneously over 28 years of a very flexible and autonomous practice of article reviewing, without any communication between the different reviewers on their respective practices.

The 19 critical points of the article on which the reviewers are spontaneously expressed are: *research questions*; research *hypotheses*; *methodological* choices; *epistemological* choices; underlying *ideologies;* methodological *processes*; *literature references*; *state of the art* and bibliographic analysis; *theoretical* and conceptual analysis; *concepts* and theories mobilized; *field materials*; *research methods* on the field and exploitation of data and materials; *interpretation*; *positioning* in relation to the research questions in the literature; explicit *generic knowledge*; *recommendations* and operational implications; *discussion* and critical analysis of results and boundaries; the communication capacity of the article as a whole; the *common thread* and the general structure of the article; conclusion and *wrapping up* with the title. Authors can use these elements to "scan" a draft article before publication, for a quality *self-control* practice.

The 10 quality criteria resulting from this content analysis are: *rigor*; *formulation*; *consistency*; *originality*; *relevance*; *clarification*; *positioning*; *contribution*; *reasoning*; and *delimitation.* The matrix analysis of the 19 critical points paired up with the 10 quality criteria made it possible to establish that the *three* main quality criteria to which the reviewers are sensitive are relevance, clarification and contribution. In addition, six *internal validity* criteria were identified: clarification, delimitation, rigor, formulation, reasoning, and consistency. Four criteria relate to *external validity*: relevance, contribution, positioning, and originality. The critical points most often reported by the reviewers are the research question, the method of field investigation and exploitation of materials, the common thread in the article, and the state of the art and the generic knowledge.

This article was published after a process of 2 1/2 years and three successive revisions. The fourth and last version contained less than 20% of the original text submitted to the journal. Looking back, the improvement of its content resulted from a genuine dialogue between the authors and the three reviewers.

REFERENCES

Boje, D. M., Oswick, C., & Ford, J. D. (2004). Language and organizations: The doing the discourse. *Academy of Management Review, 29,* 571–577.

Esterby-Smith, M., Thorpe, R., & Lowe, A. (2002). *Management research.* London: SAGE.

Golden-Biddle, K., & Locke, K. (1997). *Composing qualitative research.* Thousand Oaks, CA: SAGE.

Gephart, R. P. (1993). The textual approach: Risk and blame in disaster sensemaking. *Academy of Management Journal, 36*(2), 705–729.

Krippendorff, K. (2004). *Content analysis: An introduction to its methodology.* Thousand Oaks, CA: SAGE.

Savall, H., Zardet, V., Bonnet, M., & Péron, M. (2008). The emergence of implicit criteria actually used by reviewers of qualitative research articles: Case of a European journal. *Organizational Research Methods, 11*(3), 510–540.

CHAPTER 11

FROM INTERVENTION-RESEARCH TO PUBLICATION

The Case of a Publication in an Academic French Journal

Véronique Zardet

In 2015, the academic journal *Gérer & Comprendre* published the results of an intervention-research led by a team of intervener-researchers between 2010 and 2012 (see Delattre, Petit, & Zardet, 2015). We chose this academic journal for its editorial stance, clearly aimed towards understanding and observing concrete management situations. The intervention had previously been presented in several papers for international congresses, before submitting a proposal for an article to the academic journal. The evaluation and correction process lasted roughly 2 years and involved three stages of requested changes from the evaluators. This chapter summarizes the intervention-research conducted, the identification of the problematic retained for the article, and finally its process of elaboration and correction.

Intervention Research, pages 189–194

ABSTRACT OF THE INTERVENTION-RESEARCH IN ARCHITECTS' PRACTICE

For one and a half years, a team of three intervener-researchers conducted an intervention-research project in 18 architect practices. Initiated at the request of a Regional Council of the Order of Architects, its objective was to help a group of small architects develop their strategic, organizational, managerial, economic, and management competencies.

We formalized a methodology involving a combination of training the architect managers and a transformative intervention-research in each of the individual practices. The training part was based on the personal and professional experience of the architect managers and focused on the activity piloting of their management. The second part, the intervention-research project, involved working with each manager and his or her entire team. One previous step was a socioeconomic diagnosis that unleashed expressions about the quality of functioning, the quality of life on the job, and the strategic development of the organization. The socioeconomic diagnosis was led through semi-directive interviews and completed with an identification of the major "hidden-costs," a significant source of value-added loss in the firms' activities as well as a loss of commercial development opportunities.

After a collective mirror-effect focusing on dysfunctions and their economic impacts measured in terms of hidden-costs, a second stage of the intervention focused on helping the managers and their employees define and gradually implement improvement actions (e.g., functioning, management, strategy). The approach took place in each architect's practice over 8 to 10 months, at a rate of one half-day per month. At the end of the process, a contradictory and participatory evaluation was undertaken to identify key achievements and measure the evolution of the economic performance based on each practice's profit and loss account, focused on revenues, variable costs, fixed expenses, and the net result. The 18 architect's practices began this process with groups of 6, one of the reasons why the project took place over one and a half years.

IDENTIFICATION OF ISSUES FROM THE INTERVENTION-RESEARCH

This engagement conducted in the 18 organizations by 3 different researchers presented a rich source of data to formalize and publish intervention-research results. In a concrete way, this research has made possible to formalize the different issues that emerged through an inductive process, each of which could produce a distinct publication. The main observations were

- the dynamics that emerge when social responsibility starts from economic empowerment;
- the influence of construction and building standards and their impact on the architectural profession;
- the evolution of the architect profession toward an architectural manager job;
- the contribution of higher technical training in the current competitiveness of small enterprises, with similar application to other small companies (e.g., medicine, notaries, lawyers, nurses, physiotherapists, judicial experts, bailiffs, veterinarians); and
- the emergence of interorganizational cooperation in the construction industry.

To this week, the first three areas have been published in the form of papers in congresses and articles in journals and book chapters, written in French, English and Spanish, depending on the linguistic skills of the different researchers on the team.

The choice of an article thematic is deeply linked to the editorial policy of a journal. Thus, issues oriented towards people management and human resources management find a place in French-language journals such as *@GRH, Revue de Gestion des Ressources Humaines, Revue RIPCO,* and *Management et Humanisme.* The issues more oriented towards strategic management could find a place in the French-language journals *Management & Avenir, Finance Contrôle Stratégie,* and *Management International.* Beyond the thematic of the article itself, an essential criterion for the choice of an appropriate academic journal is its interest in qualitative research and research-intervention methodologies. It should be noted that some journals are more welcoming than others, because they are more open to mix-methods and a variety of methodologies deployed; in fact, some journals are specifically interested in these methodologies. We particularly think of French academic journals such as *Gérer & Comprendre, Finance Contrôle Stratégie, Recherche en Sciences de Gestion, @GRH,* and *Management & Avenir,* to name just mention ranked journals (FNEGE 2016 rankings). Conversely, other academic journals are much less welcoming for this type of methodology. The researcher-intervener should not waste time in submitting a draft article to these journals.

We decided to propose an article to the academic journal *Gérer & Comprendre* for many reasons: we did not have recent publications in this journal, we had a positive appraisal *a priori* to its editorial policy, which was oriented toward the distanced observation of managerial practices:

> The journal *Gérer & Comprendre* focuses on a human approach of companies and organization through analyses which are not based solely on man-

> agement tools, but also borrow from sociology as a means of understanding which [perspectives] are essential to company leaders. Its functioning is that of an academic journal with a reading committee.

Finally, this academic journal is edited by colleagues with an engineering background, and we thought they would be interested in the evolution of a technical profession toward a managerial role.

BUILDING THE ARTICLE FOR THE TARGETED ACADEMIC JOURNAL

We began framing the article by reading various pieces published in the journal *Gérer et Comprendre* in order to get a sense of the journal's editorial focus and possible ideas for designing the article. It soon became clear that the journal accepted various articles designs, which included a presentation of the issue, a theoretical framework of reference, a precise statement of the research methodology, a presentation of the results, and their interpretation.

The issue we chose—*how the introduction of management tools in architectural firm raises questions about the nature of the architect's current and future profession*—emerged from contrasts observed in the different practices. The few management-oriented articles available on the architectural industry struck us as an auspicious opportunity. The social utility of this issue also seemed to us as an *a priori* fit with the dual purpose of the journal reflected in its title, *Gérer & Comprendre* (Managing and Understanding).

The team of intervener-researchers which worked on the project decided to collectively write this article. The methodology consisted of jointly establishing a written outline of the article, then selecting the materials among the abundance of available data. One of the greatest challenges was selecting a relatively small number of relevant materials as a way of maintaining the focus of the article—as well as being conscious that this one intervention-research project could provide the basis for several articles. Thus, we decided to focus on 6 of the 18 cases in which we had complete data and an evolution of their strategic path for 2 years.

Once we decided on the article's focus, a detailed outline with key ideas (Savall & Zardet, 2004) was jointly developed by the coauthors. The drafting stage was then divided among the three coauthors, before proceeding to the final phase, which included cross-reading aimed at checking the consistency between the different parts of the paper and to adjust to the size of the article as prescribed by the journal. This laborious phase required negotiations between authors.

The article was structured as follows:

- A brief description of the research-intervention method, from the negotiation stage to the intervention's main results.
- An exposition of the problematic, showing how this reflection and contrasting evolution of managing architectural firms emerged through an inductive process.
- A presentation of the results in chronological form in order to restore to the reader the main phenomena of longitudinal research and intervention.
- Finally, our interpretation of the data, focused on creating a reading grid of the evolution of the role and profession of the architect manager, endeavoring to show the diversity of situations encountered.

INTERACTIONS WITH THE EDITOR-IN-CHIEF AND REVIEWERS

The article publishing process took a long time—the initial submission of the article was in December 2012 and it was finally published in mid-2015, roughly 2 1/2 years of work, alternating between periods of silence on the part of the journal and receiving reviewer comments together with a request for modifications and changes within a relatively short period of time. The article was the subject of 3 successive revisions before being accepted for publication. As is often the case, the evaluations submitted by the two reviewers were mixed: a rejection and a rather favorable opinion; the editor-in-chief played a decisive role in accepting the article subject to the required changes.

It is not uncommon for authors to feel resentment and aversion after reading an evaluation which they consider overly severe, considering that they have been misunderstood after spending so many hours in writing the article. As part of the rather arduous publication process, these sentiments must quickly be overcome. One should consider that reviewers act in good faith and that their criticisms should be carefully scrutinized and analyzed in order to provide a substantial response. In case of the divergence between the reviewers, we took a position and explained it in a consolidated document that was sent with the revised version of our article. This document had a point by point response to the criticisms and suggestions by the reviewers, summarizing the nature of the changes made as well as, in some cases, the reasons why we did not make any changes. The second and third reviews allowed us to see that the reviewers had positively evaluated our modifications and that we were likely to arrive at a final published version.

The main changes expected from the reviewers concerned the need to better clarify the link between the longitudinal research process and the results achieved. Thus the last part on the evolution of the trajectories of the managers-architects was significantly transformed between the first and second version of the paper—a reality that we have found to be very typical in the publication process.

REFERENCES

Delattre, M., Petit, R., & Zardet, V. (2015). Architectes et management: Histoires d'introduction d'outils de management chez les architectes [Architecture and management: A history of the introduction of management tools within Architect's practices]. *Annales des Mines-Gérer & Comprendre, 2,* 4–15.

Savall, H. & Zardet, V. (2004). *Recherche en sciences de gestion: Approche qualimétrique, observer l'objet complexe* [The qualimetrics approach: Observing the complex object]. Paris, France: Economica.

CHAPTER 12

PUBLISHING AN EPISTEMOLOGICAL REFLECTION ON ETHNOMETHODOLOGY-BASED INTERVENTION-RESEARCH PROJECTS

The Case of a Publication in *Journal of Business Ethics*

Jean-Michel Plane

In 2000, I published an article in the *Journal of Business Ethics* (Plane, 2000), an "A" rated journal by the High Council for Evaluation of Research and Higher Education HCERES, the French Foundation for Management Education (FNEGE), and the French National Centre for Scientific Research (CNRS). The paper focused on the contribution of ethnomethodology to the analysis of organizations and its methodological and epistemological implications.

Intervention Research, pages 195–202

A PUBLICATION BASED ON INTERVENTION-RESEARCH AND EXPERIMENTATION CARRIED OUT IN MULTIPLE ORGANIZATIONS

The article discusses the epistemological and methodological problems that arise from an ethnomethodological approach to the observation of strategic management practices in companies and organizations. With this in mind, our understanding of ethnomethodology regarding the management of organizations and the complexity of researcher involvement are analyzed through the lens of researcher neutrality and the inevitable immersion-distancing dialectic toward the studied object. The objective of that article was to examine the epistemological benefits of intervention-research in management. The aim of this chapter is to highlight the interaction processes that can occur between researchers and actors in the context of interventions performed within several organizations. It is based on experimentations that the author performed over a 10 year period (1990–2000). The in-depth nature of these interventions is apparent from the diversity of different missions and the time spent on them. The approach is mainly based on observations performed in an array of organizations: an insurance company, pharmaceutical research laboratory, two public service organizations, one association, and 4 small- and medium-sized businesses (an audiovisual production company, a company specialized in electronic components, an organization consulting company).

Reflections on the Fundamental Principles of Intervention-Research

The concept of intervention-research, despite its underlying complexity and challenges in the way it combines theory and organizational improvement, appears to be growing in importance within the social sciences in general and the management sciences in particular. The human sciences find themselves in an epistemological situation with methodological problems more a less unique to them (Piaget, 1972). Indeed, the sciences of humankind are placed in this peculiar situation of depending on people as *both* subjects and objects, which raises specific, difficult, and complex questions. In summary, it is hard to deny that there is *subject in object.* In terms of these complex problems, one can note that this complexity is strongly linked to the fact that subjects who observe or experiment on themselves or others can be influenced by the phenomena observed as well as be at the origin of the very nature of the changes and how these phenomena play out.

In the context of an intervention, the researcher is an actor in a process where there is concurrently and simultaneously a creation of knowledge and change. In this light, it seems that the *active participation* of the actors in these organizations in the research itself can occur, with variations. Often, actors do so unknowingly because researchers use the action they are driving in order to produce knowledge, but the people in the field are not aware of it (nor is it necessarily a worry of theirs). In other less frequent situations, the actors contribute to the very research process. With this approach, the actors of the organizations are considered to also have some of the knowledge and relevant views on the issues being investigated (Bournois et al., 1993). This conception is the closest to what we call ethnomethodology (Garfinkel, 1967), an approach that calls for a partnership between the intervention-researchers and the actors of these organizations (CARGESE-CNRS, 1990).

Researcher-Field Relations in Interactive Research

The nature of researcher-field relations has been theorized for a long time, notably by researchers in the context of psychosociological interventions (e.g., Dubost, 1987). The well-known work of Elton Mayo is far too nuanced to briefly summarize (see Plane, 2017), especially in a chapter focused on some of the founding principles of this type of research rather than an exhaustive overview. In terms of methodology, relations between researchers and organizational actors manifest themselves through strong interactions. As such the research can be significantly influenced or even shifted toward more fertile directions than initially planned. This methodological choice is at the very core of the heuristic process. In terms of epistemology, the experiment done in Chicago's Western Electric's Hawthorne Works shows that researchers favored a phenomenological approach by studying the observed phenomena based on actions intended to improve the observed objects' working conditions. This epistemological option seems to be at the heart of transformative research in organizations.

Researchers in those interventions appear to have progressively favored a paradigm of interaction with the actors, which has led them to a more transformative approach to research of the observed objects. With this in mind, researchers in the Hawthorne studies called for a new conception of human relations, which has been discussed many times since (Sainsaulieu, 1987). Kurt Lewin's (1959) approach to action research goes in the same direction, insofar as Lewin shows that it is by working alongside people who want to produce change that researchers will be able to observe, measure, and understand processes that were otherwise not available to them. Moreno (1934), founder of the sociometric school, considers that social facts must be understood as *interaction phenomena*. In the context of his research, Devereux (1980), psychoanalyst and ethnologist, discusses this question and observes, through examples, that any foreigner to a human group sees him or herself assigned a status and occupies a role in the social structure of the group. Devereux shows that researchers must make explicit the position they hold in the social structure, insofar as what he observes has a *"fragmentary"* nature, *"based on what the observed subjects think he is."*

In terms of transference, this analysis of the system of representation of the actors is incomplete if it isn't coupled with an analysis of countertransference. Indeed, Devereux shows that researchers must treat their personal reactions to the studied object as fundamental data in order to keep their conclusions as objective as possible. In psychoanalysis, transference refers to any psychological process, linked to repetition mechanisms, that redirects emotions and attitudes present since childhood onto seemingly neutral people or objects. To the analyst, it is therefore the most powerful of therapeutic instruments (Lappassade, 1971).

In the course of psychoanalysis, a psychoemotional exchange is established between the therapist and patient, through which communication passes. The therapist, despite wanting to, is therefore never the perfect mirror he or she would like to be. If the patient expresses friendly feelings towards the analyst, that person will likely respond in a favorable way; similarly, if the patient's transference is negative, the analyst may react with some sort of rejection. This behavior and attitude in response to the patient is called *countertransference.* On the issue of the interaction between researchers and actors in organizations, any researcher must occupy a position listed in the observed group's structure, in essence, an imaginable position in the group's representation system (Matheu, 1986).

Ethnologists such as Favret-Saada (1977) have noticed that phenomenological observations became possible as soon as they were able to hold an imaginable position within the observed group. Indeed, Favret-Saada was able to observe the phenomenon of sorcery in Normandy's wooded pasturelands once she realized that there is *"no place in the field for non-invested observers."* She shows how farmers made her *a space* within the system of sorcery. The author explains in that respect that she was able to enter the "system of places" created by the "autochthons" and relative to the phenomenon in question (Favret-Saada, 1977). These complex epistemological and methodological problems also led to a number of scientific discussions in the management sciences.

The depth of reflection of Girin (1986), former director of the Center for Research in Management (CRG) at the Ecole Polytechnique, is intellectually stimulating and is based on the idea of what he calls *"interactive research."* It is based on four key points: (a) the knowledge that is developed is based on field work; (b) the field work adjusts to facts and situations that can influence it; (c) the autochthons, the people in the field, have an important role on how the research proceeds; and (d) but researchers are ultimately responsible for the interpretation of information and theory-building that result from it. This conception is strongly linked to the logic of knowledge endorsed by Levi-Strauss (1950, pp. i–x) that shows that *"in a science where the observer is of similar nature to its object, the observer becomes part of the observation."* This epistemological option amounts to attempting to provide answers to the following central issue: "Can valid knowledge be gained from subjective data collected in that moment?" Given this issue, Girin's (1981, 1986, 1990) attempts to respond to this issue on an epistemological level, in the manner of Levi-Strauss (1950) or Deveureux (1980), amounts to stating that it is possible to extract knowledge from the field by *objectivizing* it, bringing it back to the situations in which it was produced. In this way, researchers don't consider phenomena of transference and countertransference (i.e., projections made by the organizations' actors on the intervention-researchers and vice-versa) as phenomena that need to be eliminated, or worse, concealed. Indeed, as soon as there is interaction, there are inevitably expectations, preferences, taboos, unsaid things that can be analyzed to gain great insight into the intimate functioning of the studied organization.

A CONCEPTION OF MANAGEMENT RESEARCH

The approach to management research that we share in this chapter lies in the context of interactive research in which the researcher produces observable transformations that create change and create knowledge. Savall (1985, 1989) has often discussed the issue of researcher-field relations in management research and has shown that the status of the field remains very vague, if not contradictory depending on the research. To summarize, we can identify two types of investigation: (a) superficial studies carried out in a number of organizations to validate pre-established models, and (b) investigations performed in several organizations considered as a field of production of concepts and methods. This conception of research assumes a strong interaction between researchers and the field in order to extract information that will later be treated scientifically. This fundamental epistemological option gives the management science researcher a societal role in improving organizations' socioeconomic efficiency. This transformative approach to the observed phenomenological field, in the context of experimentations, facilitates the study of different stages of transformation to produce theories and methods with scientific intentions. However, as stressed by Bonnet (1987), the bias linked to observation and the risks of researcher contamination are high and deserve to be mentioned. The researcher in socioeconomic management carries out experimentations while being a particular type of actor. With this in mind, researchers form opinions on their observations based on their expertise. Researchers therefore confronts their own hypotheses to those of the different actors in a way that highlights the agreements and analyses the disagreements. It is those interactions and their multiplicity that generates progress in knowledge (Plane, 1994). The creation of new hypotheses requires taking a step back from the field (introspection) and requires nearly as much work as the actual presence in those organizations. Finally, intervention-research appears to be a legitimate scientific research method in the constructivist epistemologies, which claim that knowledge only comes from intentionally-built artificial representations and that the observer cannot be separated from the observation (Le Moigne, 1990).

Experimenting With an Evaluation Chart of the Real: Ethnomethodology

An ethnomethodological approach to organizations leads to thinking about their functioning from an ethnomethods (Garfinkel, 1967) point of view, which consists of the methods and common knowledge used by actors to manage their social practices. The field of research that is analyzed leads to discussions over ethnomethodology's pertinence in strategic management with this human aspect integrated.

Using this type of evaluation chart for the management of these organizations can be discussed based on four key concepts. The first notion is *practical accomplishment.* This constructivist concept leads us to consider that social facts don't impose themselves on individuals objectively from the outside. They are formed in the practical interactions of the individuals who accomplish them. With this in mind, a process of intervention-research leads to making explicit some implicit yet mainly socialized management practices.

Reflexivity constitutes the second original concept and can be defined as the way in which actors report their activities. In other words, it is this skill that the researcher can discover without superimposing scientific sense onto common sense.

The third concept reflects *tacit knowledge and resources.* To understand the true meaning of practical accomplishments, the intervention-researcher can highlight the knowledge and resources that are inherent to performing those actions. Finally, the fourth notion is *indexicality.* This concept implies that the meaning of language can only be understood if it is brought back to the concrete situations in which it was used. Words are somewhat indexed based on the specific context in which they were expressed. On the field, we as researchers have been confronted with the difficulty of understanding intersubjectivity between actors, in essence, the meaning given to actions of collective regulation based on verbal exchange.

CONCLUSION

This chapter is an epistemological reflection on intervention-research and the potential benefits ethnomethodology brings to the analysis of organizations. The epistemological and methodological challenges discussed this text are fundamental and can contribute to further knowledge in management. Overall, papers published on these subjects are reviewed very favorably (working papers, conferences and congresses, French and international publications), due to crucial questions of validity and validation of knowledge produced by the intervention-research process as well as the status and position of the researcher-practitioner relationship.

REFERENCES

Abel, A. (1981). L›intervention [Intervention]. *Actes de la recherche en Sciences Soiales, 38*(May), 42–48.

Avenier, M.-J. (1989). Méthodes de terrain et recherche en management stratégique [Field-based Methods and Research in Strategic Management]. *Economies et Sociétés, série Sciences de Gestion, 14,* 199–218.

Berry, M. (1981). Le point de vue et les méthodes de la recherche en gestion [Methods for research in management sciences: Point of view]. *Annales des Mines,* (July–August), 19–29.

Bonnet, M. (1987). *Liaisons entre organisation du travail et efficacité socio-économique: Analyse d'expérimentations dans des services de fabrication en milieu industriel* [Relations between work organization and socio-economic performances: Evidence from the industrial sector]. Doctoral thesis, d'Etat ès Sciences de Gestion, Université Lumière Lyon 2 (January).

Bournois, F., & Brabet, J. (1993). Les nouvelles perspectives de la recherche [New perspectives for the research in Management]. In *Repenser la GRH?* (213–247). Paris, France: Economica.

Devereux, G. (1980). *De l'angoisse à la méthode dans les sciences du comportement [From anxiety to methodology in behavioural sciences*]. Paris, France: Flammarion.

Favret-Saada, J. (1977). *Les mots, la mort, les sorts* [Words, Death, Spells]. Paris, France: Gallimard.

Girin, J. (1990). L'analyse empirique des situations de gestion: éléments de théorie et de méthode [Empirical analyses of facts in management: Elements of theory and method). In *Epistémologies et Sciences de Gestion* (pp. 141–182). Paris, France: Economica.

Girin, J. (1987). L'objectivation des données subjectives [The objectivation of subjective data]. In *Actes du colloque FNEGE-ISEOR de novembre 1986: Qualité des informations scientifiques en gestion. Méthodologies fondamentales en gestion* (pp. 170–186). Lyon, France: ISEOR éditeur.

Garfinkel, H. (1967). *Studies in ethnomethodology,* Englewood Cliffs, NJ: Prentice-Hall.

Lapassade, G. (1971). *L'analyseur et l'analy*ste [The analyser and the analyst]. Paris, France: Gauthier-Villars, série Recherches Institutionnelles

Le Moigne, J.-L. (1990) Epistémologies constructivistes et sciences de l'organisation [Constructivist epistemology and organizational sciences). *Epistémologies et Sciences de Gestion* (pp. 81–140). Paris, France: Economica.

Levi-Strauss, C. (1950). Introduction à l'oeuvre de Marcel MAUSS [Introduction to the works of Marcel Mauss]. In M. Mauss (Ed.), *Sociologie et anthropologie* (pp. i–x). Paris, France: Presses Universitaires de France.

Lewin, K. (1959). *Psychologie dynamique: Les relations humaines* [Psychological dynamics: The human relations]. Paris, France: Presses Universitaires de France.

Matheu, M. (1986). La familiarité distante [Distant familiarity]. In *Gérer et Comprendre* (pp. 81–94). Paris, France: Annales des Mines.

Moisdon, J.-C. (1984). Recherche en gestion et intervention [Research in management and intervention). *Revue Française de Gestion, 47–48*(September–October), 61–73.

Moreno, J. L. (1934). *Fondements de la sociométrie* [The foundations of sociometrics]. Paris, France: PUF.

Piaget, J. (1972). *Epistémologie des sciences de l'homme* [Epistemology of human sciences]. Paris, France: Gallimard.

Plane, J. M. (2000). The ethnomethodological approach of management: A new perspective on constructivist research. *Journal of Business Ethics, 26*(3), 233–243.

Sainsaulieu, R. (1987). *Sociologie de l'organisation et de l'entreprise* [Sociology of organization and firm]. Paris, France: PFNSP.

Savall, H. (1985). Où va la recherche en sciences de gestion? [Where does the research in management go to?]. *Revue Française de Gestion, 53–54* (September–December), 242–253.

Savall, H. (1989). Professeur-consultant: Le bilan d'une expérience [Professor-consultant: Results of experimentation]. *Revue Française de Gestion, 76*(November–December), 93–105.

Villette, M. (1988). *L'homme qui croyait en management* [The man who believes in management]. Paris, France: Seuil.

CHAPTER 13

PUBLISHING THE RESULTS OF INTERVENTION-RESEARCH IN HUMAN RESOURCES MANAGEMENT

The Case of a Publication in *Human Resource Management*

Florence Noguera

In 2012, we published an article in the journal *Human Resources Management* (ranked "A" by the High Council for Evaluation of Research and Higher Education (HCERES), French Foundation for Management Education (FNEGE), and the French National Centre for Scientific Research (CNRS) on the subject of the standardization of human resources management through an analysis of independent professions (Cappelletti, Noguera, & Plane, 2012). This chapter reflects on that publication, deconstructing the underlying process followed in creating the intervention and writing the article.

Intervention Research, pages 203–210

The paper was the result of an intervention-research project carried out in 250 notary public offices between 2004 and 2010, creating a sample of 420 notaries and more than 1,700 salaried employees. The issue raised in the paper focused on the extent to which the management of such organizations becomes more a matter of standardization than managerial innovation. This somewhat provocative issue has emerged in contemporary debates concerning the changing role of management (see, for example, Hamel, 2008). To ensure customer satisfaction, product compliance and organizational efficiency, even very small companies such as independent professions like law firms and notary public offices are increasingly using a quality management system that leads to a standardization of their human resources management (HRM; Igalens & Joras, 2002). In this regard, the first international standardization study on HRM began in 2010. At that time, the French committee ISO TC 260, known as X563, was created to deal with the development of international standards in the HRM field. The study was requested by the U.S. Standards Organization ANSI (American National Standards Institute, whose counterpart is AFNOR for France) and supported by the Society for Human Resources Management (SHRM), which in early 2011 proposed the for a new standardization program focused on HRM in ISO countries.

In this context, the article proposed to study the issue of HRM standardization in independent professions through the case of the implementation of the ISO 9001 quality standard in French notary public offices. Indeed, this question is of a great importance for independent professions that employ more than 2 million employees in France, compounded by the fact that management researches have rarely made this sector a field of scientific investigation. Within this context, the notarial profession is quite representative of an independent profession and its managerial constraints. Like other independent professionals who are business leaders, such as lawyers, pharmacists or architects, notaries are neophytes in management because they have not had any training on this subject during their studies. Their confrontation with HRM is therefore carried out on the ground, in a very empirical way, even though they have been subject to new strategic constraints since the early 2000s: a growing responsibility in the courts, increased customer demands, expectations of employees in terms of career planning and training, intense inter-professional competition, threats of deregulation by the European Commission, and so forth. Consequently French notary public offices must now improve the quality of their strategic management as well as their HRM to ensure their survival-development capacity.

This general issue raises a series of questions that were also addressed in the paper: How should firms standardize HRM in independent professions in general and notarial offices in particular? Is there a paradox in harmonizing HRM practices in an independent profession whose "raison d'être" is precisely the autonomy of the actors? Is managerial innovation possible in such small companies even after a standardization process?

To address these issues, an intervention-research program was conducted by a team of 15 researchers in response to a 2003 research call by the French Superior Council of Notaries (Conseil Supérieur de Notariat [CSN]), the political body of the profession, to develop the quality and management of human resources in notarial offices (Cappelletti, Delattre, & Noguera, 2007; Cappelletti, Khouatra, & Noguera, 2011).

A LARGE INTERVENTION-RESEARCH PROGRAM

A sample of 250 offices agreed to take part in the intervention. The sample was representative of the total population of the 5,000 French notarial offices, in terms of size, geographical character, and nature of activity. The offices making up the sample had between 1 to 55 staff members, with an average of 8 employees (which reflects national figures). The offices in the sample were both city-based (urban) and country-based (rural) offices. The sample contained equal numbers of traditional practices, focused primarily on monopoly business (mainly family law), and more innovative practices involved in significant levels of competitive business (mainly real estate negotiation). During intervention planning, trends were identified illustrating the operating and HRM practices of notary offices in terms of HR management, working conditions, and job definition. The intervention-researchers also made it possible to identify the impacts of a standardization approach on HRM practices in these independent companies. To implement a notarial quality approach through an IR process, the CSN laid out a progressive, 4-step that was adapted the particularities of the notary offices (see Figure 13.1).

The process for implementing the notarial quality approach was organized in these 4 steps that were put together end-to-end with the intent of

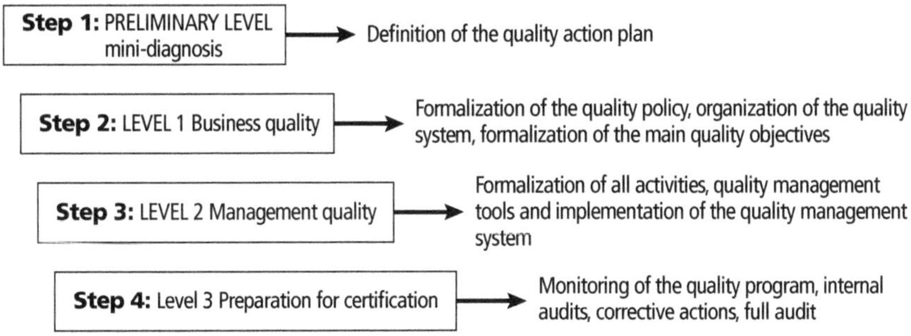

Figure 13.1 The 4 steps of the Notarial quality approach.

leading to ISO certification in 12 to 16 months, although it not an obligation for any office to go through all 4 steps). The first step consisted of performing a self-diagnosis of the firm's structure and work flow to identify major process failures, including HRM processes and the quality of customer service.

The second step consisted of standardizing the main processes that made up the core of the notarial profession, that is, the drafting of acts, the related formalities, and the classification of acts. The third step consisted of standardizing the support processes of the notary offices, such as HRM and accounting, and activating the quality system. The fourth step was used to prepare the certification, notably by carrying out internal audits and formalizing processes according to ISO requirements.

The notarial quality approach was implemented in the 250 offices using an adapted intervention-research methodology called the *Multi-SB* (Small Businesses) *HORIVERT* approach (Cappelletti, Delattre, & Noguera, 2007; Cappelletti, Khouatra, & Noguera, 2011). In the same region, offices were grouped into several clusters of five to six offices. Each office in the clusters was involved in an intra-company (work within the office) and inter-company framework. The intervention was coordinated in each region by a steering group composed of notaries elected to represent the region. To summarize, the Multi-SB HORIVERT approach comprised three dimensions: (a) bringing about change through intra-company action plans; (b) collaborative training in the use of socioeconomic management tools through inter-company action plans; and (c) the development of an overall synchronization policy (Savall & Zardet, 2008). The Multi-SB HORIVERT method followed the same principles as the SEAM method (see Buono & Savall, 2007), but used action plans that were scaled down to suit small businesses and professional offices (see Figure 13.2).

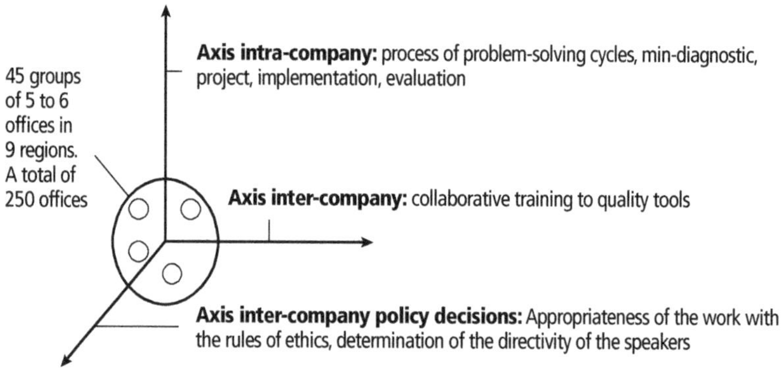

Figure 13.2 The general framework of the intervention-research methodology applied to notarial offices.

Intervention-Research Protocols Combining Intra- and Inter-Company Research

Intra-company interventions were similar in all 250 offices. They consisted of carrying out a mini-diagnostic focusing on the problems that were disrupting office effectiveness, efficiency, and HRM-related practices. In each notarial office, notaries and salaried employees were interviewed separately, focusing on their views on these dysfunctions. The results of the mini-diagnostic served as a working platform for focus groups. The focus groups alternatively gathered *restricted groups* that included the notary(s) of the office to identify priorities, define project objectives and constraints, and summarize these analyses to be shared with plenary groups. *Plenary session groups*, which included the notary(s) and office employees, were then used to cooperatively conceive and create improvement action proposals (Savall & Zardet, 2008).

The personal assistance sessions were designed around the management tools introduced in the collaborative training sessions, which were combined with the intra-company focus group sessions. Each of the 250 offices was also involved in an inter-company framework built around groups of 4 offices of different sizes. The purpose was to organize collaborative training sessions focusing on the six basic tools of socioeconomic management: time management, the competency grid, internal-external strategic action plan, priority action plans, strategic piloting indicators, and the periodically negotiable activity contract and fundamental tools of quality (e.g., process mapping, formalization of procedures, definition of indicators, measuring customer satisfaction, internal auditing). Each office was represented by the notary public and one to three staff members depending on the size of the office.

A steering group of between 4 to 6 Chamber-appointed notary publics and one Superior Council (*Conseil Supérieur du Notariat*) representative was set up in each of the 9 regions. The interveners were responsible for leading these steering groups and presenting anonymous assessments of the work accomplished in the offices.

The specifically scaled-down Multi-SB HORIVERT method was designed to optimize the effectiveness and efficiency of these initiatives in each office. It was felt that for each office in a group of 8, the involvement should be spread over a period of 8 to 12 months to allow for the integration of management and design tools and the implementation and evaluation of the selected improvement initiatives. For each group of offices, 4 inter-company collaborative training sessions on socioeconomic management tools were held every 2 months, alternating with 5 intra-company diagnostic sessions, followed by focus group and tool implementation sessions. Each office in every group of 4 was involved in the same number of inter-company sessions as intra-company sessions (2 1/2 days). Three steering group sessions also provided the opportunity to monitor how work was progressing in the various groups of offices within the region.

The scientific observations that form the basis of the study were carried out during the diagnoses carried out in each of the 250 offices in the sample, which mobilized roughly 2,100 people, notaries, and collaborators (see Table 13.1). These data were complemented by the observations made during

TABLE 13.1 Characteristics of the Scientific Observation Sample

Regions	Number of Offices	Geographical Location of Offices	Number of Notaries	Number of Employees	Total Sample
Region 1 (34)	33	10 urban 10 suburban 13 rural	68	198	266
Region 2 (69)	18	10 urban 4 suburban 4 rural	38	147	185
Region 3 (41)	19	5 urban 9 suburban 5 rural	32	133	165
Region 4 (45)	14	4 urban 6 suburban 4 rural	29	110	139
Region 5 (73–74)	61	15 urban 31 suburban 15 rural	97	414	511
Region 6 (25)	65	17 urban 30 suburban 18 rural	91	413	504
Region 7 (26)	20	5 urban 10 suburban 5 rural	28	126	154
Region 8 (78)	5	3 urban 1 suburban 1 rural	12	110	122
Region 9 (22)	15	5 urban 7 suburban 3 rural	25	103	128
9 Regions	**250**	**74 urban** **108 suburban** **68 rural**	**420**	**1,754**	**2,174**

the intra- and inter-company training sessions and the implementation of the notarial quality sessions, which involved notaries and employees of the 250 offices for a period of 12 to 16 months (Noguera, 2007, 2011, 2012).

CONCLUSION: THE IMPACT OF INTERVENTION-RESEARCH

The intervention-research program described in the chapter standardized the operation and HRM practices of the notary firms, with a view to ISO 9001 certification. The intervention had a significant and positive impact of these notary offices—but it also had raised a number of rich teaching lessons. The basic storytelling, results, and perspectives about this intervention was the core of the paper published in the journal *Revue de Gestion de Ressources Humaines* (Cappelletti, Noguera, & Plane, 2012).

To summarize the paper in broad terms, the observations made it possible to make an initial contribution to the underlying problematic, which has been little dealt with in the literature, of HRM practice and its standardization in independent professions. Drawing on this engagement, the intervention-research project illustrates how a quality management system can be enhanced in very small companies, based on appropriate methodology, a well-structured intervention team, and a favorable strategic context. With regard to this latter point, it would seem that mobilizing political representatives of a profession to sustain management control tools could be a success factor, especially in regulated professions. One could perhaps distinguish a "political" *Hawthorne effect* that could characterize the introduction of management inside regulated enterprises. For notary publics, the fact of being observed by representatives of their political authorities doubtlessly played a role in the intensity of their involvement. Yet, even within this constraint, the results show that a standardization approach can be a factor of progress for management and HRM in small professional companies. This progress can be seen in improved professional dialogue, the teamwork that was developed, and the introduction of basic HRM systems into structures that had previously lacked them. Finally, it would seem that standardization of management and managerial innovation can be compatible with the nature of these independent enterprises.

It is also apparent, however, that an ISO standard-setting approach alone is not sufficient to steadily establish regular HRM practices without connecting social and economic performance. The results of this intervention-research project show that the involvement of the notary executives is indeed central to implement and perpetuate the quality schemes developed in the process. However, the long-term involvement of the notary requires tools that ensure traceability between the investments made and the creation of value generated. In the absence of such tools, the risk is that over time the notary emphasizes current operations that directly generate results to the detriment of actions of HR development. These results contribute to the theories of standardization in small, professional companies.

These insights confirm, like the works of Vigour (2011), the driving role of the intervener who helps to translate ISO standards and the congruence of those standards with the specificities of the organization. Without this function played by the intervener—in essence, adapting organizational norms to the specificities of a particular office—the ISO standard can indeed fall short in its capacity to create social innovation for these small structures. The research perspectives generated by these initial results also call for further investigations as to whether the standardization of HRM and management practices in the notarial sector has broader ramifications for other independent professions as well as more traditional small enterprises.

REFERENCES

Buono, A. F., & Savall, H. (Eds.) (2007). *Socio-economic intervention in organizations: The intervener-researcher and the SEAM approach to organizational analysis.* Charlotte, NC: Information Age.

Cappelletti, L., Delattre, M., & Noguera, F. (2007). Introducing the first management control system in independent professions: A qualimetric enquiry. *Tamara Journal for Critical organization Inquiry, 6*(3), 23–42.

Cappelletti, L., Khouatra, D., & Noguera, F., (2011, August). *Management consulting in independent professions: Evidence from the law-related sector.* Paper presented at the Academy of Management Annual Meeting, San Antonio, TX.

Cappelletti, L., Noguera, F., & Plane, J.-M. (2012). La normalisation du management des ressources humaines: Le cas des professions libérales réglementées [The Standardization of HRM: Evidence from Independent Professions]. *Revue de Gestion de Ressources Humaines, 82,* 36–52.

Hamel, G. (2008). *La fin du management: Inventer les règles de demain* [The death of management: Inventing the rules of tomorrow]. Paris, France: Vuibert.

Igalens, J., & Joras, M. (2002). *La Responsabilité Sociale de l'Entreprise* [The corporate social responsibility]. Paris, France: Les éditions d'organisation.

Savall, H., & Zardet, V. (2008). *Mastering hidden costs and socio-economic performance.* Charlotte, NC: Information Age.

Vigour, C. (2011). *Un changement sous contrôle: L'introduction de la démarche ISO 9001 dans la justice* [A change under control: Introducing ISO within the law and justice sector]. Paper presented at the Congrès AFS, réseau thématique Sociologie de la gestion. Grenoble, France. June.

CHAPTER 14

PUBLISHING THE RESULTS OF A RESEARCH-INTERVENTION

The Case of a Publication in *Management Accounting Quarterly*

Laurent Cappelletti

In 2009, we published an article in the ranked journal *Management Accounting Quarterly*—"Performing an Internal Control Function to Sustain SOX 404 and Improve Risk Management: Evidence from Europe." The publication was based on an intervention-research project conducted in the early 2000s in a company referred to as "GDP," an intermediate size firm with a staff of 900. The company was in the surveillance and security sector and located in the south of France. The research allowed us to observe the implemented devices focused on enhanced management of the internal control and risk management system. Outcomes of the project also included a proposed model for managing the internal control function based on our observations within GDP by convergent and complementary analyses carried out in previous case studies focused on the same object. In order to be successful in this publication, we defined a strategy for targeting a relevant

Intervention Research, pages 211–216

journal and constructed the article based on the ten generic qualitative research criteria defined by Savall, Zardet, Bonnet, and Peron (2008; see Table 14.1 & Chapter 10). We believe that the process explained in this chapter provides a useful source of inspiration for successfully publishing in an international journal based on an intervention-research case study.

THE INTERVENTION-RESEARCH AND OBJECT OF INVESTIGATION

GDP sells, installs, and maintains surveillance and security systems with French companies. The company was challenged in the early 2000s to improve its

TABLE 14.1 The Grid of the Ten Evaluation Criteria for an Article Based on Qualitative Research

Criteria	Corrections Made
Rigor	The article explains more clearly that it consists in completing the works of Wilkins & Gupta: page 2, 2nd paragraph, 7th line: "Wilkins & Gupta suggested..."
Formulation	The problem and the hypotheses were clearly formulated: page 2, 2nd paragraph "Thus, the question..."
Coherence	The article has been reorganized into four parts: I. Backgrounds, II. Investigated company, III. Methodology of research, IV. Results, Discussion about the proposed model
Originality	Part 4 on page 13 explains precisely how the proposed model is original and complements the work of Wilkins & Gupta
Relevance	In the introduction, a brief history of internal control failures at EADS in 2006 and Société Générale in 2008 was added to highlight the relevance of the subject: see the first paragraph of the introduction
Explicitation	The model was better explained both on page 12, just after Figure 2, in part 4 and in conclusion.The explicit research methodology is that of intervention-research. The reference to the case study was dropped so as not to disturb the reader.
Positioning	The work was better positioned in relation to the main work on internal control, mainly in part 1 (Holt, 2008, Coso 2006, 2007, Wilkins & Gupta, 2007)
Contribution	The contribution of the work to the reflection on the management of internal control was more clearly explained in the introduction and in conclusion
Reasoning	The structuring of the article (introduction, conclusion + 4 parts) seems more relevant in terms of reasoning
Delimitation	The delimitation of the subject around the concepts of SOX, internal control and management of internal control must now clearly appear

Source: Savall, Zardet, Bonnet, & Péron (2008).

internal control and risk management system. This subject of investigation was a sensitive subject of investigation in the field of control and audit, especially with the implementation of new laws on internal control, particularly Sarbanes-Oxley (SOX) in the United States and internationally and its French substitute named the Law of Financial Security (LSF in French).

The Case of an Enterprise Subject to New Internal Control Constraints

During the intervention, GDP counted approximately one hundred managers, supervising teams of five to fifteen people. The staff was divided into four main areas of activity grouped into departments: (a) a technical area responsible for the installation and maintenance of the systems sold; (b) a commercial area in charge of the sale of surveillance systems; (c) an administrative area in charge of personnel management and sales administration; and (d) an accounting and IT department with the internal audit department. The technical and commercial staff worked in technical-sales agencies positioned throughout France; the other staff members were based at the company's headquarters. GDP's core business was to sell surveillance equipment to companies in the form of 4-year subscription contracts with monthly payments. The sale of equipment to new customers was done according to a so-called "one shoot" technique, consisting of signing the contract in a single appointment. Once the contract was signed, the client company became part of the "customer park" and benefitted from the advice and maintenance of the technicians. At the end of the 4-year contract, the client companies were negotiated to renew their contract.

The Intervention-Research Protocol Used for the Case Study

The research method chosen to develop the case study was intervention-research, which emerged as a method that was well adapted to the objectives of the research, namely to observe and describe (a) an internal control system before the implementation of SOX/LSF and (b) the actions taken to implement this law and improve the quality of internal control. The necessarily longitudinal nature of this approach (before/during/after) practically required an intervening-research method. Indeed, it is a technology of research exploration and confirmation, which consisted of penetrating the company concretely, not as a mere observer but as a player in the corporate game in charge of conducting a process (see Chapters 1, 2, 3, and 4). The intervention-research protocol confirmed the company's organizational dimension of internal control, describing it before the implementation of SOX/LSF and making initial assumptions about organizing the internal control function in the context of the implementation of SOX/LSF. The procedure of the intervention-research was carried out according to the following steps:

- In the first half of 2003, dysfunctions disrupting the achievement of objectives and the development of activities were identified during individual interviews with the management of the company. This diagnosis allowed us to describe the internal control of the company, which was not organized as a function, and to identify its dysfunctions.
- Then, twice-hourly individual interviews were conducted with management to assess qualitatively (what regulations?), quantitatively (how often over 1 year?), and economically (what loss of value added over a year?) the impacts of dysfunctions.
- The regulations were grouped into two types of activity: human activities and consumption of products (goods or services). The quantities of consumption of products or services were evaluated on the basis of the costs actually incurred by the company. Human time was valued at the hourly contribution to value added on variable cost (CHVACV). The CHVACV is equal to the ratio of the margin on variable costs over the expected number of hours, the margin on variable cost being equal to the difference between the turnover realized and the variable expenses with the level of activity.
- In the second half of 2003, as a result of this diagnosis of dysfunctions, project groups were set up in the four main departments of GDP to propose solutions to reduce dysfunctions and improve internal control through the implementation of SOX/LSF. The project group was a hierarchical working group led by the head of department, called the project leader. Four monthly project group sessions were organized in each department. These sessions included carrying out a financial study made by the project manager with the help of the controller (referred to as the economic balance) to assess whether the proposed solutions would generate sufficient profitability in terms of the means required for their implementation. The solutions chosen to reduce the dysfunctions and standardize internal control fueled the priority action plans of the four departments of the GDP company in the first half of 2004.
- During the second half of 2004, an action to evaluate the implementation of the priority action plans was carried out in the four departments concerned. Through interviews with management and departments, the level of implementation of the priority action plans was assessed. The impacts of the actions implemented

in terms of reducing dysfunctions and improving internal control were then measured qualitatively and economically, through the reduction of the costs of dysfunctions. In particular, this evaluation made it possible to observe and describe the organization of the internal control function in the context of the implementation of SOX/LSF.

STRATEGY FOR SUBMISSION

Based on this research and intervention, we developed a strategy to target an international journal for the submission of an article based on this material. We also adopted a strategy of building the article to maximize our chances of publication.

The Choice of a Relevant International Journal in Accounting and Audit

Initially, we presented our work as a professional paper at French and international congresses, in particular the American Accounting Association (AAA) in 2007. The presentation of work during such academic conferences begins a process of improvement, potentially drawing the attention of editors-in-chief of journals or colleagues who are members of a scientific committee of journals who may be asked for advice. This is what happened at the 2007 AAA annual meeting, where our accepted paper was of interest to the chairman of the AAA's Management Accounting Section. Following informal discussion (with a beer at the end of the day)—which is part of conference networking activities— we were advised us to seek publication in an American review of management control, focusing on mid-range classified journals for a first attempt and then seek to publish in top ranked journals later on relying on previous mid-ranking publications (a so-called "staircase" publication strategy). We were also recommended to look for journals that were open to field research and interested in European work—which led to the suggestion that we target the paper to *Management Accounting Quarterly* (MAQ), which met these criteria.

I was then introduced to the editor-in-chief of the journal, who attended the AAA annual meeting, and after a conversation about the research, encouraged me to submit the paper for publication review. In essence, the choice of MAQ was influenced by the advice of experienced advisors.

Using the Grid of Evaluation Criteria

To build our submission to MAQ we examined copies of the journal to assess its standards and typical article format. We also ensured that our submission corresponded to the ten generic criteria for evaluating an article based on qualitative research identified by Savall, et al., 2008; see Table 14.1) Once the submission was completed we used these ten criteria as a self-checking quality grid before sending it to MAQ in early 2008. We also had the article corrected by an Anglo-Saxon copy editor to secure the level of the English language used. Three months after submission, the reviewers suggested an acceptance of the paper subject to minor modifications, proof that the publication strategy we had followed worked well. The modifications that were requested reflected the need for more precise information on each of the ten criteria summarized in Table 14.1. We therefore explained the corrections made to the reviewers using the ten criteria grid and submitted our corrected text for a second evaluation in mid 2008.

CONCLUSION

The revised paper was accepted and published in MAQ in the summer of 2009, for an intervention-research project carried out in 2003–2004, communicated in 2006–2007, and submitted for article at the beginning of 2008, which basically, with the hindsight, is a fairly conventional timeframe for intervention-based work. The intervention also provided the framework for subsequent publications based on other data and observations that were submitted to other journals in 2008, 2009 and 2010 (see Chapter 5). Thus, although this may be a lengthy process from initial conceptualization to publication, it can also provide the basis for a stream of research that builds on and extends the initial project.

REFERENCES

Cappelletti, L. (2009). Performing an Internal Control Function to Sustain SOX 404 and improve risk management: Evidence from Europe. *Management Accounting Quarterly, 10*(4), 17–27.

Savall H., Zardet V., Bonnet M., & Péron M. (2008). The emergence of implicit criteria: Case of a European Journal. *Organizational Research Methods, 11*(3), 510–540.

CHAPTER 15

FROM NEGOTIATION TO PUBLICATION

The Case of an Intervention-Research Project in the Small- and Medium-Size Enterprise Sector

Thierry Nobre

This chapter presents the entire research and publication process starting from the negotiation of an intervention-research project to a scientific publication through a case study in the small- and medium-size enterprises (SMEs) sector. The discussion identifies the different stages of the process, from the first contacts with the actors on the ground to the eventual publication of the article (Nobre, 2006) in a top ranked Francophone journal in management control, *Revue Comptabilité, Contrôle, Audit* [Accounting, Control & Auditing Review]. The focus of the chapter is on the link between negotiation, intervention-research, and ultimate publication, capturing the different stages of the process of knowledge production and illustrating the observations formalized through the metaphor of the reading of organizations in hypertext during an intervention-research project.

Intervention Research, pages 217–222

The process of the research is presented in the chapter and publication of the studied article is divided into three phases. The first one describes the emergence of the problematic stemming from the negotiations of intervention-research projects, in which one was a failure. It appeared that this failure played a central role in validating the relevance of the problematic. The second phase describes the operationalization of the problem to convert the initial idea into a research design arriving at a first draft of the article. The last step sheds light on the dialogue between the researchers and the journal reviewers to modify the submission, responding to reviewer comments and recommended changes to warrant publication in the targeted journal.

The discussion emphasizes the decisive methodological conditions to facilitate the academic acceptance of an intervention-research article. Our intent is to provide a general guideline for the publication process, focusing on one of the main pitfalls pinpointed by editors for this type of research, namely the low readability of the submission's research question or problematic. As a prerequisite, it is important to note that the readability of a research question can be enhanced by the principle *one paper = one central idea*, which should guide the process of designing the article. Such a principle may prevent the author from dispersions and overblown contributions, which do not fit the requirements of academic journals and the expectations of their scientific committee. Indeed, acceptance of intervention-research in scientific journals can be particularly difficult due to this challenge, (the premise of "one paper = one central idea"), due to the richness of the data in this type of research. It is not easy for researchers to walk away from observations made on the ground, excluding data which may be tangential to the problematic of the article. We are often drawn to such interesting but peripheral phenomena. For the publication process, it is therefore fundamental to shape one problematic and to identify the specific data that are necessary for its treatment, whatever the richness of other observations. Indeed such a choice may engender a bit of frustration on behalf of the researcher that must be overcome on an individual basis.

FROM INITIAL IDEA TO FORMALIZATION INTO A PROBLEMATIC

To explain the genesis of the central idea developed in the article analyzed in the chapter, we would like to refer to the concept of *central hypothesis*, which draws out the researcher's intuition for the problematic of the paper, which must be validated through the chosen data from the ground. On this point, we are in line with Lorino (2008) who takes the image of the survey to detail the stages that lead from the emergence of a central idea or central hypothesis to the validation of this central hypothesis for the production of knowledge. Thus, we explore how an intuition/idea may arise stemming from immersion on the ground, then how convergent facts can be accumulated, and finally how the tangibility of observations can be confirmed by interviews with actors.

An Initial Idea for Writing a Paper: The Impact of the Introduction of Management Control on Power Relations in SMEs

The intervention-research project that is the focus of the chapter was conducted in seven small companies. Its scientific objective was to analyze the process of improving the functioning of each company. During the initial interactions with the managers and staff, a seemingly counter-intuitive phenomenon appeared. Despite convergent appeals for the need to introduce management control tools (mainly costing methods and budgetary approaches), it seemed that the behavior of the managers and CFO was not necessarily aligned and that the role of the accountant was ambiguous. This intuitive observation did not have immediate scientific consequences except the awakening of suspicions and the awareness of something probably interesting to explore.

A Bundle of Convergent Facts

A few years later and after having conducting several intervention-research projects in SMEs on the topic of management control, we wrote a pedagogical case study. In the course of collecting data for the case study, based on our distanced analysis of the data, we observed that the role played by the managers, CFO, and the accountant in the introduction of management control tools was always specific. Consequently we linked this finding to shape a central hypothesis on the role of these three actors, focusing on their relationships during a process for introducing management control tools in SMEs.

To deepen this hypothesis we engaged additional intervention-research negotiations with the SMEs. One of them was focused on the question of instrumenting its management control system. The negotiation phase with us was mainly conducted by the CFO of this SME. Soon there was a conflict between the manager and the CFO that led to a negotiation failure. Nevertheless, the negotiation conducted with the CFO clearly validated the hypothesis expressed in the previous cases. Moreover, the CFO had clearly expressed what would later become the central hypothesis of the selected article: the introduction of management control tools depends on the relationship between three actors—the manager, CFO, and the accountant. As we found these relationships were often conflictual with respect to appropriate management control tools. Unfortunately, the negotiation had failed and it was not possible to collect empirical data to validate this hypothesis. The experience did, however, allow us to concretize an intuition and convert it into a central hypothesis.

Concretization of the Research

Subsequently, during a laboratory seminar, a doctoral student presented a paper in which he questioned the theoretical framework in developing his thesis based on case study research. In the presentation of the empirical material, there appeared to be a strong similarity between points he presented and the findings of our own work. This convergence engendered a scientific partnership for sharing experiences based on a similar problematic concerning the role of the three actors mentioned above. This exchange made it possible to quickly identify the appropriate theoretical framework to raise the problematic, treat the central hypothesis, and serve as a reading grid to analyze the phenomena observed—Crozier and Friedberg's (1980) "Strategy of the Actors." Both of us had chosen to focus our paper on a longitudinal case study. We capitalized and classified the raw data accumulated in the different intervention-research projects and, based on these elements of the research, structured the central hypothesis, problematic, theoretical framework, and field materials for the paper. This step demonstrates the importance of raw information collected through the intervention (e.g., research journals, recordings, meeting reports, memos, document collection, etc.), which allowed us to undertake a hypertext reading across the organizations to produce knowledge. This process led to a draft of the article that was submitted to the *Accounting, Control, & Auditing Review.*

AN IDEA THROUGH A COLLABORATIVE OPPORTUNITY: A DIALOGUE WITH JOURNAL REVIEWERS

The phase between the first submission and eventual publication of the article reminds us that the underlying process must be seen as a dialogue, which is established and develops with the reviewers to refine a proposal. For instance, the reviewers stressed "the relevance of the subject, with a case that seems rich for teaching and probably quite exemplary." They emphasized that "the research results in an interesting result of an original sociopolitical resistance emanating not from the employees but from the chief accountant, although he is at the origin of the approach of introduction of tools." It was therefore the richness of the ground that allowed to go through the evaluation process to ultimately publish the article. The central hypothesis captured by the researchers was what attracted the attention of the reviewers. However, they requested some modifications, a process that is quite common in academic journals in general and with respect to intervention-research in particular.

These requested modifications included: (a) the readability of the methodology, (b) deepening the use of the theoretical framework to better operationalize the concepts of Crozier and Friedberg and mobilize them in the case study, and (c) the use of concepts in a way that could lead to confusion. The revision process required two additional versions after the initial resubmission. The reviewers, who should always be thanked for their effort and contribution, allowed us to "step back" and prioritize our contributions. It was a true scientific discussion and exchange, one that must be experienced as part of the production of knowledge.

CONCLUSION

This example of a scientific article highlights several features of the intervention-research publication process. First, the temporal dimension allowed different projects to be complementary and resonant, enabling the researcher to mobilize a project to propose publications, provided that the problematic and collected data are different. The intuitions also encompassed different temporalities, ranging from the fastest in the case of well-identified projects to the most tortuous paths. Then, the collaborative approach through the exchanges that it initiated intensified the capacity of the researcher to contribute to the production of knowledge. Definitely, the richness of the ground is a source of opportunity for the researcher, one that requires an open-minded posture as well as an appetite to meet the actors on the ground. These individuals, in general, have significant expectations in terms of being helped as they are also well-positions to innovate their managerial practices based on the outcomes of the intervention-research project.

REFERENCES

Crozier, M., & Friedberg, E. (1980). *Actors and systems: The politics of collective action.* Chicago, IL: The University of Chicago Press.

Lorino, P. (2008). Méthodes de recherche en contrôle de gestion: Une approche critique [Methods of research in management control: A critical perspective]. *Finance Contrôle Stratégie, 11,* 149–175.

Nobre, T. (2006). Pour une lecture en hypertexte des organisations par la recherche action: Le cas du changement à l'hôpital [For a hypertext reading of organizations thanks to action-research: The case of change process in a hospital]. *Finance Contrôle Stratégie, 9*(4), 143–168.

Nobre, T., & Zawadsky, C. (2013). Stratégie d'acteurs et processus d'introduction du contrôle de gestion en PME [Strategy of the actors and implementation of a management control process; Results from the SME sector] *Comptabilité Contrôle Audit, 1*(19), 91–116.

CHAPTER 16

PUBLISHING ACADEMIC PAPERS DRAWING ON INTERVENTION-RESEARCH-BASED DOCTORAL DISSERTATIONS

Marc Bonnet[1]

Today, more and more doctoral dissertations are written by experienced practitioners in the context of academic programs such as DBAs or executive PhDs. This kind of research is quite impactful because there is an urgent need to address complex management issues through experiments and transformative processes. In particular, doctoral dissertations can be value added for the various stakeholders of management research. For example, for doctoral candidates, writing a dissertation based on intervention-research enhances reflexivity, which is a key success factor for managers facing a blurred and complex business environment. In particular, it enables stepping back and taking distance from the field to conceptualize hands-on experience, test innovative solutions, and bring practice knowledge to a theoretical body of information. For directors of research, it is

Intervention Research, pages 223–233

an opportunity to capture high quality data through in depth and up-close scientific observation of complex managerial phenomena, which are intangible and transient. It is just the opposite of traditional research carried out by researchers who do not have sufficient managerial background and who try to process rigorous research with superficial methods and unreliable data captured through questionnaires and databases bought in the academic marketplace. In the companies and organizations where research takes place, it is an opportunity for innovation of management practices, which is an underpinning condition for differentiation and agility in a hyper-competitive business environment.

THE "PUBLISH OR PERISH" DILEMMA

A challenge for doctoral candidates is that publications are required in order to gain academic recognition for their research. Indeed, most academic publication outlets in the field of management are focused on specialized domains—often referred to as "silos"—while intervention-research

Figure 16.1 Cunning as a fox intervener-researcher facing the challenge of publishing relevant and rigorous research in a highly specialized ranked management journal (as sharp as a stork's beak).

is system-wide and cross-disciplinary in its very nature, taking into account the need to address the complexity of organizational transformation phenomena. As a result, doctoral candidates feel more comfortable in submitting their research to practice-oriented journals, and often ill-at-ease when required to publish in specialized academic journals. Such an awkward situation may be compared to an Aesop fable, also rephrased by La Fontaine, where a stork invites a fox for dinner—but the food is served in a vase appropriate for the stork's beak, not at all for the fox's muzzle, as shown in Figure 16.1. Therefore, doctoral candidates practicing intervention research have to resort to a number of machinations to work through the difficulties of publishing highly rigorous scientific observation in specialized academic journals in the field of management. This paper is aimed at illustrating such tactics through the case of an article published on overall performance measurement in a "B" ranked international journal (Voyant, Bonnet, Tabchoury, & Datry, 2017), and drawing on an intervention-research process carried out with doctoral candidates.

SETTING THE SCENE OF AN INTERVENTION-RESEARCH PROJECT IN A HOSPITAL IN THE MIDDLE-EAST

Intervention-research took place in a Middle-Eastern hospital facing the challenge of cutting costs while enhancing health-care healthcare and investing in cutting edge medical equipment. This general hospital operated 180 beds and admitted 38,000 patients, including 4,800 surgeries per year. It employed 350 nurses and 45 equivalent full-time medical doctors. The intervener-researcher was the CEO himself assisted by the ISEOR research center. The CEO had completed his doctorate, with a dissertation on socio-economic management control in this hospital.

The objective of the intervention-research was to experiment replication of innovative management control to steer overall performance, as opposed to short-term financial performance, as advocated by ISEOR's qualimetrics research methodology. The intervention process followed the rules of the socioeconomic approach to management (SEAM): mirror-effect based on field-note quotes of all the categories of actors, along with calculation of hidden costs; a socioeconomic project including the economic balance aimed at demonstrating the conversion of hidden costs into value creation; and implementation of socioeconomic management tools such as piloting log-books, internal and external strategic planning, and priority action plans. The implementation of the intervention-research spanned over more than 1 year, as shown in Figure 16.2. This figure shows how data was captured through the qualimetrics method consisting of three main pillars (Savall & Zardet, 2004):

	Première Année				Deuxième Année											
	September	October	November	December	January	February	March	April	May	June	July	August	September	October	November	December
STEERING COMMITTEE	1		2		3		4		5		6		7		8	
DIAGNOSES AND PROJECT GROUPS	X	X	X		X		X		X							
COLLABORATIVE TRAINING OF MANAGERS TO DESIGN INNOVATIVE MANAGEMENT CONTROL OF OVERALL PERFORMANCE	1		2		3		4		5		6		7		8	

Figure 16.2 Capturing reliable and relevant data through in-depth and up-close scientific observation over a more than 1 year longitudinal process.

- *Interactive cognitivity*: Diagnoses and projects required raising collective cleverness through semi-directive interviews and focus groups aimed at designing innovative solutions.
- *Contradictory inter-subjectivity*: Implementing the socioeconomic management control tools required that all actors come up to an agreement on the data, e.g., financial figures regarding the short and long term performance of the strategic action plan.
- *Generic contingency*: The steering committee made sure that the process could be replicated in other hospitals owned by the same group, while the objective of the research center was to make sure that the socioeconomic method could be applied in this very specific context in the Middle-East, after hundreds of similar experiments in 40 countries.

It should be mentioned that the outcomes of this intervention-research project were quite impressive: 47% increase in revenue and hourly margin on variable costs raised from $17 to $24, in addition to qualitative and quantitative positive impacts (e.g., improved working conditions for all employees and medical doctors, wage increase, enhanced patient satisfaction and image of the hospital).

THE PUBLICATION PROCESS

The discussion now turns to the publication process itself, beginning with the choice of an appropriate journal for submission, to framing the problem statement and phrasing hypotheses, to the intervention methodology and positioning the paper.

Journal Choice

The first step consisted of selecting an appropriate publication outlet. It was wise to choose a journal that would be open to non-positivist research, like the *Academy of Management Journal*, nor to interpretive research or organization theory, like *Organization Studies* or *Academy of Management Review*. *Society and Business Review* (published by Emerald) was selected as it was a journal open to themes related to impactful research. It could also have been *Action Research* or *Organizational Development Journal* or *Engaged Management Review*, but these journals were even ranked in the field of management science, which may seem strange in the case of a scientific community advocating management science as a research domain focused on action and decision-making (Byington & Felps, 2017). Following oral advice given by Ann-Wils Harzing, "don't take care of the level of ranking of the journal, just publish meaningful articles in ranked journals that fit with action research and intervention-research," *Society and Business Review* was considered the best outlet, as it was listed by ABS and by the Australian Business Deans Council (ABDC Journal Quality List), and reachable on electronic libraries. It was useful to have a close look at the editorial policy, in order to take into account the specificities of the journal, with its particular focus on social responsibility issues. Checking out the lay of the land and having a look at the publications of editors and the journal's scientific committee also permitted us to make sure that there was a good match between the objectives of the paper and the focus of the journal. Some of the papers published in the journal on similar themes were also downloaded to compare approaches and results with the objectives of the paper to be submitted.

Focusing the Problem Statement on a Specific Issue

Most journals are specialized, which conflicts with the ideal of system analysis, requiring a comprehensive description of the intervention-research process, the "ins and outs" of all the actions, and the monography of the longitudinal transformative process (Pettigrew, 2001). Of course, a doctoral dissertation (or a book) is much more appropriate to report on the outcomes of an intervention-research process than a 10-page article. A trap would be to attempt putting the entire dissertation into little more than a "nutshell." Indeed, the socioeconomic intervention-research in the hospital had addressed the entire management system, not only management control, from strategic management and human resource management, to marketing management and quality management. Therefore, it was necessary to cast light only on one of the aspects of the multi-faceted intervention-research process that was of interest to the journal (i.e., overall

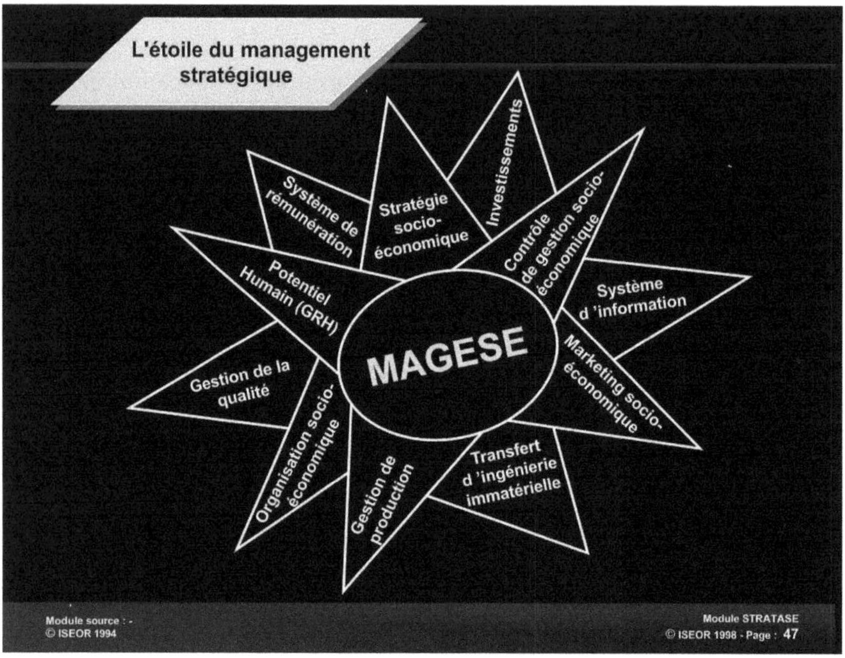

Figure 16.3 The socioeconomic intervention-research "star."

performance management control) and to discuss it through an analysis of the extant literature (e.g., observation was made by many authors that validity and reliability of overall performance reporting was eagerly awaited by investors in order to enhance trust, but management control systems were not sufficient to be up to the marks, hence hindering the development of socially responsible management control practices).

Figure 16.3 presents the socioeconomic intervention-research "star" (Savall & Zardet, 2008). It shows that the intervention carried out for the sake of doctoral dissertations is multi-dimensional, while the academic paper is only focused on the interaction between the core of the star and the socioeconomic management control ray.

Framing Hypotheses

Likewise, it was necessary to adapt the body of hypotheses created through the intervention-research process in order to only focus on the specialized theme of the article. In this case, the core hypothesis regarding management control of overall performance was phrased as below:

> Existing approaches to management control are more juxtaposing approaches than integrating methods. They are not comprehensive enough as they downplay the hidden financial impacts and hidden costs and performance stemming from informal powers. As a result, there is a need to better measure overall performance through performance metrics that include both visible and hidden costs and performance.

Such an adapted wording doesn't consist of twisting the core hypothesis, which stated that there was a need to transform the whole system through socioeconomic intervention. It only meant that the paper was aimed at focusing on one specific aspect of a multi-faceted intervention-research process.

Positioning the Research Method

As opposed to mainstream research methods in the field of management research, action research and intervention research are still considered as fringe methods by top ranked journals, even when the same journals envision moving to impactful research in a desired, but unpredictable future. The tipping point has not yet been reached, and truly impactful and scientific research is still considered at the moment as nonscientific "applied research" as opposed to the so-called "academic research," which has been criticized as drawing on less than high quality data (Gephart, 1988) but still accepted in top ranked journals due to mimicry and isomorphism (see Powell & DiMaggio, 2012) in management research. Such a differentiation between applied and academic research doesn't exist in the field of medicine or engineering, but social science has not yet moved to a philosophy of science (Van de Ven, 1987) aimed at healing organizational diseases and alleviating painful situations in companies. Therefore, there is a need to argue for the appropriateness of intervention-research, as the burden of proof is required for this kind of research method. Hopefully, as the field continues to evolve and gain acceptance, this type of burden won't be required in the future as intervention-research becomes mainstream research.

The main features of a qualimetrics-based intervention-research were described above. This methodological approach is highly relevant in the context of complexity, taking into account the "heap of variables" in the situation. The research contract process was also described, along with the need for the involvement of all parties in the research process to come up with the requirements of "contradictory inter-subjectivity" (Savall & Zardet, 2011). The merit of scientific rigor of intervention-research is that it is supported by a variety of well-established theories (Argyris et al., 1985; Collier, 1994; Pettigrew, 2001; Ullman, 1985).

Field Data

The richness of intervention research required the authors to select a few relevant and striking examples of the outcomes of the experiments regarding the subject of the paper. In this case, excerpts of the field materials were presented, such as an economic balance in the hospital showing that improving healthcare performance was not conflicting with financial objectives in the context of overall performance (see Figure 16.4). Each illustration had to be properly introduced and commented in order to articulate field materials with the hypotheses.

Positioning

Academic journals insist on the contribution to literature. Therefore, the review of the extant literature on the specialized topic broached in the paper is key. Description of the debate regarding management control of overall performance was developed in the first part of the paper and mentioned a variety of contributions considered as the milestones of research output regarding the specific topic (e.g., Butler et al., 2011; Cheng et al., 2014; Elkington, 1997; Figge et al., 2002; Freeman, 1984; Kaplan & Norton, 2001; Jensen, 2003). The last part of the paper focused on discussion of the results in order to compare scientific observation carried out through intervention-research with statements existing in the management research literature. It was an opportunity to clarify the contribution of socioeconomic management control to theories such as the sustainable balanced scorecard and triple bottom line. An example of the discussion was focused on the need to enable connection between economic, social, and environmental performance; it required shedding light on hidden costs and performance. It can't be achieved only through juxtaposing indicators, like in the case of triple bottom line theory. Intervention-research showed that it requires negotiation with the variety of stakeholders to agree on a relevant set of indicators.

CONCLUSION

This kind of publication may be considered as an example of a possible response to the growing concerns mentioned by Van de Ven (2016) regarding the output of management research. As he suggested, too many research papers are:

- *Contestable* (outliers thrown out)—the content of this paper was accepted by both academics and practitioners.

COSTS				PERFORMANCE	
	Total Amount	Number of Years for Depreciation	Costs/Year		Value Creation per Year
Creation of a specific ward for orthopedic surgery	$300,000	20 years	$15,000	20 minutes decrease in time needed between two surgeries, enabling 130 more surgeries over 6 months ($500 each) due to surgeons and nurses experiencing improved working conditions	$65,000
Specific training for orthopedic scrub nurses	$2,040	3 years	$680	Decrease in nosocomial infections	$7,500
Recruiting an additional nurse			$34,000	20 more surgeries per month	$60,000
OVERALL AMOUNT			$49,680	OVERALL AMOUNT	$132,500
				Net value creation per year	**$82,820**

Figure 16.4 Economic balance of the operating room redistribution project (©ISEOR).

- *Unreliable* (few replications, low construction validity)—in this instance, the intervention was validated by all stakeholders, including managers, medical doctors, and nurses. The method was also replicated in other hospitals and healthcare organizations.
- *Unusable* (not grounded, irrelevant)—the experiment and evaluation took place prior to publishing.
- *Overly narrow* (theory fetishism)—this article was cross-disciplinary.
- *Careerist* (instrumental, self-serving)—the first objective of the paper has been to serve the common good, before any selfish objective.

Publishing articles based on intervention-research can contribute to the challenge proposed by Byington and Felps (2017), consisting of encouraging credible research for the field, and decreasing the value of non-credible self-interests through publishing replication results, enabling robustness checks with data access, and adopting open credibility-boosting practices.

NOTES

1. The chapter is based on a paper copresented at the Academy of Management Annual Meeting (Doctoral Consortium Sessions, Management Consulting Division, 2017, Atlanta, GA) with our colleagues Olivier Voyant, Patrick Tabchoury, and Frantz Datry.

REFERENCES

Argyris, C., Putnam, R., & Smith, D. M. (1985). *Action science.* San Francisco, CA: Jossey-Bass.

Byington, E. K., & Felps, W. (2017). Solutions to the credibility crisis in management science. *Academy of Management Learning and Education* (in press).

Butler, J. B., Henderson, S., & Raiborn, C. (2011). Sustainability and the Balanced Scorecard: Integrating green measures into business reporting. *Management Accounting Quarterly, 12*(2), 1–10.

Cheng, M., Greeen, W., Conradie, P., Konishi, N., & Romi, A. (2014). The international integrated reporting framework: Key issues and future research opportunities. *Journal of International Financial Management & Accounting, 25,* 90–119.

Collier, A. (1994). *Critical realism: An introduction to Roy Bhaskar's philosophy.* London, England: Andrew Collier.

Elkington, J. (1997). *Cannibals with forks: The triple bottom line of the 21st century business.* Oxford, England: Capstone.

Figge, F., Hahn, T., Schaltegger, S., & Wagner, M. (2002). The sustainability balanced scorecard: Linking sustainability to business strategy. *Business Strategy and the Environment. 11,* 269–284.

Freeman, R. E. (1984). *Strategic management: A stakeholder approach.* Marshfied, MA: Pitman.

Gephart, R. P. (1988). *Ethnostatistics: Qualitative foundations for quantitative research* (No. 2). Thousand Oaks, CA: SAGE.

Jensen, M. C. (2003). Paying people to lie the truth about budgeting process. *European Financial Management, 9*(3), 379–406.

Kaplan, R., & Norton, D. (2001). *The strategy-focused organization: How balanced scorecard companies thrive in the new business environment.* Boston, MA: Harvard Business School Press.

Löning, H., Malleret, V., Méric, J., & Pesqueux, Y. (Eds). (2016). *Performance management control.* Paris, France: Dunod.

Pettigrew, R. (2001). Management research after modernism. *British Journal of Management, 12,* 61–70.

Powell, W., & DiMaggio, P. J. (Eds.). (2012). *The new institutionalism in organizational analysis.* Chicago, IL: University of Chicago Press.

Savall, H. (1975). Enrichir le travail humain, l'évaluation économique [Work and people]. Préface de J. Delors. Paris, France: Dunod.

Savall, H., & Zardet, V. (2011). *Qualimetrics: Observing the complex object.* Charlotte, NC: Information Age.

Savall, H., & Zardet, V. (2008). *Mastering hidden costs and socio-economic performance.* Charlotte, NC: Information Age.

Savall, H., Zardet, V., & Bonnet, M. (2008). *Releasing the untapped potential of enterprises through socio-economic management.* Geneva, Switzerland: International Labor Organization.

Ullmann, A. R. (1985). Data in search of a theory: A critical examination of the relationships among social performance, social disclosure and economic performance of U.S. firms. *Academy of Management Review, 10*(3), 540–577.

Van de Ven, A. H. (2007). *Engaged scholarship: A guide for organizational and social research.* Oxford, England: Oxford University Press.

Van de Ven, A. (2016). *Saving social science.* Address to the Department of Organization, Copenhagen Business School, November 18, Copenhagen, DK.

Voyant, O., Bonnet, M., Tabchoury P., & Datry, F. (2017). Contribution of the socio-economic management control to steering balanced and sustainable company overall performance. *Society and Business Review* (in print).

CHAPTER 17

PUBLISHING INTERVENTION-RESEARCH

From Academic Articles to Social Networks

Isabelle Barth

Although publication is not research per se (see Chapters 1 & 5), they are like the two faces of a ring of Moebius—one cannot exist without the other. There can be no published peer-reviewed scientific intent without robust and validated research, as research needs to be visible in publications that narrate it by presenting its methodology, issues, outcomes, and limits. Intervention-research (IR) is no exception since it needs scientific publication for its recognition within the academic community. But its richness also opens the way to other types of valorization dedicated to pedagogical, managerial, or even public audiences. It is what we call the "radiation" of an IR, its impacts for the society.

Over the last few years, we have noticed an international movement that has led management researchers to the question of the "impact" of their work—what are the outcomes for companies? Does it participate in the

Intervention Research, pages 235–244

progress of the world? Is it able to propose actionable knowledge? In order to respond to these questions, it is necessary to demonstrate and evaluate such impact. This challenge raises the question of measuring impact with the search for indicators that are extremely varied—for example, a blog held by the researcher, the audience of a post on a site, the number of interviews or citations in the media as illustrations of indicators increasingly used by teaching and research institutions.

We propose an overview of such processes for publishing IR in the chapter. In the first part, we analyze the writing of an article based on an IR project led by an internal intervener-researcher (see Chapter 7). In the second, we present other ways of valorization, pedagogical manuals, popular books, blogs, videos, posts on social networks, and conferences, which allow to evoke the emergence of an "omni-channel researcher."

FROM AN IR PROJECT TO ACADEMIC PUBLICATION

In 2011, the management of the EMS management school (a well ranked French business school in Strasbourg) included in its strategic action plan the implementation of management of diversity. Sabrina was recruited as a project manager to lead this project, in direct relation with the CEO of the management school and in collaboration with the quality and accreditation department. Very quickly, the choice was made to use the diversity label to guide this change based on the ISO standard NF X 50-784, "Promotion of Diversity–Human Resources Policy for the Promotion of Diversity and the Prevention of Discrimination." The labeling was intended to guarantee equal opportunities and to prevent discrimination within organizations, distinguishing those whose practices are considered exemplary. To receive a positive assessment, companies are expected to meet a precise specification including five reference areas. As regards the EMS management school, the specifications were for "Public Functions," which means specifications for business schools being a component of a public university (like EMS that is a component of the University of Strasbourg). The operational objectives of the Sabrina's mission was therefore to bring the EMS management school to this diversity label with a deadline of 2 years.

The Intervention

The intervention conducted by Sabrina followed the specifications of the ISO standard, which proposed five areas:

1. An inventory of the diversity in the organization that must be communicated to the representatives of the staff or bodies representing

employees and trade unions. This inventory was conducted in the spring of 2010 with the detailed establishment of a risk discrimination map updated in February 2013 and March 2015.

2. Documentation of the commitment of the board of directors of EMS in the form of a policy with measurable objectives. This was reflected by many actions, including: the setting up of a "diversity referent" and a cell for listening and dealing with complaints concerning alleged or proven discriminations; the recruitment of a person with disabilities at the beginning of 2012; the recruitment of a diversity manager in 2013; the recruitment of a diversity mission officer in early 2015; and the installation of a diversity committee analyzing and taking decisions as regarding discrimination and the promotion of diversity.
3. Developing internal communication, information, awareness, and training with a focus on: sensitization of stakeholders (staff, students); recruitment guides and recruitment charters; diversity days (large-scale events to raise awareness among students); implementation of an adapted training plan; and thematic workshops with the Bureau of Diversity (a student association).
4. Consideration of diversity in the activities of the organization: integration of the diversity policy in the welcome booklet, integration notes, and school presentations; post-college competitions; scholarship policy; and communication of the diversity policy to suppliers whose services have an impact on the EMS functioning. In addition, other actions included: (a) implementation of E-learning and a catalog; (b) research on diversity within the EMS laboratory of research (six theses were defended and height others are in progress); (c) partnership with companies via the Diversity Management Chair created in March 2009, bringing together twenty companies; (d) a scientific meeting in December 2009 focused on "Diversity: Questions for the social sciences—Equality in employment, Discrimination in the workplace and Management of diversity" (which resulted in a book); and numerous publications and participations in symposia and conferences.
5. Assessment of the improvement of diversity: definition and implementation of appropriate tools to measure and improve diversity (e.g., legal indicators, indicators to monitor the effectiveness of the diversity policy, follow-up of complaints); and establishment of an annual review of the implementation and follow-up of the diversity policy.

The audit took place in February 2012 with a report of which abstracts are summarized in Table 17.1. EMS management school became the first French institution in higher education to have obtained the diversity label

TABLE 17.1 Abstracts From the Diversity Audit Report

"EMS is a true living laboratory of diversity.
• EMS, through this approach, reinforces the value of diversity both for its staff but also for students. The scope of labeling takes into account all the activities of the MS: a unique and virtuous approach (from the upstream to the downstream).
• A strong investment is visible in terms of diversity (resources made available, communication, partnerships, BDD, etc.) and leads to positioning the School as a reference in this field.
• However, the culture of results should be strengthened in order to measure returns on this intangible investment, to reinforce the tools, to channel actions, to define objectives, and to reinforce internal communication."

issued by ISO and renewed in June 2016. Sabrina's mission was there deemed successful. But what about her research?

The Restitution of Research

This restitution of the research was initially made in a doctoral thesis. The research was comprehensive and aimed at interpreting observable phenomena during the implementation of the ISO diversity standards. The architecture of the research was transformative in nature and captured in a monograph (see Table 17.2). The planning of the research presented in Figure 17.1 reflects an IR process based on altering the phases of immersion and withdrawal and drawing upon the abductive principle.

The results of the research mainly consisted of presenting a model for developing diversity within a business school as well as its integration in the policy and strategy of the organization to obtain the ISO diversity certification. The results where obtained by following the Lewin's change

TABLE 17.2 The Architecture of the Research

• An innovative research object: The integration of diversity in the policy and the strategy of a French business school
• An iterative research process: Altering phases of immersion and withdrawal based on the principle of abduction
• A single case study: The monograph of a French business school during the implementation of a diversity label
• A qualitative study: An intervention-research project in line with the generic constructivism paradigm
• Transformative research: A project for creating actionable knowledge
• Coproduction of sensemaking with the actors: A comprehensive approach based on an ethnomethodologic process

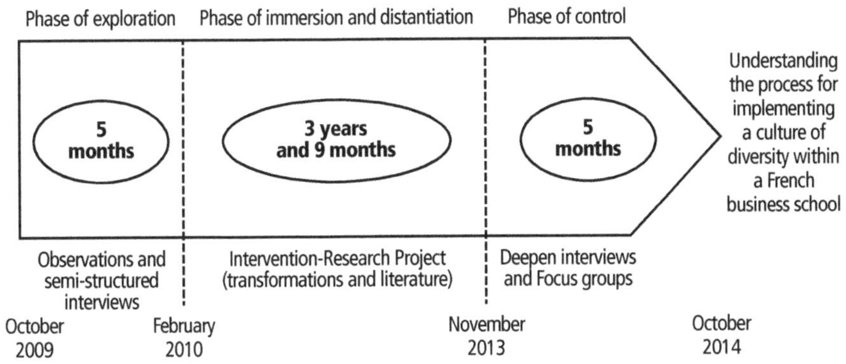

Figure 17.1 Planning the research project.

framework of unfreezing, changing, and refreezing (1948; see Figure 17.2) and Reynaud (1988, 1994, 1995) focused on social adaptation in the context of the studied business school (Figure 17.3).

In broad terms the research made a number of contributions to our understanding of organizational change. First, conceptualizing the challenge as a "project culture of diversity" allowed the development of social intelligence, proposing the transmission of "diversity capital." Second, the intervention enabled us to model the process of emergence of new behavioral rules during the introduction of a culture-project of diversity. Third, there was discovery of a positive link between diversity and three types of performance—in the human Resource function, at the organizational level, and broader social/societal performance. Fourth, we developed a fuller understanding of the behavior and role of the actors in the diversity aspect of a business school. Finally, the managerial implications go through the restoration of a process of organizational transformation around diversity.

	Phases of Lewin's model	Identification of the Change Dynamic
Phase 1	Unfreezing	The need for a new organizational culture integrating the management of diversity
Phase 2	Changing	The implementation of a diversity label (AFNOR–ISO)
Phase 3	Re-freezing	The integration of diversity within the policy and the strategy of the organization

Figure 17.2 Lewin's change framework.

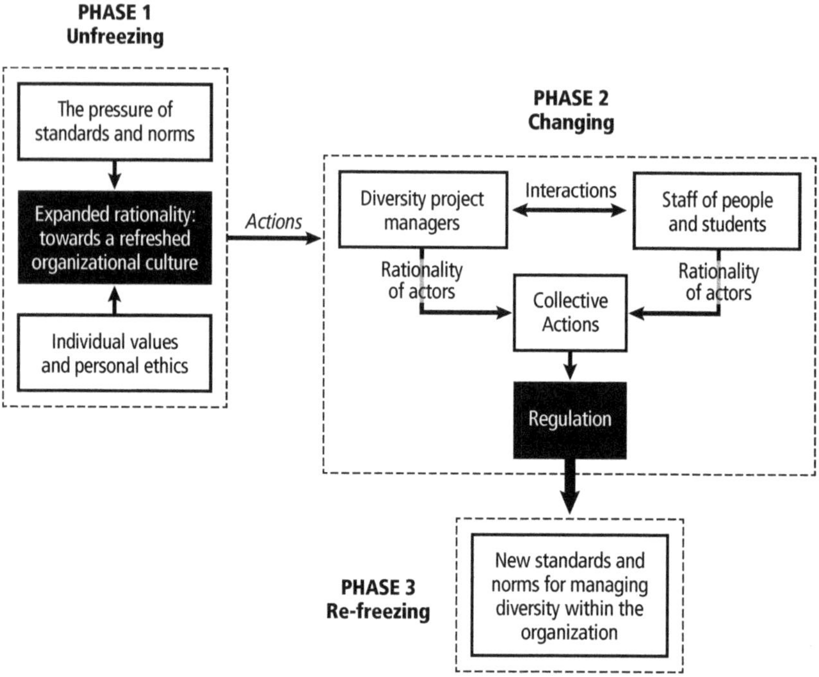

Figure 17.3 The theoretical framework of the research.

This research brought to light practices introduced in this strategic conversion to diversity.

Writing a Research-Based Publication

The first article published in an academic journal based on this research was based on a case study entitled "For the implementation of a management of diversity: How can a school be a school?" (Barth & Perugien, 2016). The article also explored broader generalizations, delving into questions about best practices and how that knowledge could be transferred to other organizations.

The plan of the article summarized in Table 17.2 illustrates the necessary "story-telling" of the intervention. A good intervention-research paper is above all a good storytelling of the intervention with an inversion of the process followed within the SOA (Scientific Observation Area) since the paper starts with the context and the state of the literature and then evolves towards the case study itself. Indeed, it is necessary to deconstruct

TABLE 17.2 Plan of the Article

1 The management of diversity a dynamic of change for organizations
1.1 Diversity: The Context of a Concept in Management Sciences
1.2 The construction of a diversity policy within an organization: the need for change
2 The question of diversity in higher education: the particular case of business schools
2.1 From the fight against social inequalities in the access to business school to the consideration of diversity
2.2 Diversity policies in the business schools sector: zoom on a new organizational behavior
2.3 Taking diversity into account in the major management schools: A strategy in line with core business?

the research process in order to follow a narrative logic responding to classical canons to enter into dialogue with the scientific community.

THE RADIANCE OF THE RESEARCH: THE EMERGENCE OF AN OMNI-CHANNEL RESEARCHER

Thanks to familiarity with companies and operational management, the intervener-researcher is able to transmit one's expertise and the knowledge acquired in an applied and popularized manner. In this respect, it is very much in line with the expectations of the professional world and, more recently, with those responsible for the assessment mechanisms of teacher-researchers and their institutions.

New Expectations

For a long time, management science sought its scientific legitimacy. Subjected to the criteria of the so-called "hard" sciences, management researchers adopted scientific criteria, emphasizing objectivity and the ability to generalize. Researchers in management, as before in economics, postponed their requirements on the method. To make the work "scientific," quantification and mathematical machinations became, in their eyes, unavoidable. We have therefore experienced decades of hypothetico-deductive research with modeling and statistical validation. What the Nobel prize-winning economist Maurice Allais (1998) has called the "blablabla mathematics." In the same movement, the level of publication became the indicator of the quality of the research, the "publish or perish" pressure and the race to become stars were the dominant model. This approach has often been denounced, but it remains the one that presides over the destinies of many scholars and their institutions. However, the reversals of this approach have gradually come to light: the sterilization of publications centered on methodology, their inability to cope with business problems, the inflation of publisher compensation and the cost to institutions to pass it on to increased tuition fees, the abandonment of pedagogy in this exclusive research, and the disaffection of companies for research in management.

All these negative effects have gradually begun to bring the institutions of teaching and research to change their strategies toward a greater balance between research and pedagogy and involvement in the institution. There is also increased attention to value the "impact" of this research on the larger society. So what are the new practices to meet these new expectations and why is IR a highly appropriate method to cope with these new challenges? A significant shift is to move from the notion of publication to that of "intellectual production," which includes: (a) written products (books, pedagogical cases, articles in professional journals); (b) oral productions such as videos, lectures, round tables, and participation in debates; (c) social network with blogs and presence in professional networks such as LinkedIn and posts on Twitter; and (d) commitment to boards of directors, creation of companies, and presence as an expert in law evaluation committees.

The Researcher-Extension

Measuring the impact of research and that of the researcher and the indicators to do that are still in the making. However, many institutions around the world have developed dashboards to do this. Examples include the number of interviews in the media, conferences participated in a year, online ticket readings, citations in the media, and organized events.

Present Your Work in 3 Minutes

Increasingly, researchers are learning to "pitch" their research in a matter of minutes. As an example, we have made a 3 1/2 minute video to convey the essential messages on the issue of discrimination for physical appearance in the work world. This research was conducted with 18 large companies over 18 months before expert hearings, working groups, interviews, and focus groups. Figure 17.4 captures the last picture of this video.

Conduct an Interview on a Publication

Companies are increasingly interested in short videos, allowing researchers to present the main results of their work. This is the case of Xerfi Canal in France—the Conversation website has specialized popular articles for which researchers are interviewed by journalists who are in charge of writing.

Figure 17.4 Capture of a video focused on the management of physical appearance.

Publish Tickets Online

Researchers can also learn how to write tickets that will be posted on blogs or social networks. These tickets can be based on the news and the angle of the sites. These are very short articles, which must be striking and catchy to solicit the attention of subscribers while the "noise" is intense and the offers are often "dizzy." It should be noted that journalists are often caught in these sources. We are then in the idea of constituting an "eco-system" media: the book carries the interview that refers to the networks that give rise to conferences—or the opposite. This is how the "personal brand" of the researcher is gradually built up, a notion that is growing in power and which is of particular interest to the scientific community.

CONCLUSION

Intervention research through the creation of actionable knowledge that it produces is particularly well adapted to the research "radiance" issue. Intervener-researchers have several advantages: a desire to produce actionable knowledge and an appetite to meet people and teach them to enter into conversation with the professional world. Indeed, to transmit, it is necessary to "upgrade" one's vocabulary, to accept to present the results before the process, to erase a certain number of references, to make the method invisible. This is just the opposite of the principles that drive a traditional scientific article.

We must also accept the need to be more assertive and to commit ourselves to produce work that has implications for manages, which means to forget the doubt that often drives the researcher. As a caution, these practices can expose the researcher to the gaze of one's peers, many of whom do not necessarily appreciate what can be called "media exposure."

The world is changing, and management research has a vested interest in enrolling "in society," with researchers committed to opening their fields, with research methods and ways of communicating that guide the resultant actionable knowledge to the practitioner world.

REFERENCES

Allais, M. (1998). Ce qui doit arriver arrive [What is about to come is coming]. *Le Monde*, Paris.

Barth, I., Perugien, S. (2016). Pour la mise en œuvre d'un management de la diversité: En quoi une école peut-elle faire école? [For the implementation of a management of diversity: How can a school be a school?]. *Revue internationale de psychosociologie et de gestion des comportements organisationnels, 54*(22), 304–324.

Lewin, K. (1948). *Resolving social conflicts.* New York, NY: Harper and Row.

Reynaud, J. D. (1988). *Les règles du jeu* [The rules of the game]. Paris, France: Armand Colin.

Reynaud, J. D. (1994). L'acteur stratégique et sa légitimité [The strategic actor and his legitimacy]. In F. Pavé (Ed.), *L'analyse stratégique: Sa genèse, ses applications et ses problèmes actuels* [Strategic analysis: Its genesis, its applications and its current problems]. *Autour de Michel Crozier.* Paris, France: Le Seuil.

Reynaud, J. D. (1995). *Le conflit, la négociation et la règle* [Conflict, negotiation and rule]. Toulouse, France: Octarès.

PART III

CONCLUDING REFLECTIONS ON INTERVENTION-RESEARCH

CHAPTER 18

RECURRENT PARTICIPANT QUESTIONS

Thoughts and Recommendations

Henri Savall and Laurent Cappelletti

As a way of concluding the volume, this final chapter will summarize and reflect on the questions asked by workshop participants—which are likely to be also raised by readers of the book—with responses by the trainers. The composition of the teacher-researchers taking part in the seminar—from Belgium, Madagascar, Morocco, Switzerland, the United States, and mostly France—give the program an international dimension, which reinforces the generic interest of the questions raised during the discussion. These questions and answers are intended to further supplement the reader's understanding of Parts I and II of the volume.

The questions are categorized into six themes that structure the chapter, with a focus on: (a) the epistemology of intervention-research; (b) methodologies, techniques, and tools of research-intervention; (c) the negotiation and sale of intervention-research; (d) publication and communication of intervention-research; (e) the framework for intervention-research work; and (f) general questions on intervention-research and evaluation.

Intervention Research, pages 247–266

THE EPISTEMOLOGY OF INTERVENTION-RESEARCH

The main epistemological questions posed by researchers wishing to carry out intervention-research for publication purposes can be summarized by the following verbatim questions:

- What is the difference between action-research and intervention-research, if there is one?
- Beyond the speeches that can be manipulative, being in action and taking a step back allows us to make quality observations. How [can we] combine the two?
- I was struck by the difficulty of understanding the actors' games because during field work [we] are not with them every day. How can we understand what is happening on the ground when we are not there?
- Is there a difference between research and intervention, which is also based on interviews?
- How can we avoid getting out of the field during research because this can happen in an intervention-research?
- Companies often work [from a] very positivist [position]. Introducing a more constructivist epistemology gives more possibilities and potential for innovation. How can you introduce such an epistemology in the field?

The responses to these questions can be summarized in the following synthetic development, which sheds light on the first two parts of the book, particularly Chapters 1 and 3.

Research-Intervention Assumes the "Non-Neutrality" of the Researcher

Macroeconomic instruments of observation may appear as being modest because "everything is more or less false" when examined through these lenses. The shift from macroeconomics to a sociology of labor, with an obsession about the quality of observations, is necessary to collect reliable data on organizations. In this vein, the socio-technical approach that comes from action-research is very important. Yet, researchers following this approach have often been disappointed because action-research still has the wish of researcher neutrality. In contrast to intervention-research, action-research is sometimes explicitly marked by this regret of neutrality. Intervention-research is based on the principle of *generic constructivism*, which assumes the "non-neutrality" of the researcher. Within this context, intervener-researchers undertake scientific work through iteration, multiplying their interviews, observations, and other forms of field data to stabilize knowledge. There may also be a sense of inferiority in action-research in terms of policy-makers in the field, as well as researchers in the hard sciences. In fact, action-researchers may even be a bit ashamed to be cast as researchers—they often remain in the middle of the watch, being quite shy about any transformations made.

Thus, action-research generally does not promise results on performance improvement. But in intervention-research, the intervener-researcher is clearly there to improve the managerial and organizational situation while being a researcher. It is a type of Aristotelian perspective: I think and I act, I do research and I help the company. There is a clear rejection of the decoupling between thought and action, with an obsession with transparency that characterizes intervention-research whose "black beast" is basically "organizational hypocrisy." In this spirit, roughly half of one's contribution as an intervener is being a methodologist, with another 30% as a mediator, and for 20% as a modest therapist. It is therefore necessary to take a closer look at action-research and intervention-research to make a difference, but in all cases the intervener-researcher is respectful of action-research, which has considerable merit in saying that it is necessary to shorten the distance between the research object and the researcher.

Obviously, intervention-research requires a minimum of longitudinal investigation. It is time-consuming, of course, but otherwise the collected data are more or less a scientific imposture. That is one of the basic reasons why we cannot undertake intervention-research without a schedule and rigorous time management. In the end, the result is not necessarily less productive than a laboratory econometric experiment, because the very rich and robust data collected provide a visible path to publication. In order to find a legitimate place for intervention-research, three key items are necessary: a research object, an intervention agreement, and an observation methodology based on the transformation of the object studied, allowing back and forth interaction between the field and the laboratory. It is this back and forth that makes the creation of knowledge possible. The interest of the intervention agreement is scientifically crucial beyond its financial interest by specifying what the researcher does in the organization, the days of intervention, and the protocol of intervention. This is where the work of the research team is important in managing the relationship with the field.

Intervention-Research Identifies Three Levels of Hypothesis: Descriptive, Explanatory, and Prescriptive

Some positivist researchers have attempted to monopolize the notion of hypotheses. This concept is nevertheless taken up in intervention-research and it becomes evolutionary with generic constructivism. The final hypothesis will be very different from the beginning of the research depending on the observations made. The notion of a hypothesis, which we prefer to that of a proposition which is sometimes advocated by constructivist researchers, is that it generates a power motive *if* we accept that it is evolutionary. The alternation between observation and distancing oneself from the field leads to the production of the themes and key ideas in which the observations (the expressions of the actors) are classified. The added value of scientific work in intervention-research, as in any form of research, is to move from a hope of rule to a scientific rule proved by the accumulation of convergent expressions. An idea will thus have two major statuses, either: (a) a hypothesis (one knows nothing about it at the start of an intervention-research or it is a hope of rule confirmed by some expressions); or (b) a proven rule of knowledge, supported by the accumulation of convergent expressions. That, essentially, is scientific progress. Thus, in an experimental approach such as intervention-research, the validation of hypotheses is not aesthetic and asks the question, "has there been a change?" Fortunately, there is the pressure of the result—transforming the organization towards a better state—in an intervention to get out of such rhetorical speculation, a pressure which can be guided by the management of time. And if there are two or three interveners to undertake the research, turning the intervention into research papers, it can be extremely productive.

An important key to intervention-research is that it identifies three levels of hypothesis. A *descriptive hypothesis* consists of describing a phenomenon observed with great modesty because another researcher could produce another description. An *explanatory hypothesis* consists of seeking explanations for the observed phenomenon. Finally, a *prescriptive hypothesis*, which is the highest level in this epistemology of generic constructivism, consists of formulating the recommendations that are reached after the description and explanation of a phenomenon. Thus, in intervention-research, a central hypothesis will be declined, framing it in descriptive, explanatory, and prescriptive terms. In the epistemological choices of intervention-research, there is therefore also a rejection of determinism, the approach is stochastic and heuristic. Each sequence is introduced with what has been learned from the prior sequences.

Authenticity Explains the Epistemological Importance of Transformation

The first reason for the epistemological importance of transformation in an intervention-research, or at least of the initial transformative intention, is to create knowledge and to move toward a better state of the organization and its members. It is in the back and forth interaction in the field that the creation of knowledge is made. Interaction with the field is unavoidable because the actor, similar to the research, carries knowledge, which explains the necessary cooperation between them. The validation of hypotheses leading to the knowledge will be done by experimentation (internal validation) and then replication (external validation). If we take the example of the intervention-researches carried out by the ISEOR laboratory since 1974, the creation of knowledge enabled the identification of 1,840 company pathologies. What can also be learned from these interventions is that these insights came out of an equal discussion between researcher and decision-maker actor. This requires great caution because what the ISEOR laboratory has learned about human actors after 110,000 interviews since 1974 is that they are intelligent, comedic, strategic, disobedient, and amnesic. This reality leads the researcher to ask himself the question of the meaning of the authenticity of the observations made—the expressions collected—behind all this: which research protocol should one use to capture authenticity (that is not sincerity)?

QUESTIONS AND ANSWERS ON METHODOLOGIES, TECHNIQUES, AND TOOLS OF INTERVENTION-RESEARCH

The main questions in terms of methodologies, techniques, and tools of intervention-research posed by researchers wishing to practice it for publication purposes can be summarized by the following questions raised during the seminars:

- What are the convergences/specificities between consulting and intervention-research?
- How do you do it when you're alone? Can it be done in one case?
- Are there any other changes than those planned in an intervention-research?
- I worked with chemist colleagues and when working with them I modified their tools. Is it intervention-research?
- Can there be external resources from the researcher during an intervention?

- What must we reveal to the field: whether we are a consultant or a researcher?
- Is it possible to refuse to do an intervention-research?
- What are the typical interview techniques of intervention-research?
- Does the intervener have to keep a field diary or logbook?
- How [should one] manage the link between literature and the field in an intervention-research?
- When building a group during an intervention, for example a project or steering group, is the operation of the company taken into account?
- Can we have interviews with actors who are not members of the organization studied in an intervention-research, such as clients?
- Can we use public data in intervention-research?

The methodological, technical, and tool responses to these questions can be summarized in the following synthetic developments, which are detailed in the first two parts of the book, in particular Chapters 2 and 4.

Intervention-Research Helps the Organization *and* Creates Knowledge

Intervention-research is longitudinal in order to observe deep changes that exceed several weeks. For example, one of our longest intervention began 31 years ago and continues today. The challenge of the researcher is then to master the tension in time between the change that benefits the company and the creation of scientific knowledge. The good news is that the intervener-research does help the company *and* create knowledge. Both are possible in the same chronology, but challenges typically come from a different conception of time between the company and the researcher. This is why the two basic tools of the intervener are the *post-it note* to constantly record remittances of the ground and the *agenda* to manage as closely as possible the programming of the devices that help the company and those that create knowledge. Indeed, the gases that are basically the ideas of the actors are explosive and accelerant if they are not converted into written notes and then reflected in actions programmed in the agenda. In this sense, intervention borrows from an ethno-methodological approach—while having an epistemology that is clearly distinct from it—the fact of considering that the actors possess knowledge which can be extracted by longitudinal observations. This knowledge takes three main aspects: (a) formal and informal; (b) visible and hidden, which does not mean that everything must be revealed; and (c) to say and to do, the deviation of which is a major cause of non-involvement.

The fables of Jean de Lafontaine and the characters of Prince of Machiavelli are therefore excellent readings to be made by the intervener to better navigate the complex world of organizations and to better deal with demands for change and improvement very varied. These range from very behavioral demands for improving the professionalism or the working environment to more structural demands, for example, the implementation of specific management tools such as dashboards, systems information, or reorganization of organizational charts.

Ideally, an Intervener-Researcher Should Never Work Alone

The starting point of an intervention is to find other people to talk to because it is the ferment of the creation of generic knowledge. This point is particularly crucial for students working on their theses that draw on intervention-research. For researchers alone in their field of scientific observation, it is imperative to make regular appointments with the thesis supervisor and have frequent presentations of his observations to research teams. In addition to such dialogue, in order to produce scientific knowledge, traceability is also required—to explain and describe the protocols implemented in a tireless and precise manner (transparency).

In all cases, the intervener must remain the sole interlocutor of his field during the research, focusing on the problematic that was asked to him. As a Spanish proverb notes, "A good doctor heals, with two doubt establishes, and with three death is assured." The technical key to good intervention is therefore its unique steering, which does not mean that the intervener who is in charge must isolate himself. The isolation of the intervener-researcher weakens him, while team work contributes to a better creation of knowledge. This is also why it is important for interveners to vary their interviewing techniques to interact, if possible, with a large number of actors in the organization being treated. For example, during an intervention in a large company located in Paris, we wanted to see the four people in the archives. In this sense, the intervention-research was part of a citizen's conception of science. There are different rationalities to be observed because the actors have knowledge, whatever their position in the company. But this conception of science implies that the intervener-researcher is conscious of the blows one is about to take—much more than if one were doing contemplative or laboratory research—and responds to the criteria of robustness of the method. In a way, "good" intervener-researchers are socially legitimate fighters. If higher education and research are to propagate scientific innovations, then they are necessarily disturbing as well.

Nevertheless, interviews with actors are not the only sources of information gathering by the intervener-researcher. One mobilizes intervention methods with expressed and observed and thus formalizes and notes of interviews and observations. This practice is called integrated observation, which combines interviews, observations, and analysis of documents. Interviews are mainly used upstream in a research-intervention to identify the dysfunctions that disrupt the organization and the attainment of its preferable state, and downstream to evaluate the result of the solutions implemented to treat these dysfunctions. Of course, for dysfunctional interviews, there is a semi-directive guide to be conducted with different themes and sub-themes that will be used to classify the expressions and which, according to the methodology of the ISEOR laboratory, requires an hour of individual interview with the members of management and 1 1/2 hours of collective discussion with staff gathered by groups of three to five actors. In both cases, at the beginning of the interview, we must reassure the anonymity of the expressions that will be noted and their systematic restitution in a specific group session of mirror effect during which the note taking will continue.

As a general rule, the interviews carried out during an intervention are exclusively with the members of the organization being treated, even if their objective is to identify what in its relation with the external environment deserves to be transformed to improve performance. For example, to identify the quality of the relationship with clients or suppliers of an organization, the intervener will not conduct interviews with clients or suppliers, but with the members of that organization on their own evaluation of this relationship. This focus is due to the fact that the members of an organization are the first bearers of traces of the external environment and they are the ones who will have to implement the actions of transformation of this relationship. As an exception, the researcher may agree to carry out specific surveys with stakeholders in the organization under review if he or she is competent with the technique. In this case, if requested by the organization, it is recommended that the investigative work be carried out by itself even if it involves external consultancy. The results obtained, as they are perceived and accepted by the organization studied, can then be more usefully used by the intervener in project group sessions with the members of the organization concerned.

Research-Intervention Is Scientific Consultancy

On the surface, the distinction between the intervener-researcher and consultant may seem rather vague. It is, moreover, absolutely not embarrassing to be perceived by the field of scientific observation as an intervener rather than as a researcher, or even, ideally, to be perceived as an agent of change in an environment that is initially enigmatic. Indeed, each field can be thought of as an enigma and that is what is stimulating. Intervention is basically an intrusion process that will simultaneously create complicities and enemies, and it is exciting to manage this dialectic. For example, during one of the last interventions we made in Africa, the CEO wanted a 3-day training course on team building to strengthen the cohesion of his management team. We discovered on the second day of the training-action that the CEO was opposed to his deputy director. We would never have discovered this critical factor without performing on the ground. A few months after this first intervention, the CEO of the same company asked us to train his intermediate management on the same subject in return for financial remuneration—which was good sign. Were these two interventions just intra-firm trainings or was it research? Or both? We helped the company change to more managerial progress *and* we also had a knowledge project in which we mobilized these interventions to produce publications on leadership in the African context.

Within this context, the intervener plows more of his field of scientific observation than a consultant or an auditor because to transform in depth he will try to go on points of innovation. And to retain the scientific intention of his approach, pretty more than a non-researcher consultant, he will have to explicitly and rigorously draw on his methods and the data collected, for example, through a logbook, which is therefore unavoidable. To capture phenomena that are not on any document of the organization and that the actors tell you, one must take notes. This is impossible because the intervener tries to detect subtle phenomena, which are often hidden. Even though exhaustive note-taking requires training, it is far better than to record without re-transcription, which forces the researcher to spend considerable time listening to the recordings for transcription. Moreover, as the intervener-researcher touches on performance, which is a highly sensitive subject, there is a risk in an intervention when it is not the question of the ethnologist or the sociologist. We are not therefore in favor of recordings for intervention-research, although they can be used without harm in sociology or ethnology.

QUESTIONS AND ANSWERS ON THE NEGOTIATION AND SALE OF RESEARCH-INTERVENTION

The negotiation and sales questions posed by researchers wishing to carry out intervention-research for publication purposes can be summarized by the following verbatim queries:

- How [should one] define the price of an intervention-research and how [should it be] presented to a client company?
- What are the rules to set up time-limits for the payment of an intervention with a client?
- Does the existence of a financial transaction between the researcher and his research object bias the results of the research?
- Can we do free intervention-research without charging the organization studied? Does [such] free search result in biased results?
- How do we find companies that are potentially interested in buying an intervention-research process?

The answers to these questions in terms of negotiation and sale can be summarized in the following synthetic developments, which are detailed in the first two parts of the book, in particular Chapters 5 and 6.

The Financial Counterpart of an Intervention Secures Its Scientific Quality if One Does Not Become Dependent on the Field

In a process of negotiating and selling intervention-research, it is necessary to underline the complex role of introducers, that is to say the person or persons who have introduced the researcher to the field and who have a positive role in the conclusion of the sale. For example, a human resources manager who introduced an intervener to his CEO to encourage him to buy an intervention. The difficulty is to be loyal to the introducer—not excluding him during the intervention once it is sold but at the same time not being dependent on him. Otherwise, the position is not tenable. To do this, it is necessary to understand the logics of the actors' actions: why did an introducer help a researcher to intervene in his company? Why did a decision-maker pay for the intervention? Beyond any formal demands, are there underlying meta-goals that should not be sought to be revealed to him but which must be realized in the intervention?

What is important is getting your client's respect, remaining a master of the methods, services, architecture, and research planning negotiated in the intervention agreement. On the other hand, financially, being scrupulous on the payment by the client of the research according to the agreed negotiated schedule. It is for this reason that you always ask for a deposit from the client before starting an intervention-research. And as long as this down payment has not been settled, the intervention does not start. Indeed, late payment is a serious indicator of a failure in the quality of the scientific relationship. In any intervention that involves a stakeholder with a company, there is in fact a hidden payment (which is qualitatively related to the researcher's work: notoriety, quality scientific materials, etc.) and a visible payment (the conventional price of the sold intervention-research). Of course, there is also a hidden payment for intervention, for instance, even in the absence of financial remuneration the researcher must qualitatively gain something in return for the transformation into a better state. Nevertheless, we advise against the systematization of apparent free research and intervention, that is to say carried out without financial remuneration of the researcher. This must remain an exception. Indeed, the apparent gratuity may have a detrimental effect on the authenticity of the data of the researcher because a question arises then on the level of commitment of the researchers in their intervention and that of the observed actors. Respect for the researcher's field of observation is necessarily greatly diminished when the researcher brings added value to the client company free of charge. The central idea of the sale of intervention-research is therefore to have a visible form of financial counterpart to guarantee the commitment of the researcher and that of the actors under study and, consequently, a good level of authenticity and robustness of coproduced knowledge.

To avoid becoming dependent on the field, the intervener must be ready to break an intervention if one loses the respect of the client. There are three main causes that can lead a intervener-researcher to threaten to stop, or even break, an intervention. The first is deontological, when the client adopts behavior that is too disrespectful of the agreement, in particular its financial elements or is excessively discourteous with the researcher. The second is when the diagnosis could not be made without sufficient construction of the company's stakeholders because the absence of a relevant diagnosis too seriously obfuscates the quality of the observations made. The third is the absence of the leader at the times agreed in the convention: steering committees, presentation of the diagnosis, project groups, etc. Indeed, the absence of the CEO degrades very strongly the commitment of the actors in the intervention-research. These causes of breakdown of an intervention must be well explained to the client during the negotiation phase of the research. If the client does not accept them, they become causes of breakdown of the negotiation itself. Once the intervention has been sold and started, the intervener must therefore monitor "as milk on fire" the indicators of these causes of intervention breakdown. Mainly by permanently cultivating proximity, complicity, and warmth with the leader of the company observed through his ascendancy, that is, by being useful to him through his methods to achieve his objectives and bring tangible added value.

In the Negotiation of an Intervention-Research One Must Distinguish Its Qualitative Sale From the Sale of Its Price

For the sake of efficiency as well as scientific reasons, there is no reason not to be paid for a research activity that leads to improvements for the company, not only to finance it but also to make it attractive. Therefore, the intervener should define his intervention rates in order to draw up estimates and propose an intervention price to his clients. It is up to the intervener to define the intervention rate. This tariff will depend on the researcher's margin objectives, market prices, and the company's ability to contribute.

Nevertheless, the sale of the price of an intervention is the last step in its negotiation process. To arrive at this financial stage, the intervener must have successfully sold the qualitative intervention-research, that is to say the accreditation by the client of the methods, services, architecture, and planning proposed to answer the client's goals. As long as there is no agreement with the client on these qualitative elements, the intervener must not talk about money with the client, repelling any questions on the subject. In a way, there is a ritual of negotiation to be respected by the intervener, who first sells methods and services in response to a request. This is the key to negotiation. Once the methods and services are well understood, accepted and desired by the customer, the sale of their price may even become a formality, provided that the intervention rates are not far-fetched. This is why the methods and services sold are the central elements of the intervention agreement that will become the managerial and scientific means that the researcher is committed to bring to the company.

The Sale of an Intervention-Research Is a Process

The rite of the negotiation of an intervention combines a technical dimension with tools and devices specific to a psychological dimension of seduction of the client. In order for a decision-maker to buy an intervention, the client needs to understand the methods and benefits, so the researcher must find the means—without denying one's ethics—to "seduce" the client in this regard. This process of seduction can be punctuated by moments of confrontation that should not be feared, because at the beginning of this process, the researcher will have allies (members of the company who want the intervention and encourage the leader to buy it) and enemies (members of the company who do not want intervention, pushing the manager not to buy). There is therefore necessarily a dialectic of confrontation and seduction in a negotiation of intervention between the researcher and the client to establish contact and then to keep it.

One of the questions often asked by junior intervener-researchers is can one attract companies, if only to initiate a negotiation process. The answer requires the intervener to define a commercial strategy: what should one do to attract requests for improvement from companies and organizations? And to attract such requests, one cannot rely solely on publications in academic journals—largely because they are not read by practitioners. There are no universal rules for the development of a commercial strategy. It is up to the intervener-researcher to define it according to one's ethics, scientific and financial objectives, time management constraints, organization of his laboratory, and so forth. Examples of possible commercial actions to attract requests for assistance include publications in professional or general journals, participation in round tables and seminars open to managers, realization of an attractive website for professionals, well referenced, intelligent use of social networks, writing reference manuals co-written with practitioners. The general tone to be adopted in these commercial and communication actions is to avoid any arrogance—leaders are often horrified by the superiority sometimes felt by certain academics—as much as any complexity of inferiority towards the professional world because the leaders only purchase an intervention if they are convinced of its discriminating added value. For the intervener, this presupposes the need to communicate the elements that make him seem ascendant while remaining humble and listening.

QUESTIONS AND ANSWERS ON THE PUBLICATION AND COMMUNICATION OF INTERVENTION-RESEARCH

The publication and communication questions posed by workshop participants wishing to carry out intervention-research for publication purposes are summarized by the following verbatim inquiries:

- How [should one] structure a research paper based on intervention-research so that it is accepted in an academic journal?
- How [should one] deal with criticisms by the evaluators [paper reviewers]?
- The link between the object of an intervention and the existing literature on this object is often complicated. How [should one] proceed?
- Should academic publications that draw upon intervention-research be systematicaly sent to the company (observation ground) that have been mobilized during the intervention? What worries me is

how long it takes to write an article. How long does it take to manage all this?

- Is there a risk of perverting [one's] thinking by sending a paper to an academic journal that obliges one to respect the guidelines (codes) of the journal? How should someone raise the contradiction—if it happens—between one's thinking and the guidelines of a targeted journal?

The answers to these questions can be summarized in the following synthetic developments, which are described in detail in the second part of the book.

To Publish in a Research Journal It Is Necessary to Distinguish the Scientist From the Academic

Publication is not just about research. At the end of an intervention, it is also necessary to "sell" the scientist. At the end of a publication, what sells the academic is essentially the rigorous "scientific" knowledge that coated in the academic codes of the targeted journal, from its favorite reference literature and generic structuring of articles, to its "prohibited" and favored methods of research, to the journal's preferred paradigms, editorial line, fetish subjects, epistemological postures of predilection, and so forth. So to be published in a journal, one must first choose one's review target and decrypt its academic codes to judge the feasibility of doing so—for it is be necessary to comply.

So publication per se is not research that is a process of generating knowledge. It is a "freeze" that takes the form of a product, which one has to learn to do without hesitation, knowledge continuing otherwise. This is why it is necessary to distinguish the academic who obeys canons and the balance of power and the scientist, who is convicted by scientific work. A publication can thus be thought of as a compromise between a research project and the objects it investigates that may be of interest to a journal. For example, in the FNEGE barometer on topics of interest to companies, the first theme that emerges is the relationship with customers—but this focus may not be viewed similarly by a number of academic journals. There are thus two universes to be distinguished: that of the "real problems," which are those of companies and organizations and that of the "other problems," which are those of the academic journals. To be published in a review, one must imperatively play his academic score, notwithstanding the scientific aspects of the submission. It is very difficult, for example, to publish an intervention-research paper in a journal whose academic DNA is opposed to such transformative research.

Drawing on a single intervention, there is a range of possible academic productions on the different objects that were observed. Once the target of the journal has been chosen, it is necessary to explain in detail the protocol of the intervention-research—the details of the field are critical to fully elaborating the methodology (presentation of the case, protocols implemented, verbatim quotes, analysis of results, etc.) for reviewers. If, in addition, the literature relating to the object of the research is properly exploited, there are no insurmountable problems to be published. In this case, the evaluators' criticisms will focus on details (e.g., integration of additional references, improvement of the explanation and justification of the research protocol), which will not be so difficult to deal with although it may take time to do so. On well-targeted open journals (being careful to avoid predatory publishers; see Chapter 9), there is less difficulty in getting published because the scientific nature of intervention-research will not typically be called into question.

Within the ISEOR laboratory, we have worked with companies of 30,000 people to small enterprises with less than 10 people. We have often found the same problems, but with very different ways to solve them. As a researcher, if we were more in the business, we would better target the literature by making better use of it. Mobilizing the relevant literature on the basis of theoretical knowledge of the company is indeed very difficult and can often lead to only using what might be thought of as the fashionable literature. Segmentation is a good way to solve the issue of literature to be mobilized for a publication, by identifying the central focus of the research problem and related keywords—then searching for the appropriate literature that pertains to the intervention in libraries or on digital bases of open archives. Closer proximities with some authors, deviations with others in the course of a solid and attractive scientific discussion, will be strongly appreciated by editors and reviewers.

A Publication Must Be Managed as a Project

Intervention-research requires a lot of time and energy and publications require deadlines. It is therefore imperative to program writing times in one's diary. As an indication, as soon as an intervention is exploitable, a publication on one of the aspects that has been observed (with a great advantage that a single intervention often produces several observations, which can maximize the number of possible publications) can easily require between 40 and 80 hours of work. The correction of reports usually require the same time frame according to their content. In summary, it takes about a month full of work to complete a paper centered on an object observed through an intervention-research. To further complicate matters, on average for a publication in a well-ranked journal, it will can take roughly 2 to 3 years between the first submission and the paper is published (if accepted). An advantage of intervention-research in terms of academic productivity, however, is that one does not have to wait until the end of the process to complete a publication. Publications are possible at the different stages of the intervention project and can be programmed on the ground.

For team-based research and intervention, team discipline can be a challenge that must be dealt with in order to avoid an anarchy in the publications of team members, each of whom may be tempted to publish in his own corner to the dismay of the others. There is then an absolute necessity to establish an agreement, in essence an ethics of publishing, before the start of the research, defining in particular the modes of relationship with the company and who will be writing what, when, were, and how.

Once a submission has been made and evaluated, it is necessary to realize that even if requested revisions can irritating, the reviewers are "always right." The main issue is then a question of pertinent correction(s) following revision—how should one overcome any aversion to negative reports? It can be a real struggle that must be carried out against oneself to say that the reviewer is right. If an author resents or resists reviewer remarks, the subsequent process rarely goes well. Once the corrections have been made following the exhaustive processing of the evaluation reports, they should be explained in a separate document in order to show that all the remarks of the reviewers have been taken into account. As an example, an article we published in *Organizational Research Methods* (Savall, Zardet, Bonnet, & Péron, 2008) went through four cycles of revisions and revised more than 80% between its first version and the one that was finally published. It is an act of respect for the reviewers and the journal to show the revisions that one has made.

An intervention-research can produce several hundred themes. In this multitude of themes, a challenge is how to choose the good ones which to publish so as not to literally get lost in the data. One should focus on the theme that is most supported by the data as well as the having the most originality—even possibly taking an opposite position from the dominant literature on the subject. Another point that should be considered is that the dominant academic ideology considers that a given theme corresponds to an investigative methodology, so one must be careful when designing the intervention. It is necessary to explain rigorously how the problem emerged from the field and why one methodology of investigation was chosen rather than another. Obviously analyzing abundant quotations with a qualitative processing software can produce quantitative results. But a reality of the publishing process suggests that the journals that are open to intervention-research are also fond of qualitative presentations of verbatim quotes. In order to quantify the qualitative, it seems wiser to maximize the results of an intervention by quantitative means (e.g., surveys, econometrics), either downstream and/or upstream, subject to defining the themes being treated.

Publication From Intervention-Research Is Not Limited to Articles in Academic Journals

Publishing in academic journals does not prevent one from using different modes of expression, for example, through a book or book chapter. There is also pedagogical publication such as case studies, which is in line with the intellectual contributions requested by accrediting bodies. There are also publishing opportunities in professional or generalist magazines as well as social networks, where an intervener-researcher can write a blog inspired by their research, for example on the *Huffington Post* or *The Conversation*. It is much shorter of course than a classic publication and one must learn to quickly clarify one's thought. Alternatively, longer videos through MOOCs or shorter ones posted on YouTube, Twitter, Facebook, or LinkedIn can be useful to broaden one's audience.

QUESTIONS AND ANSWERS ON THE FRAMEWORK FOR INTERVENTION-RESEARCH WORK

The questions concerning the supervision of work by researchers wishing to carry out intervention-research for publication purposes are captured in the following questions:

- How can we create a framework based on intervention-research, both theoretically and methodologically?
- Can we intervene in the field with the student whose work is supervised? How should one manage the relationship in the laboratory and the field?

The answers to these questions are summarized in the following synthetic developments, which are detailed in the first two parts of the book, in particular Chapters 7 and 8.

From a legal point of view, there are no rules concerning the management of appointments between the director of a scientific work and the student. There is, however, a moral and efficiency contract between the two, one that obliges a regularity of meetings. For a Doctorate in Business Administration (DBA) thesis or PhD, regularity is typically a monthly meeting between the director and student to ensure that the field work, with its many phases and dimensions, is on track. In these appointments, an underlying challenge is that the supervisor must be vigilant not to confuse the field with the object of research, helping the doctoral student take a step back (a "safe" distance) from one's observations. The capacity for reflexivity is an enormous advantage here in that it helps to reduce the risk of getting bogged down in the field of observation. The challenge of intervention-research is indeed not to tell everything, but to find a focus, a specific object. The research director is there to clarify the choice of the relevant focus and then help classify the raw data extracted from the field into relevant boxes and position them theoretically.

The research director should also be aware that the intervention is relevant only when it is transformative (or has transformative intent) and alert the supervised student on possible field attempts that resist transformation. Our advice is that the director of research should not intervene directly on the ground; instead the supervisor should provide the tools and the methods for his or her doctoral student to better negotiate in the field. Let us not forget that two thirds of young researchers do not remain at the end of their thesis in their field of observation because they have changed themselves, and that, the ground being systemic, the insights extracted from the ground for a publication should be spread to the other elements of the system.

Another concern is that research itself tends to have a longer-term horizon, while the corporate strategist operates generally on a shorter time span. In the case of an intervention-research methodology, contracting with doctoral students can be problematic because it is a challenge to supervise a thesis for 3 years. All this should lead doctoral candidates to sufficient spend time with the research manager, attempting to fully understand his or her objectives, field of influence, and sources of funding during the research, before moving forward with a project.

In our opinion, a supervisor should not impose a problematic on a candidate because, especially in the case of intervention-research, it will necessarily depend on the phenomena observed on the ground. The aim is to help the supervised student bring out pertinent issues that are of interest to the supervisor and then to accompany the student on a scientific level. It is thus important to establish clear milestones and deadlines with doctoral students to avoid a significant loss of time in the project. If carried out in this manner, there should not be any gap between the director's plans and those of the student who must be negotiated upstream. That's why, as a research director, we suggest to negotiate with the students about the risks and the issues, and then to give them 3 months to reflect.

EVALUATION OF THE SEMINAR: "FROM INTERVENTION-RESEARCH TO PUBLICATION"

As a way of concluding the volume and reflecting on the workshop series that inspired it, the following is a verbatim synthesis of the evaluations by the trainees in FNEGE's seminar. These evaluations will allow the reader to better understand the expectations of a researcher attracted by intervention-research and the elements to be emphasized in order to consolidate their motivation towards this form of research.

- I have better understood the difference between intervention-research and contemplative research. I have enough to read for several months on the question.
- Personally, I am reassured because I am not next to the plate in terms of intervention-research.
- What surprised me was the possible link between intervention-research with anthropology and sociology. I can only be delighted.
- I want to continue in this logic of intervention because the consideration of the human [factor] and the [potential] return to the company contributes to a more citizen science.
- I greatly appreciated the advice given to convert an intervention into academic publication on disciplines as varied as marketing, human resources management, accounting, and strategy.
- The seminar allowed me to validate that attitudes are changing towards more openness to transformative research that helps companies to evolve into a preferable state... [it] is rather reassuring.
- I appreciated the methodological observations on how to carry out intervention-research because often the books devoted to the question are more conceptual and epistemological than instrumental.
- I have to submit my thesis based on intervention-research in a few weeks and the seminar allowed me to better understand what I have done and to take a step back which will be useful for the defense.
- The seminar made me want to write from my field materials. On the other hand, the financial aspect of an intervention [left me with] questions... because I was not used to selling my research.
- The seminar was very interesting in that it set the framework for a research-based publication, whether it be a thesis, a book, or an academic article.
- I was very pleased to see that there was a community of intervener-researchers so that we are not isolated and that we can have scientific legitimacy with intervention-research.

- I have a much better understanding of intervention-research. It will help me publish because the seminar will prevent me from making mistakes.
- I drew on the seminar, the different perspectives it proposed on intervention-research and the publication strategies that it explained.
- The seminar showed that intervention-research and qualitative research are not declining. The contracting aspect of intervention is a very interesting aspect that I hope to be able to apply.
- The seminar gave me a lot of insight into my position as a consultant versus that of a researcher and how to move from single consultancy to science.

On behalf of the team of intervener-researchers that have taken part in the seminar, we hope that the reflections on participant questions summarized in this concluding chapter will further help clarify the nuances and subtleties associated with conceptualizing, implementing, and publishing intervention-research.

REFERENCES

Savall, H., Zardet, V., Bonnet, M., & Péron, M. (2008). The emergence of implicit criteria actually used by reviewers of qualitative research articles: Case of a European journal. *Organizational Research Methods, 11*(3), 510–540.

GLOSSARY

Academism: Confined conception of the scholar and research activity, which favors the almost exclusive study of texts as a basis of knowledge rather than the observation of real situations. This distortion of academic activity leads to conceptual and theoretical sclerosis, particularly in human and social sciences, as well as to ideological hypertrophy and so-called theoretical models that are not validated by experimentation. The risks of academicism are elitism, corporatism, and the rejection or delay of innovations (see Chapters 1, 3, 9).

Action-research: See Chapter 1.

Artificial Intelligence: A set of theories and techniques in cognitive science that proposes three interesting concepts for intervention-research: the *knowledge base* consisting of a *base of facts* and *a rule base.* Indeed, knowledge consists, most often, in establishing a link between different elements constituting the material or intangible object studied by the researcher or mentioned by the actors. The simple statement "if A then B" is useful for representing a structure of scientific knowledge (see Chapter 1).

Authenticity: The epistemological importance of transformation in an intervention-research is explained by its purpose of creating knowledge and moving towards a preferable state of the organization. The validation of the hypotheses leading to the knowledge will be done by experimentation (internal validation) then replication (external validation). This leads the intervener-researcher to ask himself the question of the meaning and authenticity of the obser-

Intervention Research, pages 267–272

vations made: "What research protocol should be used to grasp the authenticity of the phenomena observed?" then becomes the central question of the intervener-researcher and no longer that of the impossible objectivity or neutrality of the researcher (see Chapters 1, 3, 8, 18).

Central hypothesis: Hypothesis that sets out the essential of the demonstration that the researcher wishes to make and which will be declined in an intervention-research into a tree of detailed hypotheses or sub-hypotheses, descriptive, explanatory and prescriptive (see Chapters 1, 18).

Cognitive interactivity: One of the three key epistemological principles of intervention-research that refers to the fact that the construction of collective knowledge results from a process of interaction between two or more actors, each carrying a fragment of knowledge contributes, thanks to successive iterations, to build a knowledge shared by the actors of a team or an organization. This justifies the need for a structured partnership between the researcher and the field of scientific observation (see Chapters 1, 2, 5, 18).

Content Analysis: The abundance of information collected by the researcher that allows intervention-research has led to the enrichment and refinement of the content analysis method. It consists, based on qualitative information, verbatim or key ideas expressed by actors or discovered in documents, to induce key ideas of synthesis then ideas-forces more and more generic and to classify them in a nomenclature developed by the researcher. In a second step, key numbers collected or developed by the researcher will be associated with generic key ideas, in a qualimetric perspective allowing a satisfactory representation of the studied object (see Chapters 1, 4, 7, 8).

Contradictory intersubjectivity: One of the three key epistemological principles of intervention-research refers to the interactive process that allows two or more actors, from different subjective viewpoints, to construct through exchanges and iterations over time an acceptable common representation. Given the impossibility of objectivity, especially in the human and social sciences, this conventional representation, if not "objective," allows the construction of a knowledge platform of scientific intent, usable in a given space of actors and for a given certain times (see Chapters 1, 2, 5, 18).

Decider-payer: Leader of a company or organization who decides to open the door to the intervener-researcher and allocate economic resources to intervention-research, in kind (time spent by the actors of the organization) or in funding for the intervener-researcher or his team (fees, travel, living expenses; see Chapters 1, 2, 5).

Descriptive hypothesis: Hypothesis that makes sense in an intervention-research and shows the modesty of the researcher in the description of an object, because another researcher could provide a significantly different description (see Chapter 1).

Enterprise client: According to the intervention-research concept, the research partner company or organization is not just a field of scientific observation that welcomes the intervener-researcher. It has expectations vis-à-vis the intervener-researcher and coproduces the intervention-research process by making available actors of the company. It expects from this intangible investment a result in terms of direct or indirect contribution to the resolution of its specific problems and, in so doing, to the improvement of its performance.

Ethnomethodology: See Chapter 3

Explanatory Hypothesis: An assumption of explaining and interpreting phenomena, which is particularly appreciated in the research community and has developed in the history of science (see Chapter 1).

Field of scientific observation (FSO): The organizations observed during an intervention-research form fields of scientific observation. The quality of the relationship between the researcher and the actors in the field of scientific observation is a key factor in the quality of research. The generation of knowledge of scientific intent results from a back and forth between the field of scientific observation and the laboratory of the researcher, an alternation between the sequences of observation in situ, and distance from the field which allows a reflection phase with a certain distance. This process involves a periodic return of the researcher within the organization, in order to organize successive iterations that progressively improve the quality of the information that he collects as well as the knowledge base that he builds up (see Chapters 1, 2, 3, 5, 9, 18).

Generic Contingency: One of the three key epistemological principles of intervention-research which refers to the fact that any situation is contingent but that a thorough analysis reveals a generic component found in other situations, as well as the same atom in a wide variety of different molecules (see Chapters 1, 2, 5, 18).

Hidden costs and performances: The observer, researcher or actor, perceives certain *visible* elements and does not perceive others, which are hidden. As research is a process of discovery of new knowledge, the exploration, identification and use of these hidden costs and performances, most often ignored by the literature of economics and management, are crucial research issues (see Chapters 1, 2, 18).

Hypothesis: A key idea developed by the researcher may have two statuses, depending on the status of the intervention-research. It can, first, constitute a hypothesis that is a tool of motor skills in the process of scientific work, a statement to demonstrate that pulls the dynamics of research. When the demonstration is complete, the key idea acquires a status of result, a scientific statement corresponding to one of the research's production objectives. An important key to intervention-research is to determine three levels of different, complementary and successive hypotheses: descriptive, explanatory and prescriptive (see Chapters 1, 8, 18).

Intervention-research: A research methodology that, implemented cumulatively and in a team, allows the creation of unpublished databases, thanks to the interaction of the researcher with the actors of the organizations during a process of knowledge coproduction. Intervention-research implies a certain longitudinal dimension, necessary for the application of the three principles that underlie its epistemological quality: cognitive interactivity, contradictory intersubjectivity and generic contingency. The transformative dimension of intervention-research involves modifying the state of the object under study to better reveal its characteristics and properties, to describe and interpret them. The analysis of the variations of this state makes it possible to extract the in-depth generic knowledge of certain properties of the studied object (see Chapters 1, 2, 3, 4, 5, 6, 7, 8, 9, 18).

Introducer: A person who puts the intervener-researcher in contact with the researched company or organization. He can be internal or external to this organization. The introducer is an important figure at the beginning of the negotiation phase of intervention-research. Nonetheless experience shows that it is desirable that he be erased later on, in order to avoid sometimes negative interference with the decision-payer (see Chapters 1, 2, 5, 6).

Managerial and societal impacts of research: See Chapters 3, 4, 7, 8, 9.

OMSP (objective-method-service-product) tool: The material form used to formalize the specifications contract of the intervention-research is that of a triptych which synthesizes the production of the researcher: products-objectives/products-methods/products services. The content of each intervention-research is therefore adapted to each concrete situation, but it always includes elements that are scientifically "non-negotiable" that should be clearly explained and justified to future partners in the intervention-research (see Chapters 2, 5, 6).

Prescriptive Hypothesis: This hypothesis is the highest level in the epistemology of intervention-research and includes recommendations that lead to scientific work. According to some academic researchers, particularly in the humanities and social sciences, this type of hypothesis, paradoxically, would not be part of scientific research. However, the prescriptive hypothesis paves the way for the process of validating knowledge of scientific intent (see Chapter 1).

Qualimetric intervention-research: Qualimetric intervention-research methodology that systematically uses the qualimetric representation to formulate the information collected as well as the results obtained by the investigation process. The qualimetric approach, as adopted by the socioeconomic intervention-research, offers a very rich range of qualitative, quantitative and financial elements which allows to better represent the observed complex and intangible objects as well as the theoretical statements produced by the research (see Chapters 1, 2, 18).

Research: See Chapters 1, 2, 3, 9.

Intervention-research contract: Specifications that determine the conditions for collaboration and the presence of the researcher within the organization. It may be either for a fee and produce remuneration for the researcher and/or his laboratory, or more exceptionally free of charge. The contract results from a respectful, peer-to-peer discussion between the researcher and the organization's leader. The relationship between the field of scientific observation and the researcher is in a framework of transparency. His presence on the field of scientific observation is neither clandestine nor erased because it has been duly contracted (see Chapters 1, 2, 5, 6, 18).

Social networks: See Chapter 17

Socioeconomic theory of organizations: Theory developed by Henri Savall and his ISEOR team who relied, particularly on the socio-technical approach, striving to complete and deepen the critical reconstructive approach of the organization of work and proposing new concepts and management models integrating social variables and economic variables of organizations. The construction of the socioeconomic theory, by means of a longitudinal scientific program of cumulative research, implied a large number of successive experiments, made possible by the qualitative method of intervention-research and a certain methodological stability (see Chapters 1, 2).

Socio-technical school: School of research which, since the Second World War, has developed a methodological approach, action-research whose object of study was the transformation of work situations. The experiments and publications were conducted using an open systems approach and mainly fed by the work of the Tavistock Institute in London as well as numerous experiments in the Scandinavian countries. The ontological dimension of research was clearly stated: the improvement of work situations. The socio-technical approach, however, had a shortcoming, namely a caricatured conception of economic performance, considered most often as a constraint and not as one of the essential dimensions of the raison d'être of the work situations studied. Hence the simultaneous invention of intervention-research and socioeconomic theory, born from the critical analysis of action-research, the critique of the macroeconomic model of the production function and the limits of accounting (see Chapters 1, 18).

Thematic periphery: Since the intervention-research favors scientific observation, the intervener-researcher is invited to draw the hard core of his research, resulting from the fieldwork and to segment it into themes and sub-themes. This is a nomenclature that allows you to look in the academic literature for materials that will position your own research results compared to those of other researchers. Around the hard core is built a "thematic periphery" of external bibliography that consists of identifying the relevant materials, relative to the object of research, extracted from the literature. The thematic periphery tool makes it possible to position the results of the researcher, by a reconciliation with the literature and to identify sometimes proximities, sometimes discrepancies or contradictions, then to elaborate a scientific discussion and to announce, in all modesty, the limits and the perspectives of research (see Chapters 9, 10, 11, 12, 13, 14, 15, 16, 17).

ABOUT THE CONTRIBUTORS

Isabelle Barth, professor of management sciences, graduated from EM Lyon Business School and holds a PhD in Management Sciences. She worked in international business before joining the university where she held many responsibilities. She was executive director of EM Strasbourg Business School from 2011 to 2016. Her researches focuses on diversity management, emerging management, and organizational behaviors. She is editor of *la Revue Internationale de Psychosociologie et de Comportements des Organisations* (*International Review of Psychosociology and Organizational Behaviors*), and vice-president of the French Institute of Psychanalysis and Management. She is the author of numerous publications, the most recent of which are *Le manager et le philosophe* (*The manager and the philosopher*) with Y. Martin (Passeur, 2014); *Voyage au cœur de l'impulsion d'achat (Journey in the heart of the impulse of purchase)*, (L'Harmattan, 2015); and *La comédie de la vie au travail (The Comedy of Life at Work)* with Y. Martin (Desclée de Brouwer, 2017).

Anthony F. Buono, RMC series editor, is professor of management and sociology and founding coordinator of the Alliance for Ethics and Social Responsibility at Bentley University, which he directed from 2003 through 2013. He is also a former chair of Bentley's Management Department. Buono's interests include organizational change, inter-organizational strategies, management consulting, and ethics and corporate social responsibility. He has written or edited nineteen books including *The Human Side of Mergers and Acquisitions* (Jossey-Bass, 1989, Beard Books, 2003), *A Primer on Organizational Behavior* (Wiley, 7th ed., 2008), and, most recently, *Consultation for Organizational Change Revisited* (Information Age Publishing, 2016).

Intervention Research, pages 273–276

His articles and book review essays have appeared in numerous journals, including *Academy of Management Learning & Education, Across the Board, Administrative Science Quarterly, Human Relations, and Personnel Psychology.* Tony holds a PhD with a concentration in industrial and organizational sociology from Boston College.

Marc Bonnet is professor of management sciences at IAE Lyon, University Jean Moulin Lyon 3, and deputy director of ISEOR Research Center (IAE Lyon, Magellan, University Jean Moulin Lyon 3). He has carried out numerous intervention-research projects in companies and organizations of various sizes and sectors in France and abroad. His research focuses on socio-economic management and the conditions of socially responsible capitalism, themes on which he has published several articles and books with Henri Savall and Véronique Zardet. He was also former president of the Association Francophone de Gestion des Ressources Humains (Francophone Association of Human Resources Management) and chair of the Management Consulting Division (MCD) of the Academy of Management (AoM).

Laurent Cappelletti is a graduate of EDHEC Business School and holds a PhD in Management Sciences. Earlier in his career he was a financial auditor with KPMG and then an assistant professor at IAE Lyon. Today, he is chair professor in accounting and management control at the French Conservatory of Arts and Crafts (Le Cnam, Paris) where he heads the master program in auditing and control. He is also a researcher at the LIRSA laboratory of research, director of intervention-research programs at ISEOR research center and coordinator of the Tetranormalization international research network. He has carried out 165 publications on the basis of intervention-research, including *Contrôle de gestion de l'immatériel (Management Control of the Intangible)* (Dunod, 2012); *Dynamique normative (Normative Dynamics)* (EMS, 2015), and 27 articles in academic journals including *Comptabilité-Contrôle-Audit, Management Accounting Quarterly,* and *Action Research.* He was twice awarded best paper award by the Management Consulting Division of the Academy of Management in 2005 and 2009. He is also associate editor of the *Recherches en Sciences de Gestion. Management Sciences–Ciencias de Gestión* Journal of Administrative Science.

Thierry Nobre is professor of management sciences and holds a PhD in management sciences. He conducts intervention-research particularly within SMEs and the health care sector in the field of change, strategic and performance management. He has held the chair in hospital management at the Ecole des Hautes Etudes en Santé Publique (EHESP) and he currently directs the Executive MBA in hospital management at EM Strasbourg Business School. He recently published a book on managerial innovations at the hospital and is the author of thirty articles in academic journals.

Florence Noguera is professor at the University Paul Valéry Montpellier. She holds a PhD in human resources management and was a post doctorate of the University Panthéon-Assas, Paris 2. She has responsibilities with the AGRH academic association and carries out intervention-research projects within professional service companies and public organizations. She currently heads both the executive MBA in leadership and the doctorate in business administration (DBA) at the University Paul Valéry Montpellier. She was a visiting professor at Unitad de Estudios de Posgrado e Investigación (UEPI) in Mexico for the animation of a conference cycle on "Process of change and role of human resources management." Her researches focuses on the measurement of performance and the standardization of management and HRM. She has produced more than a hundred publications presented at conferences in France and abroad (AGRH, Academy of Management, IFSAM, AAA, ACFAS), including "Measuring and Developing Human Capital" which received the 2009 best paper award by the Management Consulting Division of the Academy of Management.

Jean-Michel Plane is professor of management sciences and holds a PhD in Management Sciences. He is the director of the CORHIS unit of research (EA 7400, Université Paul Valéry Montpellier) and honorary president of the AGRH academic association. He has expert and advisory responsibilities in sub-Saharan Africa and Europe and works primarily on leadership development and organizations. He is also head of the research master in science of organizations and institutions at the University Paul Valéry Montpellier, and author of numerous publications including *Management des organisations: Théories, Concepts, Performances (Management Organizations: Theories, Concepts, Performances)* (Dunod, 2016) and *Théorie des organisations* (Theory of Organizations) (Dunod, 5th ed., 2017), which sold more than 60,000 copies throughout the French-speaking world.

Henri Savall is an emeritus professor at the Institut d'Administration des Entreprises, University Jean Moulin Lyon 3, where he was the founder and codirector of the Centre EUGINOV (Ecole Universitaire de Gestion Innovante) and the socioeconomic management master's program. He is the founder and president of the ISEOR Research Center. Professor Henri Savall has a multidisciplinary education and his fields of interest include management, accounting, finance, political science, linguistics, economics, and economic history. His current research interests are socio-economic theory, strategic management, qualimetric methodology (a hybrid of qualitative and quantitative approaches), and tetranormalization. He has authored and coauthored 53 books, 98 articles, and 300 Conference papers in French, English, and Spanish. His main books are: *Enrichir le travail humain* [Work and People], *Reconstruire l'entreprise* [Reconstructing the Firm]; and coauthored with Professor Véronique Zardet seminal books among which are *Maîtriser les Coûts et les Performances Cachés* [Mastering Hidden Costs], *Ingénierie stratégique* [Strategic Engineering], *Tetranormalization,* and *Le capitalisme socialement responsable existe* [Socially Responsible Capitalism and Management] coauthored with Michel Péron, Véronique Zardet, and Marc Bonnet. His core objective is to explore and demonstrate the compatibility between social and economic performance within firms and organizations. His research methodology is referred to as "intervention research" and "qualimetrics" as it goes beyond traditional action-research. He supervises one of the largest research team in France (125 senior and junior researchers) and conducts approximately 20 intervention-researches each year, in which he gets directly involved in various companies and organizations. Henri Savall (together with the Professor Véronique Zardet) has been awarded the famous Rossi Award by the Academy of Moral and Political Sciences (Institut de France, Paris) for their work on the integration of social variables into business strategy, as their socioeconomic approach to management (SEAM) received international recognition through a joint publication with ILO, Geneva. For the past 40 years, Savall has been the co-founder and editor of the *Recherches en Sciences de Gestion. Management Sciences—Ciencias de Gestión* [Journal of Administrative Science], Paris and Lyon. He holds two doctoral degrees in economic sciences and in management sciences from the University of Paris. In 2017, he has been distinguished Chevalier (Knight) of the Legion of Honor, on a proposal of the Ministry of Higher Education and Research, France.

Véronique Zardet is a professor at the Institut d'Administration des Entreprises, University Jean Moulin Lyon 3 where she is the director of the Centre EUGINOV (Innovative Management University School) and the socioeconomic management master's program. She is also the director of the ISEOR Research Center. She holds two doctoral degrees in management sciences from the University of Lyon. Her research is centered on qualimetrics and intervention-research methodology, applied to the conduct of strategic change and the improvement of socioeconomic performance in private enterprises and public services. She received, together with Henri Savall, the famous Rossi Award from the Academy of Moral and Political Sciences (*Institut de France, Paris*) for their work on the integration of social variables into business strategy. She is the associate editor for the Spanish series of *Recherches en Sciences de Gestion—Management Sciences—Ciencias de Gestión* [Journal of Administrative Science].

Lightning Source UK Ltd.
Milton Keynes UK
UKHW05f0720130818
327034UK00018B/117/P

9 781641 132886